D0218189

Twentieth-Century Women Novelists

Twentieth-Century Women Novelists

Feminist Theory into Practice

Susan Watkins

palgrave

© Susan Watkins 2001

All rights reserved. No reproduction, copy or transmission of this publication may be made without written permission.

No paragraph of this publication may be reproduced, copied or transmitted save with written permission or in accordance with the provisions of the Copyright, Designs and Patents Act 1988, or under the terms of any licence permitting limited copying issued by the Copyright Licensing Agency, 90 Tottenham Court Road, London W1P 0LP.

Any person who does any unauthorized act in relation to this publication may be liable to criminal prosecution and civil claims for damages.

The author has asserted her right to be identified as the author of this work in accordance with the Copyright, Designs and Patents Act 1988

First published 2001 by
PALGRAVE
Houndmills, Basingstoke, Hampshire RG21 6XS and
175 Fifth Avenue, New York, N.Y. 10010
Companies and representatives throughout the world

PALGRAVE is the new global academic imprint of St. Martin's Press LLC Scholarly and Reference Division and Palgrave Publishers Ltd (formerly Macmillan Press Ltd).

ISBN 0–333–68345–5 hardback
ISBN 0–333–68346–3 paperback

This book is printed on paper suitable for recycling and made from fully managed and sustained forest sources.

A catalogue record for this book is available from the British Library.

Library of Congress Cataloging-in-Publication Data
Watkins, Susan, 1967–
    Twentieth-century women novelists: feminist theory into practice/Susan Watkins.
      p. cm.
    Includes bibliographical references and index.
    ISBN 0–333–68345–5 – ISBN 0–333–68346–3 (pbk.)
    1. English fiction–Women authors–History and criticism. 2. Feminism and literature–History–20th century. 3. American fiction–Women authors–History and criticism. 4. American fiction–20th century–History and criticism. 5. English fiction–20th century–History and criticism. 6. French fiction–Women authors–History and criticism. 7. French fiction–20th century–History and criticism. 8. Women and literature–History–20th century. 9. Feminist fiction–History and criticism. I. Title.

PR888.F45 W38 2000
823'.91099287–dc21   00–055676

10   9   8   7   6   5   4   3   2   1
10   09   08   07   06   05   04   03   02   01

Printed and bound in Great Britain by
Creative Print & Design (Wales), Ebbw Vale.

For my daughter, Amy Rose

Contents

Acknowledgements

This book would not have been written without two periods of study leave. While at Chester College of Higher Education I was awarded a grant which released me from teaching in the summer term of 1997. I made substantial progress with the first half of the book during this period. Leeds Metropolitan University awarded me a University Sabbatical which relieved me of all teaching and administrative responsibilities in semester one of 1999–2000, during which time I was able to finish the book. I would like to thank both institutions for their support of this project and the School of Cultural Studies for endorsing my application for a sabbatical. I would also like to thank Rachel Hutchings and Harriet Simpson for their initial help with researching the book. My colleagues on the English team in the School of Cultural Studies – Pieter Bekker, Christine Bousfield, Nick Cox, Tom Herron and Jago Morrison – took me out for drinks and meals during the rather pressured period of my sabbatical and kept me sane. They also helped me with numerous specific queries and general discussion of relevant issues. I would like to thank the anonymous reader of the typescript whose response was so encouraging and helpful, and Margaret Bartley for her interest in the book from start to finish. Lastly, my greatest debt is to Ian Strange, whose support, encouragement and advice, both practical and conceptual, were always vital.

S.W.

Introduction

This book tells two stories: a story about twentieth-century women novelists and a story about feminist theory. Although it may seem odd to describe an academic book as 'telling stories', I do so to point out the fact that all narratives, whether explicitly coded as fictional or not, construct a particular version or account of their subject(s). This book, like any other, is partial and specific, marked by the choices, aims, successes and indeed failures of its author. Bearing this in mind, it seems appropriate to begin this introduction by describing those choices and aims that make this book distinctive. Some of the consequent problems will then be considered. Baldly stated, the aims of the book are these: first, to introduce feminist theory to readers unfamiliar with this body of work; secondly, to suggest approaches to twentieth-century women's novels; thirdly, to make possible connections between the two. The last point should alert readers to the subtitle of the book, 'Feminist Theory into Practice', which makes it clear that it provides a model of how to use theory when reading literature. More specifically, its methodology suggests ways to use feminist theory when interpreting (since all reading is necessarily interpretative) twentieth-century women's novels. Each chapter discusses a different 'type' of feminist theory and uses two or three articles or books to illustrate a particular theoretical perspective. In every chapter one literary text is analysed. All the chapters discuss twentieth-century novels by women, except the first, which focuses, for partly pragmatic reasons, on a short story.[1] The chapters are generally organised as follows: the first section establishes an intellectual context for the specific theoretical works which are being discussed. The main arguments and innovations of those works are then described. A short section introduces the author and novel discussed in the chapter and considers some of the ways in which that author's work has been interpreted in literary criticism. The following section, 'Theory into Practice', applies the insights of the theoretical works just discussed to the novel in question. The next section, 'Practice into Theory', uses the novel to question some of those insights and raise issues ignored by those theorists.

1

The preceding account will no doubt raise a number of issues in the reader's mind which I now want to discuss. This book discusses fiction (and mostly novels) rather than a wider range of literary genres. This may imply a number of things: first it may suggest that women can only write decent novels and that their poetic and dramatic production is inferior. Secondly, it may create the impression that feminist theory is *automatically* applicable to women's novels and collapse important distinctions between the two. This book does not endorse either assumption: women writers have clearly used just as many genres as men; equally, women's novels are not necessarily feminist novels.[2] However, the book does suggest the importance of the gendering of particular genres. From its inception to the present day, the novel has been a feminised genre in terms of readership, authorship, content and narrative structure. The appearance of the novel as a distinctive and recognisable literary genre in the late seventeenth and early eighteenth centuries accompanied an increase in literacy (especially among women), and the rise of middle-class ideologies such as separate spheres for women and men and women's confinement in the home. The novel was considered an appropriate genre for women writers to use because it dealt with ordinary life and tended to use a realist mode which relied on the creation of verisimilitude and careful observation of character. It required no special education in the classics to write a novel, unlike poetry. The traditional account of 'the rise of the novel' in the eighteenth century therefore links it to the gradual imposition of realism as normative. It emphasises those male novelists, such as Fielding, Richardson and Defoe, who shaped the genre in this way.[3] This tradition of the novel continues into the nineteenth century in the work of canonical male novelists such as Dickens and Thackeray. Women are often the intended readers of these works and they are frequently the subjects. Courting and marrying them is a significant narrative thrust of such novels. However, it is also important to recognise that revisionist feminist work on eighteenth-century fiction has emphasised the resistance to realism and the greater ingenuity and flexibility in women novelists' use of the genre.[4] Women have not merely been the passive subjects and recipients of the genre, but have also shaped and formed it in ways which challenged masculine fictional conventions. In the nineteenth century, for example, women novelists such as the Brontës, George Eliot and Elizabeth Gaskell worked within and subverted the dominant realism of the novel, relying on such elements as romance, melodrama and gothic to upset their readers' expectations.[5] It is this that allows Virginia Woolf to state that 'the novel alone was young enough to be soft in her [the woman writer's] hands'.[6] While this statement certainly exaggerates somewhat, it does make an important point: the gendering of the novel as feminine allowed women to contribute to and shape it in ways that are distinct from other genres. This book discusses women writers' ambivalent position in relation to the novel genre and argues that this flexibility does have a relationship (although clearly it is not a simple one) with their gender. In the twentieth century it is women writers who have made real innovations in the genre of the novel, particularly in the connections they have made between shape, form and gender issues. The novels the book discusses have been chosen partly on the grounds of their particular concern with these matters and partly because of their popularity with students and teachers alike. Obviously my judgement here is subjective and based on my own teaching experience. However, I am not prescribing a syllabus so much as choosing ways into an always contested debate about the relationship between twentieth-century women's fiction and feminist theory. Therefore, the novels have also been chosen because they 'fit' with the theory enough *and not enough* to be interesting and provocative.

This metaphor of a 'fit' between theory and literature suggests one way of perceiving the relationship between feminist theory and women's writing (in this case, women's novels). Does the book imply that there is an obvious connection between the two? If so, what is it? I certainly would not wish to suggest that anatomy, for example, provides a causal link here. Such an interpretation would claim that all feminist theorists and women novelists share a female body which necessarily links them. Clearly it would be difficult to argue that one can be a feminist just by virtue of having a female body; as difficult as it would be to claim that it is impossible for a man to be a feminist because he does not. This is because feminism is about political aims and objectives rather than 'essential' physical identity. In other words there is no automatic relation between feminist theory and women's novels based on biology. Equally, feminist theory can be applied to any literary or cultural product, whether created by a man or a woman. However, this book does claim that there is a similarity between the critical, ambivalent relationship women novelists have to the novel genre and that between feminism and other theories. Both novelists and feminist theorists have raised similar issues about identity, the body and essentialism, issues that are of interest to these writers because they stem from occupying a similar position which might be described as one of marginality. To be on the margin or borderline is to be simultaneously away from the centre and yet essential to defining where that centre is: Julia Kristeva claims that such a position is characteristic of femininity.[7] This book argues that such a double perception of marginality is also important for twentieth-century women novelists and feminist theorists.

A more fundamental problem arises from this discussion: the relationship between theory and practice. Is there an obvious difference between the two? Does it make sense to treat a literary text as a crude 'demonstration' of a theory? It has been claimed that 'this separation of the way of knowing from the object of knowledge is itself ideologically produced and serves to re-secure an idealist understanding of theory as meta-discourse and an empiricist notion of history [or, in this case, literature] as data'.[8] It should be obvious that all texts contain ideas and theories and the demarcation of some as 'literary' and others as 'theoretical' may have more to do with commercial considerations than with the presence or absence of any 'literary' or 'theoretical' elements intrinsic in the text itself. It is impossible to isolate any single feature present in 'literary' language which is absent from non-literary language. Equally, all theoretical texts use 'literary' devices for rhetorical purposes: to persuade. Some of the texts in this book, for example Hélène Cixous's 'The Laugh of the Medusa', are extremely lyrical and some of the novels, such as Virginia Woolf's *Orlando*, are extremely theoretical. Feminists are right to be suspicious about the masculinist bias of theory, but this is not well countered by a refusal to engage with theory at all. The distinction between theory and practice in this book, while admittedly crude, serves a pragmatic and pedagogic purpose. Indeed, this distinction is deliberately broken down and questioned in the last chapter. Also, the work of one writer, Virginia Woolf, appears twice, as both 'theory' and 'practice': her essay *A Room of One's Own* is considered in Chapter 1 and her novel *Orlando* is discussed in Chapter 5. This provides the opportunity to compare an ostensibly literary text with an ostensibly theoretical one and consider the ways in which both texts play with these definitions.

As is obvious from a glance at the contents page, the organisation of this book appears to tell an extremely simplified 'tale' of feminist theory this century, which seems to move forward smoothly (and always progressively). The discussion of first-wave feminism in Britain and France in Chapter 1 considers its concern with legal and material improvements in women's situation but also argues that it anticipated more recent interest in issues of language and identity. The chapter debates whether or not the term 'first-wave' is useful or restrictive and shows it to be culturally and socially specific. In Chapter 2 the strengths of liberal feminism as a popular movement which began the second wave are discussed. Its weaknesses in terms of adherence to culturally acceptable ideas about the individual's relationship with society, normative models of gender difference and conventional ideas about political action and change are also considered. Chapters 3 and 4 discuss the attempts to link feminism with Marxism and psychoanalysis respectively. Chapter 3 demonstrates the analytical purchase of Marxist feminism when considering historically specific instances of the intersection between class dynamics and patriarchal structures. Marxist feminism accounted for the significance of women's work inside and outside the home in explaining their subordinate position and debated the impact of ideology on sexuality and identity. The strengths and weaknesses of an insistence on a materialist analysis are also considered. The next chapter discusses whether or not psychoanalytic feminism is limited by dependence on conceptions of normality and adjustment and asks if it fully embraces a conception of the subject as inevitably fractured and diffuse. Poststructuralist feminism, the subject of Chapter 5, certainly does. This chapter discusses how poststructuralist feminist theorists have focused on the position of the sexed body in culture, language and politics. It considers whether or not their writing of a stereotypical language of feminine difference is successful as a strategic attempt to insert woman as positive presence into patriarchal language and culture. Chapter 6 situates this debate in the wider context of postmodernity and postmodernism, which dismantled those ways of conceptualising identity, representation, history and philosophy characteristic of the modern period. The chapter discusses the extent to which feminism as a movement shares these concerns and considers whether or not feminism should align itself with, or distance itself from, postmodernist theory.[9] In Chapter 7 the places lesbianism occupies in feminist theory are discussed and the relationship between gender and sexuality is compared to that between queer theory and feminism. The interaction between heterosexism and patriarchy is analysed. The final chapter considers the subordinate position black feminism has had in feminist theory, which has often been implicitly white. It analyses the strategic use of essentialist theories of black female identity in black feminism and argues that such theories are put in dialogue with anti-essentialist accounts of the intersection between race and gender. This conversational model is also used to describe the relationship between black feminism and post-colonial theory.

As this short account of each chapter suggests, the book creates a particular history, or narrative, of feminism and feminist theory. It aims to provide the reader who has no experience of feminist theory with a fairly widely accepted version of it. The book also debates and complicates at appropriate points the categories used, the order in which things are placed and the way in which things are defined, indicating that all these issues are matters of debate to which the reader is invited to contribute. A deliberately schematic outline is thus contested and my decisions are made apparent to readers so that they may disagree with them as they wish. The book's organisation is not meant to imply a *simple* historical sequence of developmental thinking. Although the teleological impulse to move forward and fulfil a purpose is present in the book and in feminist theory itself, it is counteracted by an equally important circular tendency for similar issues to recur in different chapters and in various feminist theories, a tendency which I have also acknowledged. The theories I have chosen to discuss in the book are those which have been of greatest significance for feminism. They are those which have been in dialogue with feminism throughout the twentieth century and have been implicated in its definition of itself as a body of knowledge, a theory and a politics. Feminism has been shaped by liberalism, Marxism, psychoanalysis and the other theories represented here just as much as they have been formed by their consideration of gender and feminist issues. It is impossible to discuss psychoanalysis, for example, without acknowledging the importance of gender and sexuality. Perhaps the only exception is first-wave feminism, which contains the seeds of all the issues and debates which can to some extent be seen as separate (though they are never entirely so) in second-wave feminism.

The book provides access to some of the ideas of those feminist theorists who have been crucially influential this century. It discusses what might be called (if it is not a contradiction in terms) feminist theoretical *classics*: those texts which are often mainstream (and have sometimes been superseded) for feminist academics but which often remain bamboozling to a less specialist readership. I do not wish to imply that these texts necessarily exemplify or even illustrate in any simple way the feminist theoretical positions they appear to represent. If they perform such a paradigmatic function they are made to do so for initial educative purposes only. I envisage them working as specific, local routes into a particular feminist debate or field of inquiry. After all, when studying a particular feminist body of work, like any other, one has to begin by actually reading something/one thing. Is my book, then, intended to substitute for reading the theoretical texts themselves? Realistically, I hope that readers will read *some parts if not all* of the theorists' works that I discuss and that this book will crystallise particular issues that are of significance in, and provoke debate about, those works, rather than summarising them in an over-simplified way. In most, though not all, cases, the works were chosen to suggest the diversity of a particular feminist theory; in the second chapter two books by the same author, published nearly twenty years apart, have been used to demonstrate the changes and continuities in one person's theoretical orientation. If the theories and theorists discussed in the book can only partially be said to form a simple historical and developmental sequence, the novels have not always been chosen for their historical appropriateness either. Their date of publication is sometimes, but not always, close to that of the theoretical texts used in any particular chapter. Angela Carter's *Nights at the Circus*, for example, was published in the 1980s, contemporaneously with many discussions of the relationship between feminism and postmodernism. On other occasions, as in Chapter 5, where *Orlando* is used to discuss feminist poststructuralist theory, the connection is explained in different terms. (In the latter case, it was interesting to examine a work by a woman often characterised in literary terms as a modernist, given that Hélène Cixous and Julia Kristeva tend to apply poststructuralist ideas to modernist literature written by men.)

The structure of each chapter does in most cases distinguish between theory and practice. This, coupled with the fact that in every chapter a number of theoretical texts are discussed alongside only one novel, may imply that the literary text is somehow superior to the theoretical texts. I have tended to emphasise the complexity and ambivalence in the literary text at the expense of that in the theoretical texts. Indeterminacy may come to function as a positive quality in novels but be merely indecisive and confused in 'theory'. This is not meant to indicate that literature is necessarily richer and thus more rewarding for the reader than theory. I would not wish to endorse such a traditional liberal-humanist approach to the literary text. All texts can be read in terms of plenitude and plurality. The emphasis is on using the novel in each chapter to interrogate the theory, not because literature is *automatically* well equipped to do this, but because it can be made to serve such a function for pragmatic, educative and political reasons. To do so is also, I hope, interesting and enjoyable for the reader! Readers should be able to unlink particular novels from particular theories once the association between the two has been made by virtue of comparative cross-referencing to other chapters.

Inevitably, the intellectual allusiveness and level of difficulty of the book are context-dependent. In the overall context of an introductory book I would expect that readers can follow my main arguments and that any over-simplification is compensated for by footnoting which refers the reader to other more detailed sources.[10] Equally, where there is difficulty, this may be because the ideas have become more complex. In these situations, readers are entitled to an account which does justice to that complexity. Terms such as 'patriarchy', 'first-' and 'second-wave' feminism and 'Anglo-American' and 'French' feminism are initially introduced in simple terms but are discussed in more detail as the book progresses so that the variety and complexity of debate about their usage is indicated. Lastly, I want to make some suggestions about how to use this book. I envisaged that English lecturers might set it as the main text to accompany a module on twentieth-century women's fiction and supplement it with advice about material which updates or develops each of the feminist theories discussed here. Readers are encouraged to read it critically and use it as a jumping-off point into more detailed research. I hope both lecturers and students use it to begin a debate or conversation about any of the feminist issues and interpretations it raises. Doris Lessing commented that literature is 'alive and potent and fructifying and able to promote thought and discussion *only* when its plan and shape and intention are not understood, because that moment of seeing the shape and plan and intention is also the moment when there isn't anything more to be got out of it'.[11] This is as true of this book as it is of the novels and feminist theories it discusses.

1

First-Wave Feminism

Introduction

The introduction has made clear both the pleasures and pitfalls involved in the too-ready use of categories like 'first-wave feminism'. With the proviso that the following definition will inevitably be subject to debate and reassessment as the chapter progresses, we may define first-wave feminism as the first organised movement with definite and specific feminist aims, which encompassed the years between 1860 and 1920. The movement strove for political and legal equality, focusing on a range of issues such as female suffrage (votes for women); women's access to educational and employment opportunities; the legal rights of married women (for example, to own property, to divorce, and to have custody of their children). Campaigns over the sexual double standard, or unequal attitudes to male and female sexual behaviour (apparent, for example, in the treatment of prostitution) were also important, as were attempts to prevent women's exploitation in employment.

It would not be an exaggeration to say, however, that feminist historians and critics have disagreed about nearly all of the above statements. If first-wave feminism was the first organised movement, then was there no feminism, and were there no feminists before it? Obviously that depends on how we define feminism. Only if we think that to be a feminist necessarily means being involved in collective, organised action for specific aims would it be the case that feminism began with the first wave. To make such a judgement may mean that we have absorbed conventional patriarchal versions of history which suggest that it is influenced only by those movements that are 'embodiments of collective action and galvanizers of social change'.[1] Equally questionable is the timing of

9

the end of the 'movement'. Most critics see the first wave concluding in Britain with the granting of female adult suffrage in 1928. They then stress the hiatus in feminist consciousness and activism until the start of the second wave in 1960 or thereabouts. However, it is certainly the case that there was important feminist work in this period.[2] This apparent 'fade-out' may be as much a consequence of our definition of feminism as was its seeming absence prior to 1860. Equally, we may need something which seems different enough from what we like to define as 'second-wave feminism' in order to reassure us of the latter's unique qualities.

Why, if we do (however provisionally) accept the dates suggested above, did feminism suddenly burst onto the political scene? Many have seen as significant those social changes related to the rise of capitalism and increasing industrialisation which made middle-class women less independent and more confined in the home. While acknowledging the importance of such changes, Olive Banks also discusses other important sources of mid-nineteenth-century western feminist thinking such as evangelical Christianity, Enlightenment philosophy, and socialism (*Faces of Feminism*, pp. 7–8). The Evangelical Movement, with its stress on personal conversion experiences and its strong moral emphasis, was very influential in the late eighteenth and early nineteenth centuries. It did not discourage the involvement of women in missionary and charity work, fund-raising, and even, in some cases, in preaching. The Evangelicals were associated with temperance and anti-slavery movements, and the increasing involvement of women in this sort of work may have made them more aware of their own position in society. Enlightenment philosophy, which stressed rationality, advocated equal rights on the grounds of humanity. Writers like Mary Wollstonecraft argued in *A Vindication of the Rights of Woman* (1792) that women should not be excluded from such rights as they shared in those qualities of reason and common humanity which justified the equal treatment of different classes of men. The socialist tradition, beginning with the Saint-Simonian movement in France and appearing in the ideas of Robert Owen in England, advocated systems of communal living and less restrictive sexual relationships. Such attacks on the conventional family unit and childcare arrangements may well have influenced some early feminists.[3]

If it is eminently possible to debate the reasons for the appearance of first-wave feminism, it is also true that the aims and objectives of the movement were extremely diverse. Then, as now, an individual woman was likely to be involved in a number of campaigns which reflected her beliefs about feminism and defined what sort of feminist she was. A good example of this diversity can be seen in the UK campaign to repeal the Contagious Diseases Acts, and in this movement's interaction with the suffrage movement. In an attempt to control prostitution, the acts allowed the forcible medical examination and treatment for sexually transmitted diseases of women thought to be prostitutes. A woman who believed that the same sexual standards of chastity and purity should be applied to men as well as women tended to support the campaign to repeal the acts. Other feminists saw this campaign as a distraction from the more important business of getting the vote for women, clearly putting greater emphasis on equal constitutional rights.[4] The aims of first-wave feminism changed over time,[5] although arguably its strength lay in the willingness of those involved to unite under the cause of the vote.[6]

One other significant matter is the exclusively western, 'first-world' focus of this discussion so far. Elizabeth Sarah comments that timing the first wave 'presupposes a particular political and economic context – the development of liberalism, capitalism and socialist movements in this period – which is only relevant for the feminist movements which developed in the western world' (Sarah, p. 521). The definitions in this chapter are culturally specific to western, 'first-world' feminism, and all of the examples so far have been British ones.[7] A related issue is that of the class background of those involved in first-wave feminism in the UK. Most of these women were middle-class in origin, although by the end of the first wave nearly a quarter were from a working-class background (*Becoming a Feminist*, p. 21). Inevitably class background had an effect on the particular campaigns in which women involved themselves. The percentage of working-class women involved in the suffrage campaign was lower than in any other (*Becoming a Feminist*, p. 54). The suffrage movement was divided on social lines between those women who were determined to wait for universal adult female suffrage, and those who were prepared to accept an age or property-owning qualification (*Becoming a Feminist*, p. 66). It is also true that those involved in the first-wave feminist movement in Britain were white. If all of the above points are important, it is because they remind us that what we conventionally think of as first-wave feminism was a culturally specific and particular movement.

Virginia Woolf, *A Room of One's Own* (1929)

Virginia Woolf's essay *A Room of One's Own* is undoubtedly one of
the most influential feminist texts written in this century. Woolf is
certainly known just as much for her criticism as for her fiction,
which will be considered in Chapter 5. Simone de Beauvoir, for
example, preferred the essays: 'Yes, Woolf is among the writers
whose works I admire and sometimes re-read, but only her feminist
writings because I don't agree with her novels. They don't have any
center. There isn't any thesis.'[8] Although we can question de
Beauvoir's judgement of Woolf as a novelist, she certainly attests to
the power of her articulation of feminist issues and claims in her
non-fictional prose. Many critics have, of course, seen more similarities between the essays and the fiction than does de Beauvoir.[9] Yet
is it possible, given many of Woolf's ambivalent statements about
feminist concerns of the first wave (such as the struggle for female
suffrage), to consider her a first-wave feminist, or even a feminist at
all? *A Room of One's Own*, which was published in 1929, the year
after women in Britain achieved the vote, began life as two lectures
on the subject of women and fiction delivered at Newnham and
Girton, which were at the time the only Cambridge colleges where
women could study.[10] The three most significant points Woolf makes
in the essay are as follows. First, women's previous lack of success
as writers proceeds not from any absence of talent, but from social
disadvantages such as: their exclusion from educational institutions; their financial dependence; their lack of personal space; the
demands of constant childbearing. Secondly, Woolf suggests two
crucial remedies: financial independence (the magic sum of £500 per
year) and personal space (represented in the room of the title) in
order for women to achieve their full potential as writers. Thirdly,
Woolf argues that 'it is fatal for anyone who writes to think of their
sex';[11] she suggests that all the greatest writers have had androgynous minds, which blended both masculine and feminine elements.

In order to establish women's material disadvantages, Woolf uses
the clever device of showing how she experienced many difficulties
in researching the subject of her lecture. Seized by a flash of inspi-
ration, she takes a short cut across the lawn of the imaginary com-
posite Oxbridge college she is visiting, only to be met by a furious
beadle, who informs her that the lawn is reserved for the male
Fellows and Scholars of the college. Woolf then heads for the library,
only to be denied entry on the grounds that women must be accom-

panied by a Fellow or provided with a letter of introduction. Having brought to the reader's notice women's exclusion from educational institutions, Woolf continues her theme by comparing and contrasting a luxurious evening meal at a men's college with a spartan dinner at a women's college. She suggests that it is only once immediate physical needs have been satisfied that intellectual work can be at its most productive, and emphasises that the finest foods and wines are more likely to produce excellence than the 'school-dinner' menu of gravy soup, beef and two veg, and prunes and custard, which she eats at the women's college. The differences in menu are clearly related to the financial situation of both colleges: the men's college has, in its long history, amassed huge wealth from the gifts of rich patrons and alumni, whereas the women's college has barely scraped together enough money to exist. This is made most apparent in the deliberately literal image of money pouring into the foundations of the men's college (p. 11). Woolf reminds us that men were able to endow seats of learning so liberally because they were wealthier than women. In contrast, women were occupied with childbearing and rearing; acquiring financial assets was impossible when in most situations all a married woman's property and earnings legally belonged to her husband.

Such material disadvantages in women's situation make significant practical differences to their lives and to their creative freedom and expression. Woolf documents in the third and fourth chapters of the essay the ways in which women who wrote in the period between the sixteenth and nineteenth centuries struggled to reconcile their social position with their literary calling. Perhaps the most poignant of stories in this part of the essay is Woolf's account of what might have happened to an imaginary sister of Shakespeare's. Although she possesses equal talents, Judith's rebellion and eventual demise symbolise for Woolf all the women's writing which we may have lost. Also important for Woolf are the ways in which women's social and material disadvantages affect how they are perceived. When Woolf visits the British Museum to research the subject of women and poverty she finds that the notes she has taken from a random assortment of male-authored books on the subject of women reveal a bizarre collection of details. Some may appear to be factual: '*less hair on the body of*'; others are more clearly laden with patriarchal value judgements: '*mental, moral, and physical inferiority of*' (p. 30). The list reveals the curious fact that men seem to be obsessed with denigrating women, that they conceal biased opinions beneath an apparently scientific objectivity, judge all women alike and make such judgements solely in terms of an assumed masculine norm: *'weaker in moral sense than'*; *'greater length of life of'* (p. 30). Woolf is ostensibly puzzled by the fact that there appears to be such a stress on confirming and documenting women's inferiority in the writings of men, who are so obviously in a position of power over women. She concludes that 'women have served all these centuries as looking glasses possessing the magic and delicious power of reflecting the figure of man at twice its natural size', or, as she elaborates: 'if they [women] were not inferior, they would cease to enlarge' (p. 37). In fictional works, however, the situation is apparently very different. Woolf stresses the 'utmost importance' of women characters in male-authored fiction, who are: 'very various; heroic and mean; splendid and sordid; infinitely beautiful and hideous in the extreme; as great as a man, some think even greater' (p. 45). Woolf slyly implies that such stereotyped and diametrically opposed versions of femininity are not as varied as they appear; there is no space between the beautiful, virtuous, angelic heroine and the ugly, wicked, demonic villainess for the diverse versions of femininity about which we may wish to read.

Simone de Beauvoir, *The Second Sex* (1949)

The date of publication in France of Simone de Beauvoir's *The Second Sex* appears to fall in the middle of the apparent hiatus between the first and second waves of feminism. To choose the book as an example of first-wave feminism is appropriate when we consider the particular situation in France in the period. In 1949 France was recovering from its occupation by Germany in the Second World War, women had only gained the right to vote in 1945, and abortion and contraception were illegal. Women's rights were not on the agenda. It is perhaps no surprise that the book caused an immediate rumpus; savagely attacked in the press, it was placed on the Vatican's index of prohibited books. In 1953, it was translated into English and published in the USA and in the UK, to a less alarmist response.[12] *The Second Sex* is a large book, both literally and conceptually. It deals with many issues, such as biology, race and lesbianism which are important in subsequent feminist writing, and discusses the connections between feminism and other theories like Marxism and psychoanalysis in ways which broke ground for second-wave feminist theory. Like *A Room of One's Own*, *The Second Sex* sees the inferiority of women as a fact related to their situation, rather than to their nature. De Beauvoir acknowledges the influence of Woolf's essay on her own work in a number of places (and, indeed, quotes from those of her novels she later claimed not to enjoy). The work is divided into two halves, or books: the first describes the ways in which patriarchy has perceived women; the second provides an account of the experience of living as a woman. Within that structure, different sections consider the following issues: philosophical and ethical discussions of femininity; the history of women; images of women in literature and culture; phases of a woman's life; ways of enduring or coping with the oppression of women in a patriarchy; ways of achieving true liberation for women.

Perhaps de Beauvoir's most famous statement in the book is that 'One is not born, but rather becomes, a woman.'[13] This important insight suggests that it is not biology or nature which makes us women: it is our situation in society. In other words, what it means to be female is, to all intents and purposes, inseparable from social, historical and cultural definitions of femininity. In a patriarchal society, such definitions position woman as the 'other' to man: as all the things which man is not: 'Thus humanity is male and man defines woman not in herself but as relative to him' (p. 16). Masculinity, for de Beauvoir, stands for the positive, the neutral, the normal, and the transcendent. In contrast femininity is perceived as the negative, the aberrant, and the immanent. The terms 'transcendence' and 'immanence', which are important ones in *The Second Sex*, can be defined, respectively, as the ability to engage in some worthwhile activity or project in the world, as opposed to being merely confined to self and routine. One of the book's most demanding and controversial suggestions, however, is that individual women can, and should, resist the situation of immanent femininity and choose to change it, despite the temptations that it offers. De Beauvoir admits that it may be easier to comply with such patriarchal definitions of woman, which may even make us happy, but she stresses that our liberty is more important than our happiness (p. 29). The early chapters reject those explanations for women's inferiority offered by biology, psychoanalysis and Marxism because they cannot account for the fact that woman is the 'other' to man. De Beauvoir sees history as the long process of developing and instituting this 'othering' of woman, and, like Woolf, finds in male-authored literature and culture an apparent ambivalence in images of women that arises from the elasticity in this concept of the other. She considers women's writing, like Woolf, to be marked by their social inferiority.

De Beauvoir's vision of woman's liberation is centred around the destruction of her situation as man's inferior other, and the creation of equality. She stresses that such a development is partly dependent on social changes such as women undertaking profitable work outside the home, the abolition of marriage as we now know it, and the provision of childcare, maternity benefits and abortion rights. Such changes must go hand in hand, however, with an alteration in the ways in which men and women perceive each other. A relationship of dominance and submission should be replaced by one of mutuality: 'when we abolish the slavery of half of humanity, together with the whole system of hypocrisy that it implies, then the "division" of humanity will reveal its genuine significance and the human couple will find its true form' (p. 741).

Doris Lessing, 'To Room Nineteen' (1963)

Of all the novelists discussed in this book, Doris Lessing has written about the widest range of subjects and done so in the most varied manner. Her experiences as the daughter of white British settlers in Southern Rhodesia (now Zimbabwe) find their way into her searing examination of its colonial society; her arrival in London in 1949 after the Second World War provides her with a curiously mixed perspective on English culture which is simultaneously that of outsider and insider; her involvement in Communist and Socialist groups in both Southern Africa and England appears in her political analysis and fascination with political involvement of all kinds, and her interest in women's lives is evident in her sympathetic yet analytical accounts of her central female characters. To say this is not, however, to assume that Lessing's (or any writer's) art can be naively read as a product of her life. Any wide reader of Lessing's texts would be struck first by their incredible generic and formal differences from each other, which are evidence of one of her greatest interests: writing itself. Lessing has written conventional realist novels, including a linked series of *Bildungsroman* (novels of development), science fiction, comic books, fantasy, and other texts which are more difficult to classify. This diversity is represented in this book by the following discussion of her short story 'To Room Nineteen', as well as the consideration of what is possibly her best-known novel, *The Golden Notebook*, in Chapter 3.

'To Room Nineteen' is the story of the gradual breakdown of Susan Rawlings, its central character. Susan is sensibly married, and has given up her job in order to care for her children. She is aware of 'a certain flatness' in her life, and when her husband, Matthew, has a casual affair, is confused and depressed. Her problems really begin, however, when her two youngest children go to school and the freedom she was so eagerly anticipating begins to turn into a threatening, malevolent enemy, only serving to remind her how thoroughly she is still tied to her responsibilities for house and children. Her tentative attempts to tell her husband about her confused feelings, in particular her desire for freedom, are not understood, as Matthew feels that his life is equally restricted. Susan tries to create a space for herself in the house, and turns one of the spare rooms into what is known as 'Mother's Room'. However, it soon begins to be used by the whole family, and Susan is forced to rent a room in a cheap hotel for privacy and her own sanity. Gradually she begins to spend more and more time there, and when Matthew has her followed by a private detective, she pretends that she has a lover to explain her behaviour. When Matthew confesses that he is having a serious extra-marital relationship himself, and suggests that they create a foursome for lunch and the theatre, Susan decides to kill herself in room nineteen.

Theory into Practice

Lessing's story echoes the concerns of Woolf's essay in various ways. Most obvious is her stress on Susan's need for a room of her own: although room nineteen is 'hideous',[14] it provides a space where she can be private, and recover what Lessing terms the 'essential Susan' from 'cold storage' (p. 359) beneath the superficial roles of wife, mother, and manager of a large house. Both Lessing and Woolf prioritise financial independence and personal space for women. Susan is forced to ask Matthew for the money to rent room nineteen, and is horrified that he perceives it as 'paying her off' (p. 378). Although she sees this as a betrayal of the once intimate knowledge they both shared of the family finances, the underlying point is to emphasise that women's work in the home is not paid for adequately by any notional family wage, which is ultimately controlled by the man. Financial independence for Susan would prevent her subordinate economic relationship with Matthew. Woolf tells us that she heard of her aunt's £500 a year legacy at the same time as women were granted the vote, and thought the former 'infinitely the more important' (p. 39). Undoubtedly one of Woolf's most controversial statements, it casts doubt on the efficacy of constitutional representation when women are not in a social position to take advantage of the vote. The number of women MPs has always been small; historically, once the vote was won, women began voting along party lines and, to an extent, lost interest in feminist issues (*Faces of Feminism*, p. 149). 'To Room Nineteen' shows that having the right to vote certainly makes little difference to Susan Rawlings. Admittedly, however, Woolf does not acknowledge that it was only as a consequence of the parliamentary process of legislative change that women were allowed to own property in their own right. If women had been part of the constitutional process earlier it is possible that such a change might have come sooner. Some readers may feel that Woolf over-emphasises the issue of financial independence, or makes too great a distinction between economic and constitutional freedoms, but Susan's situation suggests that being legally permitted to earn and control your own money is not the same as creating a social situation where doing so is normal for married women with young children. Woolf's argument that £500 per year (the contemporary equivalent is about £25,000[15]) provides valuable space and security for creative endeavour is clearly a powerful one. However, 'To Room Nineteen' makes clear that if she decided to return to work and became economically independent the fact that Susan assumes total responsibility for all aspects of her children's care would not alter.

Woolf's understanding of human nature as basically androgynous is also apparent in the story. The terrible fears and resentments which Susan experiences are visualised by her as 'some sort of demon ... thinnish, meagre in build. And he had a reddish complexion, and ginger hair. That was he – a gingery, energetic man' (p. 367). One day when Susan is in her garden she sees this figure torturing a snake with a stick. Neither Susan nor the reader understands at first whether he is real or a figment of her imagination, yet it becomes clear that he represents a double, or *alter ego*, who possesses all the energy, power and control that Susan lacks. Lessing was undoubtedly very much influenced by the psychoanalyst Carl

Jung, who believed that all women have a masculine element to their personality, which he called the animus, and all men have a feminine aspect, known as the anima.[16] Her point is that if a person is only allowed expression of one aspect of their personality, then the repressed part will cause psychic disturbances. In the sharply sexually segregated society in which Susan lives, it is not surprising that her rebellious impulses should erupt in an aggressively masculine image.

The insights of de Beauvoir's *The Second Sex* can also be fruitfully applied to Lessing's story. 'To Room Nineteen' bears out the statement that 'One is not born, but rather becomes, a woman'. Before her marriage and the birth of her children, Susan is much more *like* Matthew than she is after these crucial events. She has a job she enjoys, and her own flat, money and friends. 'Becoming' woman, for Susan, is a process that is instituted by her occupation of the role of wife and mother, a position that establishes her as Matthew's 'other'. While he goes out to work and is the financial provider and head of the household, Susan assumes those responsibilities (for children and house) which are left over. It is clear, despite the lip service paid to the notion of separate, but equal and complementary spheres, that Susan's position is the inferior one, because the tasks with which she is occupied do not fulfil her: they encourage, in de Beauvoir's terms, immanence rather than transcendence. Although Matthew argues that he is no more free than Susan from 'bondage' (in his case, that of turning up for work), it is clear that his job provides more opportunities for self-fulfilment than her role as housewife and mother. Even if it is 'scarcely a reason for living', and he is not 'proud' of the newspaper he works for, it is 'interesting' and he 'took pride in doing it well' (p. 354). It also allows him to maintain contact with the world, and people, outside the home, unlike Susan, who is remarkably lonely and isolated. Like de Beauvoir and Woolf, Lessing clearly suggests the limitations of childcare and management of the home when they are assumed to be all-sufficient for a woman's personal enrichment.

Lessing's story makes a similar connection between adultery and marriage to the one made by *The Second Sex*. De Beauvoir argues that adultery and marriage are mutually sustaining because conventional monogamous marriage inevitably leads to boredom with one's partner. Only the abolition of marriage and its replacement by partnerships which last as long as both parties wish will prevent this situation arising. De Beauvoir follows Marxist theory when she suggests that most marriages are merely economic unions designed to serve the purpose of passing on property to legitimate heirs (see Chapter 3). Lessing's treatment of adultery also recognises that it is about much more than sex. Matthew's first, casual affairs are deemed 'banal', 'not important', and 'inevitable' (p. 356). The marriage moves into 'a different phase' (p. 357) for which both recognise that Matthew's adulteries are now necessary. Susan is forced to pretend that she has accepted this situation by inventing her own lover. Her inability to cope with this pretence forces her suicide, because she recognises that the degree of change she requires of her relationship with Matthew is beyond him.

Practice into Theory

While the story raises many of the same feminist issues as Woolf's and de Beauvoir's texts, it can also be used to explore some of the contradictions and ambiguities in their arguments. The room in Lessing's story is much less clearly positive than in Woolf's. Arguably, it becomes a prison from which it is difficult for Susan to escape. Its freedoms are never more than temporary and must at some point be exchanged for the restrictions of the surrounding world. The only alternative to this fact is death, and how we respond to Susan's suicide (which will be discussed later) obviously has a bearing on our interpretation of the room. Woolf's use of the image of the room leads her to make some problematic judgements about women's writing. The figure of Jane Austen, who wrote her novels at the parlour table surrounded by family, ready with a piece of blotting paper to cover her work if visitors arrived, is used to emphasise the necessity for privacy, security, time and independence for women writers. Yet one of the contradictions in *A Room of One's Own* lies in the fact that Austen *did* write her novels in inauspicious conditions. If one brilliant exception does not disprove Woolf's general rule, there may be a sense in which Woolf has absorbed patriarchal judgements about women's writing of previous centuries to her own. In seeking to explain the scarcity and inferiority of women's writing as a consequence of social disadvantages, Woolf still accepts that it *is* scarce and inferior, and the exceptions she does make resemble to an extent those she implies men might make in the opening paragraph of the essay: 'When you asked me to speak about women and fiction I ... began to wonder what the words meant. They might mean simply a few remarks about Fanny Burney; a few more about Jane Austen; a tribute to the Brontës ... a respectful allusion to George Eliot; a reference to Mrs Gaskell and one would have done' (p. 5). Although she considers and rebuts the argument that 'talent will out' (regardless of circumstances) (pp. 105–6), it may be that her essay unintentionally suggests something similar.

Although Lessing's story explores those repressed aspects of Susan's personality which can be culturally coded as 'masculine', there are ways in which it questions Woolf's valorisation of the androgynous text. Her suggestions that people are made up of both male and female elements and that the best writers are those who forget their sex and allow androgyny full reign in their work appear to provoke some oddly traditional aesthetic judgements. Charlotte Brontë is castigated for allowing anger at the situation of women to 'tamper' with her integrity (p. 73), and Coleridge and Shakespeare (both male, and highly canonical writers) are held up as examples of the great androgynous mind (p. 97). 'To Room Nineteen' is certainly an angry text, but not, I would argue, a flawed one because of that. It is its odd combination of anger mixed with resignation which gives it its curious power. While some have seen Woolf's preference for androgynous writing as an evasion of her own situation as an oppressed woman (*A Literature of Their Own*, p. 264), others have regarded it as an attempt to question, destabilise and subvert conventional, binary gender stereotyping and categorisation.[17] There is one writer, however, whom Woolf finds difficult to fit into her views on androgyny: Jane Austen. Paradoxically, she argues that Austen's brilliance lies in her creation of a distinctly *feminine* sentence (p. 77), one that is closely linked with the female body (p. 78). She is therefore more reluctant to sever the connections between the female body, women's experience and women's writing than the concept of androgyny may at first suggest. Lessing similarly emphasises for the reader the importance of such links, seen in the close bond between mother and child in the scene where Susan returns unexpectedly to her house and sees her daughter, Molly, sick and wanting comfort. The description of Susan's feelings – 'The child's listless face, the dark circles under her eyes, hurt Susan' (p. 381) – stresses the immediate physical way in which Susan experiences her child's pain. At this point, however, the au pair picks up the child and comforts her, and Susan concludes that her maternal role could be filled by anyone. The reader wonders whether she is correct to think this. The possibility that mothering is something unique and precious remains as a troubling remnant in the story.

If Lessing's story points out such contradictions in Woolf's text then we can view them in two ways. They could be evidence of serious flaws in Woolf's arguments which invalidate them for us as readers. Alternatively, they could be read as part of her stylistic strategy in the essay, which, in its tone, language and narrative technique, deliberately attempts to resist the logic, linearity and rationality of patriarchal discourse, in order to suggest the importance of the connections between gender and language.[18] I have deliberately been writing as if the narrator of *A Room of One's Own* is Woolf herself, but if we read carefully we find this not (necessarily) to be the case. At the beginning of the essay 'Woolf' writes: 'Here then was I (call me Mary Beton, Mary Seton, Mary Carmichael or by any name you please – it is not a matter of any importance ...' (pp. 6–7). We might see in this passage a wish that the narrating voice in the essay might be simultaneously representative and various; inclusive and inconsistent. Woolf's strategy for dealing with her subject – women and fiction – is similar. The essay is about the process of writing an essay on the subject of women and fiction just as much as it is about women and fiction; in other words it is metadiscourse: writing about writing. In her use of these amongst many other strategies (for example the use of irony and parody) Woolf draws our attention to language; she asks us to question the value of masculine discourse, which she associates with binary logic. This is apparent, for example, in the opening sentence of the essay, which begins with 'But', and in her way of representing the beadle's outrage when she walks on the lawn: 'he was a Beadle; I was a woman. This was the turf; there was the path. Only the Fellows and Scholars are allowed here; the gravel is the place for me' (p. 8). The short sentences divided into neat and opposite halves by the semi-colon emphasise her point. A similar strategy is apparent in Woolf's depiction of women characters in male-authored literature: 'heroic and mean; splendid and sordid; infinitely beautiful and hideous in the extreme' (p. 45).

Lessing's text achieves similar effects to Woolf's in the way it is written. 'To Room Nineteen' is narrated in the third-person mode and uses at different points both an omniscient point of view and the device of focusing exclusively on Susan's perspective. When using the latter technique Lessing uses free indirect speech, which hovers between direct and indirect speech and moves in and out of a particular character's voice to create its effects. In the opening of the story the narrator's tone is flat, even world-weary, as if to suggest that there is nothing unique about the story being told. The characters are always the pink and pattern of convention, responding to ideology disguised as received wisdom: 'Children needed their mother to a certain age, that both parents knew and agreed on, and when these four healthy, wisely brought-up children were of the right age, Susan would work again, because she knew, and so did he, what happened to women of fifty at the height of their energy and ability, with grown-up children who no longer needed their full devotion' (p. 355). This tone creates an incredible narrative pressure, which is never released, but is instead intensified by disturbing images, such as the sudden appearance of the red-haired demonic man, and by extremely violent language. A good example is the description of the holiday Susan takes alone, remaining in regular contact with her family by telephone: 'Susan prowled over wild country with the telephone wire holding her to her duty like a leash. The next time she must telephone, or wait to be telephoned, nailed her to her cross' (p. 371). Susan is here compared to a wild beast on a lead, and to Christ crucified.

The use of such devices as complex point of view and tone and disturbing imagery serves a number of purposes. They appear to exaggerate, almost to parody the typical strategies of realism, such as narrative omniscience and free indirect speech, which can allow a reader to assume an unproblematic relationship between literature and reality. Lessing highlights the tensions involved for any writer in producing a text which attempts to be 'lifelike' in order to make us question exactly what such a process might involve. Her stylistic strategies also make her characters into little more than victims of the social situation they are in; the oppressiveness of the language leaves them no choice about their lives, or only the illusion of significant choices. More importantly, perhaps, her style, like Woolf's, associates rational, logical, 'intelligent' discourse with masculinity.[19] Lessing opens her story with the words, 'This is a story, I suppose, about a failure in intelligence. The Rawlings' marriage was grounded in intelligence' (p. 352), which 'logically' leads us to assume that this is a story about the failure of a marriage. (Yet the parenthetical 'I suppose' implies that it may be about much more than that.) Susan continually attempts to use her intelligence to analyse and understand her situation, and the word is repeated many times. Lessing's point is that rational intelligence is not enough, and that its failures are connected with the fact that it is associated, culturally, with masculinity. In making this point stylistically, she uses the same strategy as Woolf does in *A Room of One's Own:* she attacks patriarchal discourse by undermining its rules from within.

The diverse ways of looking at Woolf's arguments provoked by an examination of them alongside 'To Room Nineteen' suggest the flexibility of her feminism. We can see Woolf as a writer who advanced the first wave's claims for equal rights to financial independence and personal space and freedom, a 'guerilla fighter in a Victorian skirt', as Jane Marcus terms her;[20] we can also see her as someone whose stress on material and economic issues over the vote might have placed her on the edge of the broadest definition of 'first-wave' feminism, although not entirely outside it. Her concern with issues of language and gender and the suggestion that patriarchal power is related to dominant masculine discourses as well as economics anticipates some of the concerns of feminists writing in the second wave. Thus she acknowledges that while equality is a laudable aim for feminism, it should not necessarily mean the denial of difference. After the experiences of exclusion detailed in the first chapter, Woolf writes: 'I thought how unpleasant it is to be locked out; and I thought how it is worse perhaps to be locked in' (pp. 25–6). In other words, she sees that a marginal position can sometimes provide a fresh, precious perspective.

Lessing's story also suggests many ways in which *The Second Sex* can be criticised. Perhaps her most powerful statement, de Beauvoir's suggestion that woman is the 'other' to man has also proved to be her most controversial. If Lessing defines femininity merely in relation to masculinity, she, like de Beauvoir, is perhaps guilty of echoing masculinist assumptions and denying woman authentic femininity on her own terms. Is there not something in women's experience (for example, pregnancy and motherhood) which makes femininity unique and not reducible to the mere opposite of masculinity? Some feminist theorists (see Chapter 5) would claim that there is.[21] While 'To Room Nineteen' considers this possibility, as we have seen, it tends to echo de Beauvoir's attitude to childcare, which suggests the absorption of patriarchal views of the female body rather than a celebration of its difference. De Beauvoir sees experiences of puberty, menstruation, pregnancy and childbirth as oppressive evidence of woman's immanence; the female body is something completely separate from the mind, which struggles, and fails, to be reconciled with physical processes. Adolescence is described as follows: 'It is a most unfortunate condition to be in, to feel oneself passive and dependent at the age of hope and ambition' (p. 382), and the depiction of pregnancy may at times suggest the invasion of the female body: the foetus is described as an injury and a parasite, and the pregnant woman is termed 'the plaything of obscure forces' (p. 512). It is possible, however, that both Lessing and de Beauvoir draw our attention to, even parody, the way the female body is perceived in our patriarchal society.[22] Lessing's reminder that Matthew feels his life to be equally restricted also questions de Beauvoir's assumption that masculinity is normative, and that a man's experience of his body is trouble-free. If Lessing seems reluctant to site the source of a unique femaleness within the female body, then this may be because she wishes to complicate essentialist ideas about the body and identity. Although Susan feels that she is 'just the same' (p. 376) beneath the roles of wife and mother when she peels off those layers in room nineteen, this is very doubtful. All Susan seems capable of in the room is what is described as 'wool-gathering': 'what word is there for it? – brooded, wandered, simply went dark, feeling emptiness run deliciously through her veins, like the movement of her blood' (p. 377). In room nineteen Susan recovers a sensuous experience of her body, but whether this can be the source of an essential female identity is debatable. Although Lessing clearly suggests that 'wool-gathering' is important because it is impossible to live by intelligence alone, the story's conclusion implies that one cannot recede into this part of the personality without leaving life altogether.

Another clear difficulty many readers experience when reading 'To Room Nineteen' is Susan's inability to act. Many find her passivity frustrating, and wish she would tell Matthew how she feels or go back to work; others see her as a victim totally without power to change her life, except through what they read as the 'protest' of her suicide, which others interpret as a flight from responsibility. The extent of her power to act suggests a crucial problem about agency which is also present in *The Second Sex*. De Beauvoir stresses the individual woman's responsibility to choose transcendence and reject immanence. Some have argued that the text, and particularly her concept of the other, are overly influenced by existentialist philosophy, itself influenced by the Hegelian 'master–slave dialectic'. Existentialist philosophy stresses that human beings are autonomous and responsible, always free to act, or interpret a situation, as they wish, even when in a relationship of unequal power, like that between a master and a slave.[23] The best-known proponent of existentialism is Jean-Paul Sartre, who was de Beauvoir's long-term partner. Much ink has been spilt (to borrow de Beauvoir's own phrase) over the question of their relationship and the extent of his intellectual influence on her, with more recent feminist critics suggesting that this was much more of a two-way process than has previously been supposed.[24] However, both de Beauvoir's dualistic concept of self and other, and her apparent stress on the individual woman's responsibility to change her own situation, may be related to her interest in existentialism. The Self/Other pair is a binary which de Beauvoir explains as constituent of our very existence:

> As I have already said, man never thinks of himself without thinking of the Other; he views the world under the sign of duality, which is not in the first place sexual in character. But being different from man, who sets himself up as the same, it is naturally to the category of the Other that woman is consigned; the Other includes woman.   (pp. 100–1)

De Beauvoir rejected historical materialist and psychoanalytic explanations for the 'othering' of woman, and did not consider the possibility that this binary is created in language itself, as many poststructuralist feminist critics were to do (see Chapter 5), and as Woolf's and Lessing's texts may suggest. She is thus forced to explain it as a philosophical inevitability, loosely related, in parts of the book, to the physical 'inferiorities' and differences of woman. It is this inevitability which conflicts with the stress laid on the individual woman's autonomy and responsibility to resist her positioning as the other. Exactly how free does de Beauvoir believe women are to change their situation? While her stress on individual liberty can be interpreted as empowering, it also denies the significance of the effects that oppressive situations may have on that liberty. Many feminist critics have been more suspicious than de Beauvoir appears to be of philosophies which stress the liberty and rationality of the individual, arguing that such freedoms have only been available, historically, to white, privileged men. (For more discussion of this see Chapter 6.) Others have argued that her work displays a more nuanced understanding of the relationship between individual freedom and social oppression in its understanding of human beings as situated in a particular context which may affect their power to act (see Kruks, 'Gender and Subjectivity', pp. 97–108). 'To Room Nineteen' demands that the reader engage with a number of different interpretations of the question of Susan's freedom, or ability to act to change her situation.

A significant response to Lessing's story is to feel a distinct lack of sympathy with Susan's middle-class predicament and to resent the privileged position she appears to occupy as a housewife with a cleaning lady, an au pair and a spacious home. After all, Susan does not actually bear the brunt of the hard work her life involves. Lessing cleverly incorporates this interpretation in the episode with Miss Townsend, who runs the respectable hotel where Susan first attempts to rent a room. Miss Townsend is a lonely, unmarried, impoverished woman; Susan has everything she wants: '"I can see from the gleam of hysteria in your eyes that comes from loneliness controlled but only just contained that I've got everything in the world you've ever longed for"' (p. 369). De Beauvoir displays no similar awareness that she is insufficiently attentive to the diversity of women's experiences. Although the style in *The Second Sex* is ostensibly very objective, pseudo-scientific and universalist, most of the accounts of women's lives in Book II are provided by white, middle-class, heterosexual and well-educated women remarkably like herself and Susan. This has led some feminists to comment on the autobiographical aspects of the book; others have suggested that it could best be described as an anthropological study of a very specific group, even if de Beauvoir does not acknowledge this herself.[25] Some of the class assumptions are best revealed by de Beauvoir's suggestion that women should liberate themselves by engaging in rewarding work outside the home. We might wonder who de Beauvoir imagines will run the nurseries and do the housework, which she perceives as necessarily immanent tasks. She does not face fully the implications that freedom for a small group of professional career women might have for other women who do their childcare and cleaning. It is in the work of Marxist feminists, discussed in Chapter 3, that issues like these are more adequately addressed. Going back to work is, of course, an option for Susan, but one which she rejects, possibly because she recognises that doing so would not actually change the way in which husband and children perceive her. So while all de Beauvoir's sympathies are for the independent woman, struggling to keep her house tidy and herself presentable as well as managing a career, Lessing's heroine appears to choose immanence deliberately, a strategy which de Beauvoir would condemn.

One of the most striking aspects of Lessing's story is that fact that her heroine has no friendships with other women. Her relationships are dominated by the 'heterosexual contract' and the women she knows, like Mrs Parkes, Sophie Traub and Miss Townsend, are in a subservient economic position in relation to her. The story certainly implies that this is one of Susan's problems. Lessing demonstrates that dividing women from each other economically and making their sexual relationships with men the most significant aspect of their lives places them in a weak position. The story offers no alternatives to this situation, except, perhaps, in the hypothetical possibility that if Susan had confessed the real reason why she needed to rent a room to Miss Townsend she may have met with more support than she imagined. Similarly, there is a hint that Sophie, the new au pair, understands her situation more than she realises: '"You want some person to play mistress of the house sometimes, not so?"' (p. 374). The possibility that alignment with other women could provide ways out of Susan's situation exists as the merest trace in Lessing's text. De Beauvoir's treatment of women's relationships with each other is also ambivalent. Her discussion of lesbianism, for example, has been extremely controversial. Setting aside the question of her own relationships with women,[26] critics have emphasised that her dualistic Self/Other model of human relationships is basically a heterosexual one. She may be guilty of supporting the institution of 'compulsory heterosexuality' and fails to establish a convincing account of lesbian identity outside heterosexual frames of reference.[27] However, seeing lesbian and heterosexual feminine identity as mutually implicated may anticipate the work of contemporary queer theorists, who see lesbian sexuality as a subversive reworking of straight and gay male sexual practices. (For further discussion of these views see Chapter 7.) Lesbianism also exists as an important trace in Woolf's *A Room of One's Own*. When reading a contemporary novel by a woman writer Woolf is struck by the sentence: '"Chloe liked Olivia"'. She continues (after checking there are no men present): 'Do not start. Do not blush. Let us admit in the privacy of our own society that these things sometimes happen. Sometimes women do like women' (p. 81). In Chapter 4 we will discuss the historical and biographical reasons for Woolf's (always implicit) interest in lesbianism. The point here is that women liking each other is something new (according to Woolf) in English literature and something potentially subversive in society. One certainly feels that liking another woman could have made a significant difference to Susan Rawlings's life and story.

'To Room Nineteen' may appear to offer very little explicit hope for achieving the liberation of women. As in *The Second Sex*, one of the key issues is the extent of the individual's freedom to resist her positioning as the immanent 'other'. If de Beauvoir argues that the individual *is* free to make such a choice, would enough women doing so in itself constitute liberation? At what point do a few enlightened individuals create enough of a critical mass to make a real change in society? Does de Beauvoir imply that liberation for women means assuming those masculine qualities of transcendence which men have regarded as their own preserve? Many readers have rejected de Beauvoir's concluding appeal for men and women to affirm their 'brotherhood' as suggesting that women should become like men, who will not need to change.[28] Lessing's text implies, however, that relying on an essential definition of womanhood based around the female body is equally problematic. Reading both texts together forces us to acknowledge that equality necessitates a redefinition of 'transcendence' in order to strip it of its masculine associations.[29] It is certainly the case, however, that neither Lessing nor de Beauvoir acknowledges the *strategic* value of separatist, or 'difference', feminism as a particular stage in feminist politics (Moi, *Simone de Beauvoir*, p. 211). De Beauvoir, who was not willing to call herself a feminist until 1972 when she joined the MLF (Mouvement de Libération des Femmes), only then recognised that the struggle for women's liberation must take place 'before our dreams of socialism come true'.[30] She prioritised socialism above feminism for many years, and *The Second Sex's* rather vague pronouncements about the relationship between feminist and socialist aims suggest in different places both that Marxism is ineffective in explaining the situation of women, and that a socialist revolution would necessarily improve the position of women. More important, perhaps, is the fact that 'To Room Nineteen' reminds us of two areas which de Beauvoir either castigates or ignores: the unconscious and language. Lessing's description of Susan's malevolent enemy forces us to see the unconscious in social terms, as responsive to cultural conditions. The story's use of language displays just how important the connections between patriarchy and language are, and its ambiguities and contradictions force the reader to consider and debate exactly those issues which remain anomalous in *The Second Sex*.

Although any text can be read in terms of its gaps, erasures and pressure points, some encourage this process. It is exactly this linguistic flexibility which remains Lessing's most useful feminist tool.

Conclusion

The Second Sex occupies a position in relation to first-wave feminism in France which resembles that of *A Room of One's Own* in Britain. Both texts were published very soon after women had won the vote in their respective countries; both acknowledge the importance of such victories, but also demand practical and material changes in the social position of women, such as financial independence and freedom from unwanted childbirth and childcare. Yet each writer recognises that such improvements are, on their own, insufficient to end women's subordination. Their answers to the question of how to change the enabling conditions of patriarchy are different: Woolf stresses the necessity of personal space, and acknowledges in her stylistic strategy the importance of undermining patriarchal language, whereas de Beauvoir emphasises that women should reject their position as 'other' to men. The degree to which the individual can actually resist the situation of oppression in which she finds herself is an issue both writers address in different, and perhaps rather confusing, ways. The example of Jane Austen suggests that Woolf's explanations for the 'inferiority' of women's writing are not always [consis]tent. Some women can write without a room of their own or [financ]ial independence. Equally, the extent of the individual's [power] to act in an oppressive situation is an issue about which *The Second Sex* is unclear. Neither writer appears to believe in an essential feminine nature, and yet parts of their texts come close to suggesting its existence (think, for example, of Woolf's feminine sentence tied to the female body, or de Beauvoir's description of pregnancy). Yet it is exactly these ambiguities that make these texts good examples of the first wave, and can simultaneously take them beyond it, when read alongside Lessing's 'To Room Nineteen', which forces the reader to confront such contradictions.

2

Liberal Feminism

Introduction

The previous chapter's examination of first-wave feminism revealed its diversity in both theory and practice. The same point can be made about second-wave feminism, with which the rest of this book is concerned. As second-wave feminism became more theoretically sophisticated and conscious of its history, philosophy and politics, its explicit formulation of the various positions detailed in this and following chapters developed apace. Although there is some debate about the role of liberal feminism, the subject of this chapter, in initiating the second wave, it is widely accepted historically as the most public manifestation of the resurgence of feminist activity in the 1960s in the west.[1] To understand liberal feminism it is firstly important to examine some of the different contemporary implications of the term 'liberal'. In common parlance to be liberal (as opposed to conservative) suggests tolerance of a variety of lifestyles, beliefs and behaviours including those which are more alternative, or threatening to the status quo. However, it is equally possible to perceive liberal perspectives as more conventional and less socially subversive than radical ones. Some of these ambiguities are apparent in contemporary UK party politics, for example, as well as in writing about feminist theory and practice. Betty Friedan considers her writing to have revolutionary implications,[2] but other commentators perceive her writing (specifically *The Second Stage*) as 'conservative pro-family'.[3] Juliet Mitchell has described the National Organisation for Women (NOW), which Friedan founded in the USA in 1967 to fight a liberal feminist agenda, as 'reformist' and 'not now regarded as a part of Women's Liberation either by itself or by most other groups'.[4]

Such ambiguities in the term 'liberal' relate to specific aspects of its history, as well as to potential contradictions in linking it with a feminist agenda. The liberal philosophical and political positions came to prominence in the eighteenth century alongside the transition from a feudal to a capitalist economy, the rise of the bourgeoisie, the fragmentation and decline of organised religion and emerging industrialisation and urbanisation. The eighteenth-century liberal tradition stressed individual liberty, the value of rationality, and had faith in the ability of reform to achieve progress for mankind. John Locke, one of the most important early liberal philosophers, engaged in seventeenth-century political debates provoked by the English Civil War and Interregnum. Rather than the king's divine right to rule, which provided a model for other hierarchical relationships (between, for example, master and servant or husband and wife) he argued that government in fact proceeded by the consent of the governed and the individual's ability to enter into a contractual relationship dependent on his ownership of property. Locke's endorsement of the new market-led philosophy and economics of capitalism was later criticised by the French Romantic philosopher and writer Jean-Jacques Rousseau, who argued that individuals should be protected from the worst excesses of the market, although he still accepted the value of private property in creating an individual's sense of self-worth. While explicitly supporting the idea of the individual human being as the possessor of liberty, rationality and the ability to succeed according to merit, both Locke's and Rousseau's philosophies contain certain assumptions which make them less egalitarian than they may at first appear to be. The emphasis (however qualified in the writing of Rousseau) on private property as a guarantee of individuality and citizen rights excludes those, such as women and the working classes, who are not property owners and ignores the power relations which are historically embedded in the ownership of property. The eighteenth-century liberal model of the autonomous, reasoning individual is therefore an implicitly white male middle-class one. Both Locke and Rousseau, for example, advocated traditional roles for women, based on their exclusion from the public sphere of the market and their confinement in the newly feminised and private sphere of the home and the nuclear family.

It is in the work of late eighteenth- and nineteenth-century writers and philosophers like Mary Wollstonecraft, John Stuart Mill and Harriet Taylor[5] that the arguments of liberal theory were explicitly extended to women. Wollstonecraft's *A Vindication of the Rights of Woman* (1792) argued that women were as capable as men of reason and self-determination, and that if educational and social disadvantages were removed women would be able to enjoy the equal opportunities which logic and justice suggested they deserved. The work of J. S. Mill and Harriet Taylor similarly argued for full equality of opportunity for women, including full citizenship rights, and rejected the idea that it was possible to make judgements about feminine 'nature', which could be used to justify women's inferior status. These writers made clear analogies between the unfairness of the arbitrary rule of one man over another based on class or privilege, and the power individual men exerted over individual women. However, their emphasis on the *irrationality* of individual men denying individual women equal rights ignores the wider structural inequalities between men and women which create unequal power relations in a patriarchal society. This is perhaps most obvious in their recourse to arguments and ideas about motherhood, which they still perceive to be a natural role for women. Indeed there is a clear stress in their work on the importance of educating women to exercise their individuality, rationality and freedom of choice, in order that they may become better mothers. This does not, however, recognise the restrictions placed on women by their automatic association with the private sphere of home and family, an association which is structurally created within patriarchy and capitalism.[6]

Ambiguities similar to those in eighteenth- and nineteenth-century liberalism and liberal feminism are apparent in contemporary western capitalist societies, such as the USA. Indeed, the discussion in this chapter of the work of an American feminist and an American woman novelist indicates a shift from Europe to the USA which is not merely accidental. It is the USA in the twentieth century which best embodies the history and contradictory ideologies of liberalism, and this is clearly related to the importance of liberal feminism in initiating the second wave in the USA. Although it is possible to point to the links between the second-wave feminist movement and the civil rights, student and peace movements of the 1960s, most commentators discuss the re-emergence of feminism in the USA at this time in terms of a liberal feminist agenda.[7] This included J. F. Kennedy's appointment of the Commission on the Status of Women (1961), the passing of the Equal Pay Act (1963) and Title VII of the Civil Rights Act (1964), the publication of Betty

Friedan's *The Feminine Mystique* (1963) and the founding of NOW (1967). The importance of Friedan's *The Feminine Mystique* for the women who read it is apparent in her account of the responses she received and the effect the book's publication had on her life (see Friedan, *It Changed My Life*). For a contemporary critic, the text is relevant because it is part of a specific social and cultural context and embodies some of the ambiguities and contradictions of that context. It also has important implications for more recent feminist theory.

Betty Friedan, *The Feminine Mystique* (1963)

The Feminine Mystique was written to identify a problem, elucidate the causes and effects of the problem and suggest solutions. It opens in reportorial guise, with an attempt to investigate a mystery: the mystery of why so many 1950s American housewives appeared to be suffering a nameless malaise characterised by feelings of depression and dissatisfaction.[8] Friedan finds the solution to the mystery in the dominance of a concept she calls the 'feminine mystique'. The feminine mystique combines two important ideas: first, that femininity is something special and precious, different from yet complementary to masculinity; secondly, that this idea of femininity is best, even *only* fulfilled through marriage, motherhood and domesticity: what Friedan terms '"Occupation: housewife"'.[9] The book explains the creation of the mystique in terms of a post-Second World War culture characterised by the return of servicemen longing for an image of 'motherhood and apple pie', the rise of consumer capitalism and suburbanisation, the increasing influence of magazines and advertising, the dissemination of popularised Freudian psychology, and the effects of functionalist models of society and culture on sex-specific higher education for women. Friedan claims that the feminine mystique is new in American history and culture: a radical departure from the assertive, career-oriented image of the 'new woman' of the early decades of the twentieth century. She argues that women's magazine articles, stories and advertisements began in the post-war period to create an image of the good wife, mother and homeworker which was dependent on the purchase of new consumer goods, what Friedan terms the 'sexual sell' (*The Feminine Mystique*, Chapter 9). The book suggests that the move away from cities to the suburbs, and to the open-plan 'ranch-style' homes they contained, also endorsed this image of woman's role, creating large, labour-intensive environments which, once left behind by the male breadwinner on his commute to the city, became an entirely feminised sphere. Popularised Freudian psychology was equally to blame, according to Friedan, for creating the mystique, because it implied that woman's true vocation was as a wife and mother, and that to aspire to anything other than conventional feminine roles was the cause of sexual dysfunction and bad mothering. Similarly, functionalist theoretical models in academic disciplines such as sociology and anthropology emphasised the study of the function of the parts of a social structure within that structure in a way which tended to endorse the status quo. In other words, if in many contemporary cultures women and men occupy separate spheres and perform different roles, then this was assumed to be the best way of fulfilling the necessary functions or purposes of that culture or society. Friedan accuses higher-education institutions of absorbing the influences of both functionalism and Freudianism and disseminating them in less intellectually rigorous, sexually specific curricula for women.

The effects of the feminine mystique are serious for both the individual and society. Friedan documents what she terms a 'problem of identity' (p. 68) experienced by many women, who are unable to develop a sense of self-worth and purpose in their lives solely through marriage, childcare and domestic responsibilities. She also argues that women's confinement in the domestic sphere puts unnecessary pressure on men to act as breadwinners, causes sexual problems in marriage, and creates bad mothering. In making the last point, Friedan opposes the child-centred theories of contemporary writers like Spock, who stressed the importance of the mother's undivided attention for the child. Instead, like Wollstonecraft and Mill, she argues that only individuals with the strong sense of 'human maturity' (p. 179) which comes from playing a full part in society can bring up children to be responsible adults capable of making reasoned choices. While admitting that 'there are no easy answers' (p. 297) to the questions posed by the problem of the feminine mystique, Friedan does suggest some concrete solutions, most of which demand changes in the individual. She argues that women must develop a new self-image involving a new 'life plan' which puts housework and marriage in their proper places, and allows time for a fulfilling, demanding career or other work outside the home. She also exhorts educational institutions to change to make it easier for mature women returners to develop and update their skills, by, for example, introducing part-time study and allowing for periods out of education.

Betty Friedan, *The Second Stage* (1981)

Nearly twenty years later, Friedan's 'sequel' to *The Feminine Mystique, The Second Stage,* was published. One of the most obvious shifts in *The Second Stage* is in the historical and cultural context: the background to the book is the economic recession and rise of New Right politics of the late 1970s and 1980s. In this environment Friedan identifies a new 'problem' with new causes and effects. The problem now is the failure of the feminist movement to transcend 'first-stage' thinking and politics, and develop 'second-stage' thinking and politics. (These categories should not be confused with what we understand as first- and second-*wave* feminism.) Friedan associates first-stage feminist activism with 'the rhetoric of sexual politics':[10] a stress on sexual and personal issues such as lesbianism, pornography and the right to abortion on demand, at the expense of the struggle for legal and political reforms such as the passing of the Equal Rights Amendment, which would make discrimination on the grounds of sex illegal. She argues that stressing sexual politics has alienated ordinary (by which she means heterosexual, married) women from the feminist movement, and played into the hands of New Right politicians by allowing them to claim the traditional family as their concern.

Friedan is also worried by her sense that women are becoming too like men: they are acquiring and endorsing conventionally masculine models of thinking, career progression, work and living patterns, and as a result they are struggling to make 'the choice to have children', a phrase which resounds throughout *The Second Stage.* Friedan believes that women also find it difficult to make this choice in a context where their work outside the home is economically necessary to sustain the family unit, and she argues that the effects of recession on work patterns and standards of living have not been reflected in a shift in gender attitudes, responsibilities and living arrangements; for example, women still do more of the routine household and childcare tasks. Both the economic and social context in which she writes, and the failings in the contemporary women's movement have conspired, according to *The Second Stage,* to create a backlash against feminism which has resulted in the polarisation of feminist and anti-feminist beliefs and agendas. Friedan uses a dialectical model to argue herself and society out of this damaging impasse: 'there is a reconciling of seeming opposites that has to take place now, a dialectical progression from thesis–antithesis (feminine mystique–feminism) to synthesis: a new turn in the cycle that brings us back to a familiar place, from a different vantage' (p. 81).

For Friedan, the solutions to the 'new problem' demand the following initiatives in second-stage feminist politics: a renewed focus on the family; the realignment of the priority accorded issues of sexuality and concerns about legal reform; an emphasis on men and masculine identity; the introduction of what she defines as 'beta', as opposed to 'alpha' thinking, and the development of new ways of planning living and social spaces. Friedan argues that the family is the most important of areas for second-stage feminism because most women still live in families and want to have children. In order for women to make a free and informed choice to have children, without worrying about the effects of that choice on their career and family finances, not only must they have access to safe abortion, but there must also be new childcare initiatives and tax allowances for childcare. Feminists must prevent the New Right from associating itself with concern for the family by resisting those elements within both right-wing and women's movement agendas which position feminism as anti-family. Equal rights for women must be divorced from anti-family lobbies associated with sexual politics such as homosexual rights and abortion on demand, and instead associated with the pro-family, pro-life position. In this way the rhetoric can become 'women *and* family' instead of 'women *versus* family' (p. 228). In order to achieve the real changes in society which would support this aim, feminists of the second stage must focus on masculine identity, which is changing in response to the increasing job insecurity of a world-wide economic recession and the economic independence of women. Men must become more involved in domestic and childcare responsibilities, which should be rewarding. Living spaces and social contexts must change to make the tasks associated with living in families such as childcare, housework and cookery less onerous. Friedan extols the virtues of early twentieth-century living experiments with shared kitchens and nurseries attached to apartments. In this way the idea of separate spheres for women and men will disappear. As a result, individual men and women, and society generally, will come to value beta (conventionally perceived as feminine) as opposed to alpha (usually regarded as masculine) thinking. Beta thinking is 'synthesizing, intuitive, qualitative ... "contextual", "relational"' (p. 244), whereas alpha thinking, which is 'based on analytical, rational, quantitative thinking' is reliant on 'hierarchical relationships of authority' (p. 244). The second-stage feminist movement must think in beta rather than alpha ways.

Alison Lurie, *The War between the Tates* (1974)

The novelist Alison Lurie could be described as a documenter of mid- to late twentieth-century American life as experienced by the white middle classes. In this, and other respects (such as her use of irony and her clever characterisation) she has been compared with Jane Austen, whose specific class focus has been the cause of similar debates about her literary merit.[11] Her popularity on both sides of the Atlantic indicates a degree of WASPish Anglophilia which links her to a Europeanised tradition of the American novel which includes Edith Wharton and Henry James. Lurie's novels are usually written in the realist mode, are often set in the academic context with which she herself is familiar,[12] and discuss the sexual and moral dilemmas of characters who are frequently (although not exclusively) university professors and faculty wives. The plots of her novels often rely on the introduction of a threat or unfamiliar context which disrupts the lives of the central characters, which is usually resolved by the novel's conclusion. Notably, however, Lurie juxtaposes the thought processes and perspectives of her characters, particularly her male and female characters, in a subtle counterpoint which creates delicate effects of irony and ambiguity. *The War between the Tates*, Lurie's fifth novel, was published in the USA and in the UK in 1974 to great acclaim. Set on 'Corinth' University campus, its central characters, Brian and Erica Tate, are a married couple with two teenage children. He is a university professor of politics, she a faculty wife. He subscribes to the ideology of separate spheres for women and men: his sphere encompasses his university career and the role of economic provider; hers involves sole responsibility for domestic and childcare tasks. The novel opens with a number of challenges to this arrangement: first, the Tates' two children are in the process of metamorphosing from well-adjusted, pleasant children into sulky, rebellious teenagers and

Erica seems unable and unwilling to control this process; secondly, Erica discovers that her husband has been having an affair with a graduate student. The discovery of Brian's affair with Wendy – who is nicely caricatured as the embodiment of hippy, alternative late-1960s youth culture – forces a series of radical alterations in both Erica's and Brian's conventional lifestyles which severely question their previously settled attitudes. On realising that Wendy is pregnant with Brian's child, and discovering that he is attempting to make her have an abortion, Erica temporarily aligns herself with Wendy against Brian, who is forced to leave the marital home. As the novel progresses, however, Wendy has an abortion and moves in with Brian, leaving Erica solitary and vulnerable. By the end of the novel Wendy has become pregnant again with someone else's child and leaves Brian for a commune. The novel concludes with Erica and Brian tentatively moving closer together. Throughout the text, chapters or sections focusing on Erica's and Brian's perspectives alternate, and the events and problems in their marriage are described using metaphors of warfare. The device of introducing oppositions and then watching them collapse applies not only to the 'separate' feminine and masculine spheres of the Tates' marriage (which the novel proves are not so separate after all), but also to other paired terms and areas in the book, such as the radical student movement versus the conservative university authorities, and the logical, rational thinking of academia as represented by the Politics Department versus the alternative, mystical philosophy of the Krishna bookshop.

Theory into Practice

Although published in 1974, *The War between the Tates* is set in 1969, six years after the publication of *The Feminine Mystique*. Although the latter text documents what might be termed a 1950s malaise, the impact of the mystique was certainly still being felt in the 1960s, judging by the response Friedan's book received. Lurie's novel shows how the heroine, Erica Tate, is defined by the ideas Friedan identifies as part of the feminine mystique. Her husband perceives her as 'gay, almost childlike, yet at the same time serious and even dignified. "A young princess".'[13] His perception of women is that they are 'essentially different from men: weaker and less rational, but also gentler, finer, more sensitive' (p. 262), although he is roundly disabused of this belief by the end of the novel. As a consequence of the special, different, precious feminine nature he believes her to share with all women, the most appropriate of roles for Erica is perceived by Brian to be the conventional one of housewife. We learn that he:

> had long subscribed to the doctrine of separate spheres of influence, both in national and domestic matters; he attributed the success of their marriage partly to this doctrine. He might advise Erica on important policy decisions, but ordinarily he would not question her management of the home, nor would she ever try to intervene in his professional life.   (p. 5)

As a result, Erica's day closely resembles that described by Friedan:

> Millions of women lived their lives in the image of those pretty pictures of the American suburban housewife, kissing their husbands good-bye in front of the picture window, depositing their stationwagonsful of children at school, and smiling as they ran the new electric waxer over the spotless kitchen floor.
>
> (*The Feminine Mystique*, p. 16)

> She is encouraged to stand up, to clear the table and do the dishes and start her day's work. She picks up the house, skipping the children's rooms; washes out two sweaters; draws for an hour and a half; and makes herself a chicken sandwich. After lunch she goes shopping and to the bank ... She drives home, puts away the groceries, makes a raspberry mousse, and is mixing some lemon cookies when Danielle's VW pulls into the driveway.
>
> (*The War between the Tates*, p. 7)

Although the children are now in their teens, Brian refuses to let Erica work outside the home as a research assistant at the university. He argues that her responsibilities to home and children are too important to sacrifice to someone else for the meagre rewards of a poorly paid job, and implies that it is wrong for her to move outside her demarcated sphere.

Some of the causes Friedan identifies for the emergence of the feminine mystique are also present in the novel. The Tates' farmhouse is surrounded by building work, which is transposing Jones Creek Road into Glenview Heights, a process of suburbanisation which alters the area into one full of expensively equipped ranch houses. The rise of consumer-capitalism provides an insidious background to the novel, which for Erica is linked with the increasing unruliness of her teenagers, and other changes in her life. The problems with the children are perceived to be Erica's responsibility by both Brian and Erica. Her explanations for what appears, in fact, to be perfectly normal teenage behaviour are suffused with the popularised Freudian psychology Friedan blames for endorsing the feminine mystique, at the centre of which is the figure of the mother, who is either remote or overprotective. Similarly, the novel shows how sexual problems are interwoven with the feminine mystique. Brian and Erica's sexual relationship has not always been satisfactory: he prefers penetrative sex; she prefers foreplay. He finds her unadventurous; she finds him demanding. Yet after he wins the argument about whether she should take the research assistant's position at the university, Brian makes love to Erica very attentively, an attention she tries to recreate by continuing the argument later. Friedan's insight that sexuality is increasingly used as an explanation for problems that are not really sexual, that would be better understood in terms of women's boredom at being confined to the home, is also endorsed by the novel. Brian's affair with Wendy, and Erica's growing intimacy with her old college admirer, Sandy Finkelstein, are not really about sexual desire as such, but are shown to be responses to problems in their self-images, gender roles and family situations.

As an admirer of the work of George Kennan,[14] Brian's adherence to the doctrine of separate spheres of influence has many points of contact with Friedan's comments about the rise of functionalism:

Functionalism began as an attempt to make social science more 'scientific' by borrowing from biology the idea of studying institutions as if they were muscles or bones, in terms of their 'structure' and 'function' in the social body. By studying an institution only in terms of its function within its own society, the social scientists intended to avert unscientific value judgements. In practice ... 'the function is' was often translated 'the function should be'. (*The Feminine Mystique*, pp. 112–13)

After a heated discussion at a department meeting Brian 'in his usual role of George Kennan' offers 'a structural analysis of the conflict and propose[s] a compromise' (p. 143). Both the Kennanite emphasis on separation and containment, and functionalist models of society, analyse a subject in structural terms which tend to endorse a strategy of inaction or maintenance of the status quo. In terms of gender relations, this means that Brian's aim in the novel is to avoid change and maintain convention wherever possible. Friedan's criticisms of functionalist and Freudian-influenced sexually specific higher-education courses for women are also apparent in *The War between the Tates*. Brian does not perceive Erica in academic terms at all: it is not clear what subjects she studied as a Radcliffe student; all we know is that she has earned money since graduating as the writer and illustrator of children's books. This is in stark contrast to the detailed information we are given about Brian's academic career. His view of Wendy, who is a graduate student in social psychology, suggests that he endorses the functionalist view of education for women as preparation for marriage:

> Wendy was intelligent enough, but her mind was not scholarly. Until very recently, girls like her, whatever their SAT scores, didn't usually go to graduate school. But nowadays, if they hadn't found someone to marry as undergraduates they continued their education and their search, often in fields like psychology or sociology which seemed relevant to their situation. (p. 31)

Brian despises the graduate programme in Social Psychology on the grounds that the courses were made up of 'equal parts of common sense and nonsense – that is, of the already obvious and the probably false' (p. 28). Although we must not assume that Brian's views remain unquestioned in the novel, it is certainly the case that Wendy is set up as a rather vague, woolly thinker, who uses passivity as a strategy, and is easily influenced. The implication is that these weaknesses are not discouraged by her academic discipline and her association with the youth protest scene and the Krishna bookshop. All three form a feminised environment which Brian finds rather threatening.

The War between the Tates shares some of Friedan's suggested solutions to the problem of the feminine mystique. There is one clear example of a marriage which takes account of her ideas: Danielle Zimmern's informal pre-nuptial agreement with Bernie Kotelchuk involves her keeping her academic job, having a separate bank account, sharing or paying for someone else to do housekeeping, cooking and cleaning, and holidaying separately each year. Erica thinks that if she and Brian are to resume their relationship then he will agree to her working outside the home, and that the idea of a marriage contract has much to recommend it. It is clear that the Tates' marriage could metamorphose in unsuspected ways to take account of the challenge the events of the novel have offered to the idea of separate gendered spheres.

While Lurie's novel makes many similar points to those contained in *The Feminine Mystique*, it also has parallels with Friedan's new position in *The Second Stage*. Although the novel precedes the late 1970s–early 1980s economic downturn and the emergence of the New Right agenda that forms the background to *The Second Stage*, it puts into practice, particularly in the second half, some of the criticisms and concerns Friedan develops in her attack on first-stage feminist thinking and activism. Erica caricatures her friend Danielle's feminist beliefs as a hobby horse: 'a large grey-white wooden nag mounted on red rockers, unattractively and aggressively female' (p. 15). She believes Danielle's new interest in feminism to be a result of resentment caused by the break-up of her marriage: an emotional response to personal issues rather than a rational system of beliefs and political actions. She comes closest to agreeing with Danielle's views only after her own marital problems emerge; in this way the novel suggests that feminism has very little to offer happily married women, and positions it as anti-family. This association is seen very clearly in the novel's perspective on abortion and sexuality. What Friedan terms 'the rhetoric of sexual politics' (*The Second Stage*, p. 49) is associated with Wendy's, and her generation of women's, sexual freedom. Such freedom is perceived to be anti-family, and it is also shown to be highly possible that men are co-opting it for their own pleasure. The former point is clear in the structural position Wendy occupies in the novel – as the threat to a (reasonably) stable marriage; the latter is most apparent in the treatment of abortion in the text. An entire chapter is given over to three conversations related to Wendy's first pregnancy with Brian's child. In the first, Erica speaks to her own doctor and attempts to get information about abortion. Her doctor assumes that she herself is pregnant, and encourages her to proceed with the pregnancy. He sternly reminds her that abortion is illegal and that if she is trying to help a friend she is accessory to a crime. It is Brian who is able to procure the assistance required, from a male friend. The irony of this does not escape the reader: men seem to control women's reproductive choices and are associated with the pro-abortion position. In contrast Erica eventually decides that Brian should marry Wendy and bring up the child. This decision emerges in a passage where she cooks Wendy some breakfast, in which the frying eggs become a clever and visceral extended metaphor for the unborn foetus. However, Brian's attempts to persuade Wendy to go ahead with the abortion eventually succeed, allowing his relationship with her to proceed in its previous fashion, and preventing resolution by the creation of a new family, consisting of Brian, Wendy and their child. When Wendy becomes pregnant again, there is uncertainty about the identity of the father, and the novel concludes with Wendy leaving for a commune with another partner, Ralph. She quotes her new partner's view that an unmarried couple '"can split any time, so if you stick it out it's because you really dig each other"' (p. 300). Erica thinks that 'not for the last time – Wendy was repeating as her own sincere opinion statements made to her by some man for selfish ulterior purposes' and adds: '"marriage is a social contract. If everyone thought like your friend, families would break up; parents would desert their children"' (p. 301). It seems clear that the text works to associate sexual freedom and sexual politics with the counterculture, anti-family positions and with the co-option by men of feminist agendas in a similar way to *The Second Stage*. This is apparent in the novel's ironic concluding image of the peace march, hijacked by a variety of groups supporting women's and gay rights, Maoist politics and even using the opportunity to advertise local businesses and services.

The War between the Tates also makes similar points to *The Second Stage* about masculine and feminine thinking. Like Friedan, Erica feels that first-stage feminists have acquired the worst of masculine traits: 'they are loud, aggressive, competitive … practice the sort of one-upmanship usually seen only in men' (p. 191) and use bad language. Similarly, the WHEN (Women for Human Equality Now) group has made the mistake of wanting to be treated like men, disapproving of gestures such as having doors held open for them. Rather than forcing women to take on conventionally masculine, or what Friedan terms 'alpha', thinking, the novel shows the importance of 'beta' thinking. Brian's ways of justifying his actions are satirised precisely for their alpha qualities: 'he stops, tries to catch his breath. He must clarify his mind, review the situation as a whole, make a structural analysis, reject extraneous data' (p. 87); the novel works by forcing him to encounter some of the domestic and emotional problems which he usually associates with 'Erica's sphere', what Friedan terms 'the new American frontier for men, this exploration of inner space, of the "messy feelings" that are the core of personhood for us all but that for too long were awesome, mysterious, forbidden territory for men' (*The Second Stage*, p. 153).

Brian's experiences of Wendy invading his space in their small shared flat, her lack of embarrassment about matters of personal hygiene, the bad effects of these intrusions on the progress of his latest book, and his worsening relationship with his children, are all evidence not only of the importance of beta thinking, but of the relevance of some of Friedan's points about the way we structure our domestic and work lives. Similarly, Erica's admirer, Sandy Finkelstein, and the Krishna bookshop he runs, although associated by Brian with sloppy, unscholarly thinking and academic failure, are a more severe, if not sustained, threat to alpha rationalism than is at first suggested. The novel certainly implies that a relationship with Sandy, who has long been hopelessly in love with Erica, might have offered her the new emotional and domestic developments Friedan argues are necessary for women and men in the second stage.

Practice into Theory

However, *The War between the Tates* also highlights some of the ambiguities and problems inherent in Friedan's analyses in both *The Feminine Mystique* and *The Second Stage*. While Friedan's description of the feminine mystique is powerful, its accuracy as an account of what was happening to American women in the late 1950s has been questioned. Her suggestion that the mystique represented a departure from the strong position women occupied in the early decades of the century has been criticised. So has the assumption that large numbers of women in post-Second World War America were not occupied in working outside the home. Leila J. Rupp and Verta Taylor argue that: 'Betty Friedan presented the feminine mystique as a new phenomenon created in the postwar period when in fact it was simply a particular version of the traditional ideal, the successor to nineteenth-century "True Womanhood".'[15] Statistically, more women were employed outside the home in the postwar period than previously (Rupp and Taylor, p. 15). Friedan's account of the causes of the mystique is similarly open to question. The culprits she identifies: the rise of consumerism and suburbanisation, the 'sexual sell' of the advertisers, the dissemination of popularised versions of Freudian psychoanalysis and functionalist social science could all be viewed as particular manifestations of mid-twentieth-century capitalist, patriarchal ideology. Friedan never clarifies the way in which this ideology (a term not used in the book) relates to economic and social factors, nor does she examine how it connects with the individual's experience of subjectivity or selfhood. Sandra Dijkstra suggests that 'Friedan limited her attack to the more superficial enemies ... themselves not the *cause* but rather the *means*, the agents by which the subordinate condition of women is ideologically maintained.'[16] Friedan does not analyse the historical reasons why a separation between the private and public spheres was created, gendered and maintained, something which would require a more thorough historical discussion of the intersection between capitalism and patriarchy. (See for example the Marxist feminist analyses in Chapter 3.) This is apparent, for example, in the throw-away remark that 'it is perhaps beside the point to remark that bowling alleys and supermarkets have nursery facilities, while schools and colleges and scientific laboratories and government offices do not' (*The Feminine Mystique*, p. 328). Clearly, this is not beside the point: it is precisely the point that the former provide childcare facilities to encourage women to *spend* money whereas the latter do not to prevent them *earning* it.

Similarly, Friedan alternates between seeing women as the unwitting dupes of powerful forces beyond their control, and blaming them for their collusion with the feminine mystique. A trend in the book is to begin each chapter with a description of the forces oppressing women, and to conclude with an exhortation to individual women to resist these forces: 'In the last analysis, millions of able women in this free land chose, themselves, not to use the door education could have opened for them. The choice – and the responsibility – for the race back home was finally their own' (*The Feminine Mystique*, p. 159). To what extent the individual is capable of awareness of, and resistance to, a dominant ideology is a question to which the book offers no clear answer. In this way, Friedan tends to prefer analysis at the level of the individual, which contradicts her implicit argument that women share a particular economic or social position because of their gender. Zillah Eisenstein suggests that

'Friedan's claim to the rights of woman as an *individual* rests on her rejection of woman being treated as a group, which rests in a sexual-class analysis she says she rejects' (Eisenstein, p. 183). Friedan's rejection of a perception of women as a sex-class is, however, an equivocal one.

The emphasis on separate gendered 'spheres of operation' in Lurie's novel appears at first to be an indisputable fact of life: in this sense the text suggests the 'invisibility' of ideology in the same way as *The Feminine Mystique*. However, it does so in a self-conscious manner which alerts readers to the questions about the mystique which are not asked in Friedan's text, and forces them to consider several possible answers. This process relies on a number of devices: first, the deliberate clash of the main characters' perspectives; secondly, the ironic commentary on the characters; and thirdly, the movement of the plot, which introduces new characters and situations, forcing the protagonists to change, develop or confront different attitudes. In the argument about Erica taking a research assistant's position at the university we follow her changing opinions. She is first persuaded by Danielle that working outside the home would be good for her self-esteem and her relationship with her children, then confronted and affected by Brian's vehement objections on the grounds of her responsibility to home and children. Finally, and ironically, she is convinced that 'she has been exposed as selfish, greedy, and thoughtless of her family's welfare: the sort of woman one cannot trust to do the right thing' (p. 64). Both the limitations in the terms of the argument itself, such as the absence of any reference to a father's responsibilities to care for his children, and the fact that the argument is couched solely in terms of the children's rather than Erica's welfare, expose the relationship between the ideology of separate spheres, a structural system of power serving patriarchal interests, and the individual's experience of negotiating around that ideology. Further plot developments introduce the characters of Wendy Gahaghan and Sandy Finkelstein as representatives of lifestyles, perspectives and values totally new to Brian and Erica. These characters and plot movements force them, and the reader, to encounter a blurring of the demarcation between their separate gendered spheres which enables the (albeit temporary) creation of new alternative spaces and theories of the relationship between gender, social roles, and family structures. Such possibilities (for example, the woman-centred alignment of Wendy with

Erica and Danielle against Brian) enable us to question the logic and assumptions which lie behind the conventional positions the protagonists occupy at the novel's opening.

In this way, Lurie's novel is particularly adept at presenting the individual as enmeshed in a social system, as responsive to ideology though not entirely coerced by it. *The War between the Tates* therefore suggests the difficulties inherent in Friedan's model of the rational, autonomous, individual self capable of making decisions which are independent of the social system. Lurie puts this in terms of identity being 'at the mercy of circumstances, of other people's actions' (p. 45). As Erica sees it, Brian's affair makes her into the spurned wife of farce; her children's behaviour makes her an unfit mother; the developers building new ranch houses make her into a suburban housewife. Although Erica's perception of this process is limited at first to the effect of other individuals' behaviour on her own, her thinking extends outwards from the individual to society:

> It was like being on stage. The lights change from amber to blue; the scenery alters behind the actors: the drop curtain showing cottages and gardens is raised. The villagers have not moved, but now they appear awkward, small, and overdressed against the new backdrop of mountains and ruins. And nothing can be done about it. This is the worst thing about being a middle-aged woman. You have already made your choices, taken the significant moral actions of your life long ago when you were inexperienced. Now you have more knowledge of yourself and the world; you are equipped to make choices, but there are none left to make.
>
> What Danielle said is true, Erica thinks: it is better for men. Brian has an important job, he makes decisions ... But for her there are no decisions, only routines. All she can do is endure.　(pp. 45–6)

This passage criticises the idea that individuals are autonomous and self-determining by showing how such an idea only really applies to men, yet it is also structurally ironic in that Erica does go on to make various important decisions in the novel which do have effects on those around her. She is not merely a member of the 'chorus of villagers'. In this way, the novel demonstrates the complex process by which any individual is embedded in particular cultural values, rather than displaying what Bowlby has termed the 'hesitation as to victimization or agency' which occurs in *The Feminine Mystique* (Bowlby, p. 69).

The text also debates more explicitly than does Friedan the issue of the gendering of the self: it questions whether women and men really are different, and if so, asks what causes that difference. Friedan argues that women are capable of sharing a full 'humanity' with men, but her definition of humanity in *The Feminine Mystique* is culturally masculinist: identified with work outside the home, rationality and independence. She suggests at one point that 'the quality of being fully human … is not quite the same as femininity' (*The Feminine Mystique*, p. 169). Although in one sense this is a pertinent criticism of the cultural coding of masculinity as normative and femininity as deviant, Friedan's argument in *The Feminine Mystique* that women need to be educated to share in masculine values means that she inevitably devalues traditionally feminine ones and does not go as far as arguing for a breakdown in such gender stereotyping. Neither does she discuss exactly how gender difference is produced. By virtue of its plural perspectives, *The War between the Tates* offers many different views of gender difference. Brian begins with a conception of women as essentially different from men which is disturbed by the end of the novel; Danielle Zimmern perceives women as an oppressed group; Sara, a student activist, lectures Brian on their innate superiority, and Erica experiences many different developments in her own understanding of these issues. The overriding metaphor for the relation between men and women is one of warfare in the novel, but this is obviously only one of a variety of perspectives from which the reader must choose in order to engage with the text.

Perhaps the most pertinent criticism of *The Feminine Mystique*, however, concerns its class, race and heterosexist bias. Friedan's agenda is to free the white middle-class heterosexual woman from her confinement in the domestic sphere by appealing to her ability to share the values and lifestyle of white middle-class heterosexual men. She ignores the fact that many working-class black women's experience was precisely *not* one of suburban motherhood and fails to acknowledge that work outside the home can be exploitative and physically demanding for those of both sexes in manual and non-professional employment. She is also rather vague about who will do the housework and care for young children if both partners are working, and does not acknowledge the existence of different sexualities and living arrangements from those in the nuclear family. Indeed, at one point in *The Feminine Mystique* she argues that one of its worst effects is to cause an increase in male homosexuality, as if this were obviously something to be avoided. Although it is obvious that Lurie's novel is set in the same white middle-class heterosexual context, this context is severely threatened by the alternative lifestyle of the student body and the existence of the Krishna book-shop, which emphasise the limitations of an environment which in Friedan's book is perceived as normative. Brian is at one point forced to confront the possibility of parenting Wendy's black baby; he encounters a much more liberal sexual scene when he begins a relationship with her, and she eventually departs for a commune. Although these 'threats' to coupledom are frequently perceived as such, and are resolved by the novel's conclusion, they retain their ability to act as an ironic counterpoint to Brian and Erica's world in the text.

Similarly, the novel suggests some of the problems with Friedan's attitudes to sexuality, motherhood and childcare. One of the contra-dictions in *The Feminine Mystique* is its suggestion that the mystique causes sexual dysfunction, and yet, simultaneously, that it uses sex-uality as an explanation for problems that are not really sexual. Sexuality cannot be both symptomatic of a wider problem and a dis-traction from a clearer understanding of that problem. An exactly similar contradiction exists in the discussion of childcare and moth-erhood: the mystique causes poor mothering, which is bad since mothering is important, and yet 'mother-blaming' is also an effect of the mystique. Erica experiences many of the same alterations in her view of her children: she feels responsible for their welfare, and oscillates between blaming herself for neglecting them and fearing that she is smothering them. While she is sometimes able to perceive the unfairness of a social system which allots childcare responsibil-ities to her solely on the grounds of her biological sex, at other times she senses something precious and unique in a woman's ability to create and nurture a life. Wendy experiences identical shifts of per-spective, agreeing to, refusing, and finally having an abortion, and then getting pregnant again. This parallel between Erica and Wendy is important in allowing the reader to sense the contradictions sur-rounding childcare and motherhood and develop a response to them. In many of their discussions about this subject, the two women reveal the terms of the arguments they have to be limited. Erica's argument that the social contract of marriage cements the nuclear family is countered by Wendy's sense that her relationship with her unborn child is instinctive and essential: '"It's really heavy; not like some guy you're not even related to. I know already I'll never leave him; I'll always belong to him completely"' (p. 300). The clash between an understanding of motherhood as biological and an appreciation of its position in a particular social and cultural context is not resolved but is forced to exist in an uneasy dialogue. That tension is, however, explicit rather than buried as it is in *The Feminine Mystique*.

The novel is much more ambiguous about solutions than is Friedan. It shows the limitations to the individual's ability to negotiate her way out of a particular ideological impasse, while not suggesting that this is impossible, and it is much less optimistic about the role of educational institutions in improving the situation of women. One of the unsatisfactory elements of *The Feminine Mystique* is its stress on the importance of education for women as a solution to the 'problem that has no name', when earlier chapters have convincingly demonstrated just how much education is embedded in the ideology of an era, and explored how it can act as an instrument of indoctrination. The conclusion of Lurie's novel deliberately leaves unanswered the question of how much Erica and Brian's relationship will have been changed by the events in the text; it shows that educational institutions are at the mercy of particular intellectual and social trends, and it demonstrates that the individual's ability to act is always in relation to her cultural context.

The Second Stage can be criticised for many of the same reasons as *The Feminine Mystique*, for example the obvious limitations of its focus on the heterosexual nuclear family and white middle-class women, its stress on acting within the existing capitalist system, and its reliance on the individual's ability to determine her own future and resist ideological 'brainwashing'. Judith Stacey terms it 'a liberal's response to the failures of liberalism and a feminist's response to the setbacks of feminism' (Stacey, p. 224). However, *The War between the Tates* also suggests flaws in three of the new arguments Friedan develops in this text. One of the most striking elements in Lurie's novel is the use of extended political and military metaphors for gender relations. Such metaphors were particularly relevant at the time of publication given the impact of the Vietnam war on American culture and society (see Newman, pp. 104–5), but the way in which they are associated with Erica and Brian's relationship and wider relations between men and women makes larger points about the impact of language on individual subjectivity and the connections between self and society. As Erica gradually acquires the discourse of warfare and uses it against Brian, we see that the personal clearly does affect the political, and vice versa. This connection is precisely the same as that made by the radical wing of the feminist movement, which Friedan blames in *The Second Stage* for hijacking the liberal feminist agenda and emphasising sexual politics (the political nature of personal, intimate and sexual relationships and behaviour) at the expense of legal reform. Friedan's resistance to one of the most important of second-wave feminist insights involves her 'bracketing off' sexuality as a merely personal issue; *The War between the Tates* shows such a stance to be naive. When Brian tells Erica that Wendy is not her concern, she replies: "'I don't agree that it's not my concern ... That's what the 'Good Germans' said''' (p. 141). This analogy is remarkably similar to one Friedan herself makes in *The Feminine Mystique*, when she hyperbolically compares being a housewife to the dehumanisation of the concentration camps of the Second World War (pp. 265–6). At least metaphorically, then, Friedan's first book suggests the pertinence of seeing the personal as political, even though her second resists the effects and implications of a feminist activism which places that understanding at the centre of its agenda. This is clear in her positioning of the right to abortion as part of a platform which would ensure that women can make 'the choice to have children' in preference to perceiving it as an issue which relates to a woman's control over her own body and sexuality. Similarly, the novel shows the pertinence of the feminist attack on the nuclear family as a potential site for women's oppression, a perception which *The Second Stage* resists.

The War between the Tates is a novel which could be seen to work either dialectically or deconstructively. If we read the text dialectically it introduces a thesis (that heterosexual married couples operate best in separate gendered spheres), sets up an antithesis (in the form of Wendy and the lifestyle she represents) which questions that assumption, and finally reaches a synthesis which includes elements of both views. The novel encourages us both to invest in this process and to view it ironically: we may feel on reaching the end of the novel that important developments have occurred in the characters' lives which reflect significant changes in society, or we may sense an ambivalence about the idea of progress and a return, instead, to the status quo. If we read the novel deconstructively, then it works by setting up binary oppositions: pairs of opposed terms which are mutually dependent, one of which has more status and power and is thus dominant (for example, Brian and Erica; men and women; the university and the Krishna bookshop). As the text progresses, these terms are shown to be less separable than at first appeared and by the end of the novel the distinctions between each term, and the hierarchical relationship in which they are placed, have collapsed. The novel can thus be seen to echo, but also to question, Friedan's dialectical model in *The Second Stage*. Friedan moves from the thesis of first-stage activism against the feminine mystique, to the antithesis that the *feminist* mystique has gone too far in encouraging women to echo alpha, or masculinist, ways of thinking and living. In its emphasis on a radical agenda concentrating on sexual politics, it has separated 'ordinary' women from the aims of the movement. Her synthesis involves an attempt to revalue the traditionally feminine qualities (associated with nurturing, beta thinking) and divorce them from gender stereotyping so that they come to be a priority for men and women. In its ambivalent conclusion, where a small child asks '"Mommy, will the war end now?"' (p. 310), *The War between the Tates* suggests the idealism involved in this progressive model of human development. It also suggests its gender bias, since the linear, rational, evolutionary implications of such a model are decidedly masculinist, and develops the contradictions between this model and the priority accorded beta (non-linear, intuitive) thinking. It exposes a similar ambiguity in *The Second Stage*'s perception of gender identity, which alternates between a dialectical model of progress towards an androgynous future world free of gender-stereotyped personality traits and lifestyles, and a positive valuation of conventionally feminine qualities.

Conclusion

The novel thus foregrounds its ambiguity on a number of issues which plague Friedan's works, in a way which avoids both compromise and the kind of contradictions which operate solely at the level of connotation or implication. Through the process of investment in different characters' clashing viewpoints and the development of the plot, Lurie's text forces us to form our own opinions about similar ideas to those in Friedan's two important liberal feminist texts. We can thus arrive at some important conclusions about liberal feminism. Its adherence to culturally acceptable ideas about the individual's relation to ideology and society, to normative (if contradictory) models of gender difference, and to conventional ideas about political action, progress and change make it clear that liberal feminism has an investment in the structure of our society as it currently exists, and is unwilling to consider moving outside that structure. While this is one of its greatest limitations, it is equally obvious that this is why liberal feminism has been the most popular and least threatening of feminist theories and political movements. This creates a situation which makes a liberal feminist agenda strategically important in order to work for specific feminist aims, such as the campaign to pass the Equal Rights Amendment.

3

Marxist Feminism

Introduction

If liberal feminism is limited by its reluctance to consider transforming the kind of society in which we live, the same certainly cannot be said of Marxist feminism. The majority of Marxist feminists believe that liberation for women will not occur within capitalist patriarchal society as we know it. They advocate a synthesis, development or transformation of Marxist and feminist theory in order to explain and end the oppression of women. The term 'Marxist feminist' is not the only one associated with this particular theoretical position: other critics and commentators prefer to define themselves as socialist or materialist feminists. This may be because they wish to align themselves with a broader tradition of Left thinking, or because they value an insistence on a materialist conception of the world, without confining their understanding of materialism to Marx's. Although such distinctions may seem insignificant, they are important, as Landry and MacLean suggest when discussing the impact of McCarthyism on terminology in the USA:

> The broader or more inclusive – but also historically less politically loaded – term *socialist* is often employed even where there is a primary, direct engagement with texts and controversies from the Marxist tradition. Whether the move to *materialist* constitutes a comparable evasion ... remains to be seen.[1]

Although by no means absent in the USA, Marxist feminism has been of more significance in the UK, as a consequence of the greater impact, organisation and political importance of the British Labour movement and socialist intellectual traditions.[2]

To understand Marxist feminism, we clearly need to begin with a discussion of those of Karl Marx's ideas which have been most important for feminists. This is complicated by the fact that Marx himself had very little to say about women, and that it was his collaborator Friedrich Engels who, in *The Origin of the Family, Private Property and the State* (1884), wrote what many consider to be the most influential text for Marxist feminism. However, much of Marx's thought has provided a basic grounding for further specific feminist work. What first strikes most readers of Marx as different from their usual way of perceiving the world is his anti-idealism. We tend to assume that human beings are free individuals who have ideas about the world around them: ideas which have an impact on the sort of society in which we live, and on the relations we have with other individuals. Marx's materialism turns this on its head; our lived experience as individuals, and our ideas about the world, are a result of the material conditions around us, or the way our society is organised economically to create the means of sustaining and reproducing itself. The theory of dialectical historical materialism argues that history demonstrates ongoing change and development in these material conditions, which occurs as a result of the inevitable conflicts created by specific modes of production, or ways of organising the economic basis of society. Marx therefore saw the transition from a feudal to a capitalist economic system to be crucial in determining the lives of individuals of particular social classes. Under capitalism, the dominant class of the bourgeoisie is engaged in a continual struggle with the subordinate working class, or proletariat. Where the profit incentive is crucial, and private ownership by the bourgeoisie dominates, a member of the proletariat has only one thing to offer: labour power. In return for his labour he receives a wage which assures his own and his family's survival, but the surplus value created by his labour is hived off by the capitalist to create higher profits. The tension between the capitalist drive to increase profits and the worker's drive to increase his share of what his labour has contributed to create will eventually result in revolution. A communist economic system of collective ownership of the means of production will then be created. At any point in history, then, an individual's sense of his own relation to the world and other individuals has more to do with his class position and his role in the economic system which surrounds him than he realises.[3] The reason why he may not be aware of this is because of the role of ideology. Ideology can be defined as the way in which ideas, beliefs and common perceptions relate to the class and economic structures of a society. Marx suggested that 'the ideas of the ruling class are in every epoch the ruling ideas'.[4] In other words, dominant ideologies maintain the interests of dominant social groups.

The fact that the male pronoun has been used throughout the previous discussion of the labourer is intentional. Marx certainly assumed as typical a male labourer working outside the home, supporting a wife and children within it. This 'division of labour' was not explicitly analysed in his own work, but was crucial to the argument of Engels's *The Origin of the Family, Private Property and the State*, which took account of the work of reproduction as well as that of production. Engels argues that men's dominance over women arose alongside capitalism with the necessity for the bourgeois class to ensure that only legitimate heirs inherited their growing wealth. Pre-capitalist societies were, according to Engels, matriarchal, with women in control of the household, their work in the home, and inheritance. His remedy for women's oppression is their entry into the wage-labour force, and indeed, this remained the 'official' Marxist line on women's liberation throughout the first half of this century.[5] A history of Marxist feminist theory is a history of the attempt 'first to include women into and then progressively to transform and ultimately to abandon much of the Marxist problematic'.[6] Marxist feminism can also be seen as part of a more general neo-Marxist tendency to question and develop orthodox Marxist tenets. Initially then, Marxist feminist work discussed the specific situation of women in conventional Marxist terms. It analysed, for example, their involvement in social reproduction: the daily and intergenerational re-creation through housework and childcare of the labourer's ability to labour. In particular, this early work was concerned with the question of whether or not women's unpaid domestic labour in the home could be said to generate surplus value (or hived-off profits for the capitalist). Did this work constitute the main explanation for women's oppression in capitalism, and should it be remunerated in some way other than through the notional 'family wage'?[7] Later theorists criticised this body of work for, amongst other failings, its lack of recognition of women's work outside the home in the wage-labour force. For many Marxist feminists, it is women's function as a 'reserve army' of cheap labour, available when necessary for capitalist accumulation but returning to the home when not, that is important in explaining their subordination to men.[8] Other factors such as job segregation by sex (the fact that women are concentrated in employment such as childcare and cleaning which mirrors the sort of work they do in the home) are also significant.[9] Some have pointed to the fact that women do a 'double day' of work, since even if they do work outside the home, they still do more of the work in it. Others have argued that women's oppression can only be explained by their interlocking roles in production, or work outside the home, and reproduction, or work within it, since involvement in both spheres tends to prevent full commitment to either.[10]

Marxist feminists have been particularly concerned to theorise the relationship between capitalism and patriarchy. While conventional Marxist thinking suggests that patriarchy is a symptom of capitalism which will disappear with communism, the most important intervention of Marxist feminists has been to argue that patriarchal social systems preceded capitalism.[11] However, Marxist feminism also rejects the simple use of patriarchy as a trans-historical term, arguing that it needs to be discussed in precise historical and economic ways to give it any analytical purchase. In other words, we need to account for how patriarchy and capitalism work together, sometimes to reinforce, and possibly on occasions to conflict with, each other in specific contexts.[12] Another way in which Marxist feminist debate has moved beyond orthodox Marxism is in its willingness to consider the roles of ideology, sexuality, race and the unconscious in explaining human behaviour. The vexed issue of exactly how independent any ideology is from the economic system of a particular society is perhaps most apparent in the case of gender ideology. As we shall see, many Marxist feminists have been willing to argue that ideology can be just as material and important as economic factors in analysing a patriarchal society. Equally, the struggle to demonstrate that gender is as important as class in any individual's lived experience has meant that other influences, such as race, ethnicity and sexuality have increasingly been accepted as playing an important part in Marxist feminist theory.[13]

Sheila Rowbotham, *Woman's Consciousness: Man's World* (1973)

In its opening discussion of Betty Friedan's *The Feminine Mystique*, Sheila Rowbotham's *Woman's Consciousness: Man's World* makes the differences between liberal and Marxist feminism particularly clear. Although Rowbotham admires Friedan's account of 'the problem that has no name' she criticises the book's weakness at suggesting remedies, terming it 'shuffling about within capitalism'.[14] In contrast, her own discussion of women's oppression and suggestions for their liberation relies on the understanding that

> while it is true that women were subordinated to men before capitalism and that this has affected the position of women in capitalist society, it is also true that the context of oppression we fight against now is specific to a society in which the capacity of human beings to create is appropriated by privately owned capital and in which the things produced are exchanged as commodities.
>
> (p. xiii)

She argues that liberal feminism ignores the need to consider the economic structure of our society, but suggests that orthodox Marxism is equally guilty of underplaying the importance of the family as a site for both the production of oppressive ideologies for women, and their exploitation through domestic labour. Only by understanding women's double role in the wage-labour force and in the home can liberation be achieved.

The importance Rowbotham accords gender ideology in explaining the position of women is obvious from the structure of her book. The second chapter discusses her own negative image of feminism as a seventeen-year-old girl, her encounter with orthodox Marxism at university, and her attempts to find a space within Marxism for an understanding of her own experience as a woman. In the third chapter Rowbotham examines some of the ways in which gender ideology operates to obscure both its own functioning, and its oppressiveness for women. She uses the analogy of the three-way dressing-table mirror, which at certain angles presents an endlessly repeating self-image of the woman looking in it, to indicate the multiple, fractured and artificial image of woman in patriarchal capitalist society. To end oppression an oppressed group must become conscious of its self-image and work to change it. Rowbotham argues that language, the unconscious, the body and sexuality are all important areas where women need to take control in order to liberate themselves. One of the great strengths of the book is this attempt to situate the personal as political in a specifically Marxist sense. The reader thus follows a process of 'consciousness raising', moving from personal to more abstract political ideas, and ultimately questioning the distinction between them. In the remaining chapters, Rowbotham examines the role of women's work in the

family, in the wage-labour force, and as consumers. Capitalist patriarchal ideology maintains that the family is a safe, feminised place
of retreat from the brutish masculine world of wage-labour. This
division of labour is seen to be a consequence of biology rather than
economics. Despite the suggestion that housework and childcare
are not 'real work' because they are not part of the commodity system, this work is actually crucial in ensuring the reproduction of
labour power, and thus in maintaining the capitalist system as it
currently exists. The struggle for equal opportunities to work outside the home, although an important feminist demand, does not of
itself adjust the structural division of labour, because women still do
most of the work in the home, and are thus left with a double load.
As a result, it is possible for the capitalist system to exploit women
as cheap labourers, segment the labour force, and segregate women
in jobs which fit with a particular ideology of femininity, or resemble their role in the home.

Rowbotham's answers to the question of how to achieve liberation for women concentrate on changes in contemporary capitalism
which force a recognition of its contradictory nature for women. The
family contains traces of earlier, feudal relations which create what
Rowbotham terms 'friction' (p. 63) in women's consciousness. The
significance of the family has become such that 'it sags with the
weight of its unrealized hopes almost before it creates itself' (p. 60).
Although it is reasonably efficient at maintaining the capitalist system in its present form, it is also 'irrational' as 'a system of organiz-
ing the reproduction of human labour which is completely designed
to produce commodities efficiently and has freed itself from all earlier property relations' (p. 66). Equally, the fact that women's work
outside the home is in tension with their work within it can be used
'like a crowbar to crank open the tender and unprotected slits in Mr
Moneybags's defences' (p. 102). Domestic labour has become less
satisfying for women because it is more commodified, involving
serving goods produced and purchased elsewhere, rather than the
home production of food and clothes. Sexuality is also increasingly
commodified, and thus has an unrealisable significance for women.
The result of all these changes is to 'produce the shifts and fissures
which make the growth of new movements [like women's libera-
tion] possible' (p. 116). In this situation working-class women are in
the most ambiguous, and therefore the most potentially subversive
position, Rowbotham suggests, and a Marxist feminist movement
must begin with them.

Michèle Barrett, *Women's Oppression Today* (1980)

The first edition of Michèle Barrett's *Women's Oppression Today*, originally subtitled *Problems in Marxist Feminist Analysis* has been termed 'exemplary of both the strengths and weaknesses of the best white British materialist feminism' (Landry and MacLean, p. 25). The aim of the book is to 'develop an analysis of women's oppression in contemporary capitalism that represents a genuine synthesis of Marxist and feminist perspectives'.[15] This task is very necessary, according to Barrett, given the rise of New Right ideology, the failure of the Left to take account of 'the political character of personal life' (p. 2), and the analytical weaknesses of radical feminism. The book begins with a rigorous consideration of 'some conceptual problems in Marxist feminist analysis' (p. 8), which includes a critique of the terms 'patriarchy', 'reproduction' and 'ideology'. While criticising the ahistoricism and biologism of radical feminist usage of the term patriarchy, Barrett accepts that most Marxist feminist discussions either assert patriarchy's complete independence from capitalism, or suggest that it is merely a symptom of it. As a result, she argues, the term is of very limited use in a Marxist feminist analysis. Equally, Barrett is sceptical about the stress in Marxist theory on women's role in reproducing the labour force through their work in the home. She argues that the domestic labour debate mixed up biological reproduction and social reproduction, and thus failed to specify why it should be women who are assigned the role of homeworker. She claims that the sexual division of labour is not merely a consequence of the requirements of capitalism, although it is now utilised by it. Lastly, Barrett concerns herself with the role of ideology, and suggests that a more flexible understanding of the concept than orthodox Marxism allows, which accords it some degree of autonomy from the economic context which surrounds it, is particularly helpful in explaining women's oppression in contemporary capitalist societies.

Having clarified her theoretical position, Barrett then proceeds to discuss women's oppression in terms of sexuality, culture, education, the division of labour, the family and the state. The discussion of sexuality in Chapter 2 rejects a radical feminist explanation for the sexual exploitation of women which points to men's attempt to gain control over women's ability to give birth. It also questions the orthodox Marxist explanation of the 'functional fit' between capitalism and the male-dominated nuclear family. Instead, Barrett argues that ideology is crucial, in intersection with the capitalist economic system which underpins it, in regulating sexual behaviour. This regulation takes the form of the close association between gender identity and sexual practice, apparent in the idea that certain types of erotic behaviour define one as a gendered being. Appropriate sexual behaviour is only that which could give rise to biological reproduction. Barrett's analysis of the cultural oppression of women focuses on literary texts, where she argues that the conditions of production and consumption are of equal significance to those of representation. In other words, we must consider the situations in which a text is written, published and read as well as what is contained between the covers of the book. When analysing a text's contents in terms of gender ideology, we need to be alert to processes of stereotyping, compensation (the creation of images of women which replace their real powerlessness with an exaggerated moral worth), collusion (the suggestion that women are responsible for, or agree with, their oppression) and recuperation (the attempt to defuse the subversiveness of ideas or individuals that threaten the status quo).

Barrett sees the education system as an agent for the reproduction of both class relations and patriarchal gender ideology. She criticises Marxist analyses which have failed to fit gender oppression into their conception of education. As a significant means by which capitalism is maintained, education serves to position women in appropriate positions within the wage-labour force, as well as encouraging them to value their role in domestic labour. These aims are achieved in a number of ways: the promotion of an ideology of appropriate feminine and masculine behaviour; the sexual segregation of the teaching profession, both hierarchically (more head teachers are male than female) and by discipline (more men than women teach the sciences); the channelling of children into subjects which reflect and promote the sexual division of labour; and definitions of 'legitimate knowledge' (p. 147) which devalue disciplines and ways of learning associated with women. According to Barrett, the family is another area where greater explanatory power should be afforded ideology. It is in the promotion of what Barrett terms an 'ideology of familialism' (p. 206) that women's oppression can be most clearly perceived. This ideology (which we might best understand by thinking of the image of the family in soap-powder advertisements, for example) bears only a loose relation to the actual organisation of most families. Women have always worked outside the home more than ideology suggests, and the family has always been more diverse than the image of it as 'a small group of co-residing blood relatives' (p. 223) implies. Barrett argues that no one particular social group benefits unambiguously from the institution of the family, and that it cannot be proved that capitalism demands the current family structure for its own survival. However, she does suggest that familial ideology and the economic organisation of the household reinforce one another, particularly in the encouragement of consumption of household goods. Reallocating childcare is seen to be particularly important in changing the structure and ideology of the family, and thus achieving liberation for women.

Barrett's argument about feminism and the state hinges on its role as regulator of the systems of oppression discussed earlier in the book. Welfare and tax legislation are designed to support the 'family wage', and the medical and social work professions tend to pathologise women's social problems, so that mental illness, rather than social subordination, becomes an explanation for criminal behaviour in women. Barrett queries liberal feminist insistence on the necessity for active involvement in national state politics. She warns of the dangers of reformism, which could involve the recuperation of the feminist agenda, the extension of control over women, and the failure to affect the real sources of women's oppression. However, she also suggests that 'to reject this level of struggle altogether is to lapse into the romance of anarchism' (p. 246). For Barrett, women's liberation and the overthrow of capitalism are linked processes which would require the reallocation of childcare responsibilities, the destruction of the dependence (real or not) of women on a male wage, and the transformation of gender ideology.

Doris Lessing, *The Golden Notebook* (1962)

Doris Lessing's *The Golden Notebook* was an extremely significant novel for many women. Gayle Greene documents some experiences of reading the book, which demonstrate that it involved a process of 'consciousness raising' about their own lives, relationships and feelings which made many women active feminists.[16] This is despite the fact that Lessing herself has never been anything other than sceptical about feminism as a movement and has been unwilling to identify herself as a feminist. Greene argues convinc-

ingly that Lessing's stance towards feminism is a consequence of
the amount of energy she expended in the communist movement in
both Southern Rhodesia (now Zimbabwe) and Britain (Greene,
p. 28). Lessing was a communist throughout her twenties and thir-
ties, and only left the Party after the invasion of Hungary in 1956.
In the preface to *The Golden Notebook* she identifies herself, somewhat ironically, as an 'old Red'.[17] The heroine of the novel, Anna
Wulf, is, as Lessing was herself, involved in the British Communist
Party. She is living off the royalties from her first novel, about her
experiences in South Africa, but she now has writer's block. She
feels that anything she could write would be pointless when there
is such horror in the world because it would merely create an
untruthful version of reality. *The Golden Notebook* is set against the
background of the emergence of the Cold War and the declining
popularity of communism. It goes into great detail about left-wing
political activism and orthodox Marxist theory, but Anna's growing
sense of disillusionment with Party doctrines is clear throughout
the text. It is related to her understanding of herself as a woman,
and her struggle to define what a 'free woman' is. Although the
novel is concerned with broad questions of political involvement,
and how the individual can have an effect on national and international events, such questions are related just as much to the politics
of gender as to those of class. The text was unique at the time of
publication in its detailed descriptions of physical processes like
sex, menstruation and mothering in women's lives, and in its
attempt to deal seriously with mental experimentation and definitions of sanity and insanity. Rachel Bowlby termed it 'the first tam-
pax in world literature'![18]

Perhaps more relevant than any thematic concerns, however, is
the shape and structure of the novel: in the preface Lessing identifies this attempt to 'talk through shape' as the most important
aspect of the book (p. 13). As well as considering thematically the
issues just mentioned, the novel is innovatively structured to make
the same points. Anna keeps four coloured notebooks in which she
writes about different aspects of her life: in the black notebook she
discusses her writing, in the red she deals with politics, in the yel-
low she experiments with possibilities for new stories and novels,
and she uses the blue notebook as a diary. Extracts from these notebooks follow each other in sequence, and are concluded by an inner
'golden' notebook, where she joins the divided aspects of her life
and writing together again. The notebook extracts are surrounded

by framing chapters which form a novel called 'Free Women'. Initially we think that 'Free Women' is an objective account of events in Anna's life authored not by her but by an omniscient narrator. However, at the end of the inner golden notebook, Anna is given a sentence by her lover Saul Green to use when writing her next novel. This sentence opens the first 'Free Women' section, so we realise that it is actually the novel Anna is finally able to write after her writer's block is over. If 'Free Women' were read on its own, it would strike the reader as a very conventional text, with a straightforward linear narrative, recognisable plot and character development, and chapter summaries to help the reader. The status of 'Free Women' within *The Golden Notebook* is thus very significant: is it a parody of the type of conventional realist novel Lessing has previously written but now rejects, or is it something to which she thinks we ultimately have to return? Related to this is the fact that *The Golden Notebook* is full of other novels within novels, and characters who are doubled fictional creations of other characters. The text's experimentation with the conventions of the novel, and its innovative shape, have encouraged many critics to align it with postmodernist fiction (see Chapter 6), although others have noted Lessing's reluctance to abandon some sort of order, morality and political purpose in the text.[19]

Theory into Practice

The Golden Notebook takes Anna through a process of discovery: the discovery that Marxism is failing, particularly in its account of women's experiences and oppression. However, it also shows Anna's residual loyalty to Marxism, and her struggle to synthesise its class-based analysis with her awareness of the significance of patriarchy. In this sense, the text enacts what both Rowbotham and Barrett attempt to theorise, as Anna tries to fit analysis of women's issues into Communist Party ideology, and reconcile an awareness of the significance of gender with what Barrett terms the 'biographically prior commitment to the struggle for socialism' (p. 3). This is particularly well demonstrated in a passage of the novel which shows Anna spending afternoons canvassing for the Communist Party in a North London by-election. Anna is joined in this task by some housewives, who are the only people available in the afternoons. A discussion follows about how to dress to visit a working-class area: is it 'cheating' to dress down, or intimidating to dress 'too posh' (p. 159)? On the doorsteps Anna is met by women busy caring for children who are better dressed than they are. All mention that they vote the same way as their husbands, who vote Labour. Anna thinks:

> Five lonely women going mad quietly by themselves, in spite of husband and children or rather because of them. The quality they all had: self doubt. A guilt because they were not happy. The phrase they all used: 'There must be something wrong with me.' Back in the campaign HQ I mentioned these women to the woman in charge for the afternoon. She said: 'Yes, wherever I go canvassing, I get the heeby-jeebies. This country's full of women going mad all by themselves.' A pause, then she added, with a slight aggressiveness, the other side of the self-doubt, the guilt shown by the women I'd talked to: 'Well, I used to be the same until I joined the Party and got myself a purpose in life.' I've been thinking about this – the truth is, these women interest me much more than the election campaign. Election Day: Labour in, reduced majority. Communist Candidate loses deposit.   (p. 161)

The passage emphasises the inefficacy of an orthodox Marxist conception of these women's subordinate position and implies that it can only be understood in terms of the intersection of patriarchy and capitalism. The women's involvement in domestic labour and social reproduction is important, but so is gender ideology, seen in the stress on clothing and appearance. They are encouraged to sacrifice their own well-being for their children's, and to perceive their dissatisfaction in terms of their own failings, or incipient mental illness, rather than as the result of a problem in society. An analysis which focused solely on their patriarchal oppression, however, would equally fail to appreciate the ways in which they are divided from each other by class, and the fact that such divisions serve to prevent women working together to liberate themselves. The passage also suggests some of the possible problems which Barrett identifies with attempts to engage in state politics. The vote has little significance in these women's lives when patriarchal convention dictates that they use it the same way as their husbands. The Communist Party candidate loses his deposit, failing to split the Labour Party vote, demonstrating the ambivalent idea of democracy contained in the 'first-past-the-post' British electoral system.

Anna's thoughts about Jean Barker, the wife of a minor Party official, make other significant points about the intersection of capitalism and patriarchy. Jean is a woman who has developed a habit of saying what, according to Communist Party doctrine, should not be said:

> Jean works as a manager of a canteen. Long hours. Keeps her flat and her children and herself very well. Secretary of local Party branch. She is dissatisfied with herself. 'I'm not doing enough. I mean the Party's not enough, I get fed up, just paper work, like an office, doesn't mean anything.' Laughs, nervously. 'George' – (her husband) – 'says that's the incorrect attitude, but I don't see why I should always have to bow down. I mean, they're wrong often enough, aren't they?' Laughs. 'I decided to do something worthwhile for a change … I mean, something different. So now I have a class of backward children on Saturday afternoons … not Party children, just ordinary children.' (p. 162)

Jean's work in the wage-labour force as a canteen manager (work which appears to fit with ideas of job segregation by sex) and in the home means that she is in effect doing a double day, but even when this is accompanied by voluntary work for the Party, she is dissatisfied. None of this work makes her feel worthwhile because in each role she remains in a subordinate position, unable to exercise her obvious talents. She resists her husband's arguments that this is the 'incorrect' attitude, stressing that men are often wrong, and questioning her own subjection to them. But she continually replaces criticisms of male domination, or communist orthodoxy, with statements turned on herself, or defuses those criticisms with laughter. It is clear in this instance that patriarchy and capitalism work to reinforce each other, and that Communist Party structures and orthodox Marxist ideology support patriarchal oppression.

The Golden Notebook makes the importance of women's interlocking roles in the family and in wage labour clear, through the device of creating a heroine who fills neither position. Anna's profits from her first book mean that she does not have to work to support herself. She is not married, nor part of a conventional nuclear family, although she does have a daughter. She speculates with her friend Molly about whether it is these unusual circumstances that constitute freedom for women, or whether she is still defined in terms of relationships with men, even if she appears to be outside them. The novel thus bears out Barrett's point that the ideology of familialism affects even those women whose lives do not conform to the orthodox Marxist definition of the family household. It also provides examples of the actual oppression of women who do fill more conventional positions in the family. Anna and Molly are particularly contrasted with Marion, the wife of Molly's ex-husband Richard, who has become an important businessman. Marion has brought up three children, cared for the home, hosted dinner parties to help her husband's career, and, after discovering Richard's affair, has begun to drink heavily. This is another example of what Barrett terms the 'insidious process by which social problems … are accommodated to a medical model of individual pathology' (p. 238). As the novel progresses she slowly extricates herself from her marriage and her dependence on men, using Anna as a role model. However, Anna is not immune to the problems which beset Marion. In caring for her daughter, and in her relationship with her lover Michael she suffers just as much from what she terms the 'housewife's disease':

> It must be about six o'clock. My knees are tense. I realize that what I used to refer to … as 'the housewife's disease' has taken hold of me. The tension in me, so that peace has already gone away from me, is because the current has already been switched on: I must-dress-Janet-get-her-breakfast-send-her-off-to-school-get-Michael's-breakfast-don't-forget-I'm-out-of-tea-etc.-etc. With this useless but apparently unavoidable tension resentment is also switched on. Resentment against what? An unfairness. That I should have to spend so much of my time worrying over details. The resentment focuses itself on Michael; although I know with my intelligence it has nothing to do with Michael. And yet I do resent him, because he will spend his day, served by secretaries, nurses, women in all kinds of capacities, who will take this weight off him … Long ago … I learned that the resentment, the anger, is impersonal. It is the disease of women in our time.
>
> (p. 298)

Anna's analysis here is particularly apposite in suggesting the weight of women's routine responsibilities in the home when contrasted with men's. She is aware that job segregation by sex, coupled with a patriarchal ideology of femininity as servile, means that other women will remove these responsibilities from Michael. She also understands that as an individual, Michael is not to blame for the structural inequalities of the patriarchal capitalist system, although he benefits from them. The metaphor of disease in the body politic is very appropriate in suggesting the individual's place in this larger system and points out the *social* causes of apparently individual problems. That the demands of childcare are particularly onerous for women is obvious in Anna's growing sense of freedom when she reluctantly lets Janet go to boarding school: 'I haven't moved, at ease, in time, since Janet was born. Having a child means being conscious of the clock, never being free of something that has to be done at a certain moment ahead. An Anna is coming to life that died when Janet was born' (p. 480).

However, the novel also suggests, like Barrett and Rowbotham, the importance of sexuality, the body and fantasy in explaining women's oppression under patriarchy and capitalism. Whereas the men in the novel share a very mechanistic understanding of sexual pleasure, the women '"have got more sense than to use words like physical and emotional as if they didn't connect"' (p. 48). Female sexual experience cannot be reduced to questions such as whether or not the vaginal orgasm exists, but is intimately bound up with issues like love and trust. In this way, Lessing divorces sexuality from procreation and essential gender identity in the way Barrett advocates, and demonstrates how it responds to social pressures. As Anna's fictional creation Ella states when failing to achieve orgasm with a man she does not love: 'for women like me, integrity isn't chastity, it isn't fidelity, it isn't any of the old words. Integrity is the orgasm' (p. 292). For women conditioned to rely on men for protection and status, it is not surprising that sexual pleasure is dependent on emotional stability. As Rowbotham suggests, 'our consciousness of our orgasms is part not only of the total relationship with the men we are with, but also of our total situation in relation to our bodies, other women, and the world outside' (p. 44). She argues that women learn to experience their bodies and sexuality in male-defined ways: 'we substitute our own experience of our genitals, our menstruation, our orgasm, our menopause, for an experience determined by men' (p. 35). Such 'colonisation' is apparent in Anna's account of a day when her period starts, and she struggles to resist feelings of uncleanliness and irritability which she is aware have more to do with social expectations than her body's physical processes. According to Rowbotham and Barrett, in order to liberate themselves, women must explore their own sexuality and the politics of the personal, and *The Golden Notebook* certainly begins this process; indeed it can be said to take the reader on the same process of consciousness raising which Rowbotham describes:

> It is one thing to encounter a concept, quite another to understand it. In order to understand a general idea like male hegemony it is necessary first to perceive in a whole series of separate moments how this has affected you. Then these moments have to be communicated. This is part of the total process of female self-recognition. It is the way through which we start to make our own language, and discover our own reflections. The confirmation of our understanding comes through our organization and our action.
>
> (p. 39)

The extent to which the ideology of femininity which surrounds Anna is shown to be independent of the economic system in which she lives is an issue which concerns Lessing in the novel. Barrett suggests that ideology, although in the last instance determined by the material basis of society, has some degree of independence and influence in determining women's lives. She also considers the related debate in contemporary postmodernist and poststructuralist theory which suggests that language and discourse do not reflect reality so much as construct our understanding of it. (See Chapters 5 and 6 for further discussion of these issues.) *The Golden Notebook* addresses the same issues in Anna's vexed attempt to overcome her writer's block and begin writing something which will be truthful and valuable. She is aware that her novel 'Frontiers of War' was an incredibly nostalgic account of her experiences in South Africa, and many of the black notebooks are filled with attempts to rewrite this part of her life more authentically. However, she acknowledges her failure in this respect: 'I read this over today, for the first time since I wrote it. It's full of nostalgia, every word loaded with it, although at the time I wrote it I thought I was being "objective"' (p. 150). *The Golden Notebook* is filled with many different texts: newspaper cuttings, reviews, drafts of novels, plans for novels, stories, plays and film scripts, which is ironic for someone with writer's block. The fact that each of these texts presents differing versions of reality could easily suggest agreement with the idea that texts, discourses and language construct our versions of reality, or that ideology is just as 'material' as economic factors in explaining the world around us. However, the novel also makes clear that the economic ultimately underpins many of these ideological and discursive practices, for example in the continual attempts of film-makers to interest Anna in selling the rights to 'Frontiers of War', with the proviso that drastic changes in plot and characterisation would be necessary to make the film a commercial success, or in the obvious point that Anna's own position is dependent on the fact that her novel was enough of a success to make her financially independent.

This last point makes Barrett's stress on the necessity of considering the conditions of production and reception of a work of literature when interpreting it appear to be extremely significant. Anna's financial independence allows her the freedom to make informed decisions about the sort of text she will write next; the attempts to 'commercialise' and commodify 'Frontiers of War' can be resisted merely because she is not in a desperate financial position; thus the writing of literature is shown to be a part of the capitalist system of commodity production. In contrast, the notebooks appear to be a privatised form of 'counterculture' which we feel privileged to read, temporarily forgetting as we do so that Lessing's novel is published by a profit-centred publishing industry, which may even use its significance for twentieth-century feminism to increase sales (see, for example, the blurb on the jacket of the Flamingo edition).

Practice into Theory

Lessing comments on the novel's 'commodification' in the preface, where she suggests that the education system is wrong to prescribe her text on reading lists: 'Why spend months and years writing thousands of words about one book, or even one writer, when there are hundreds of books waiting to be read. You don't see that you are the victim of a pernicious system' (pp. 16–17). However, it is equally possible that the experience of reading the text could be a transformative one which alerts students to exactly those economic and ideological processes of oppression which Marxist feminists criticise. The conclusion to the preface offers a more optimistic perception of literature as 'alive and potent and fructifying and able to promote thought and discussion *only* when its plan and shape and intention are not understood, because that moment of seeing the shape and plan and intention is also the moment when there isn't anything more to be got out of it' (p. 21). Lessing suggests that struggling with meaning and interpretation is positive, and that by engaging in this process, the individual is able to question and possibly come to resist her positioning by ideological and economic pressures. In this way, Lessing addresses a central problem for both Rowbotham and Barrett: the extent of individual agency in a capitalist patriarchal system, and the efficacy of such a system's attempts to sustain itself. This problem tends to be discussed in one of two ways: either the system is completely flawless and thus there is little freedom for individual resistance, or the system is imperfect and its 'mistakes' provide opportunities for individual subversion. Rowbotham gives both answers at different points in her text. Barrett's position is to acknowledge the power of the system over the individual while suggesting that social changes in late capitalism may encourage some degree of liberation for women. Lessing sees her text (or, more accurately, an 'open minded' reading of it) as fulfilling a conventional liberal humanist purpose: to make its readers think, improve their self-awareness and thus encourage their individual growth. Her perception of the relationship between the individual and the economic and ideological systems which surround her is therefore profoundly different from Rowbotham's and Barrett's. Rowbotham and Barrett are much more doubtful about the extent of the individual's freedom to act and think in ways which are unaffected by those systems. Although initially profoundly pessimistic about this issue, *The Golden Notebook* finally moves forward from an apparent nihilism to suggest that as an individual Anna is ultimately capable of having ideas and making decisions which can affect her environment. (This is seen, for example, in the position and importance of the inner golden notebook and the self-realisations contained within it in relation to the other component parts of the novel.)

The scepticism with which Anna tackles issues of moral, political, and literary responsibility in the main body of the text is certainly significant, however. The novel's experimental shape and technical innovations arguably prioritise text and ideology to the extent that they question Barrett's ultimate adherence, however qualified, to materialism and economism. If we choose to read the novel as a postmodernist text (and there are problems with such a reading which have been discussed earlier), then we can see it as endorsing the view that our understanding of the world is intimately related to our immersion in different textual or discursive versions of it. When Anna pastes a series of newspaper cuttings into her diary she is pointing out not only the casual way in which the horrific world events they contain are discussed, but the possibility that our relationship with these events is an entirely textual one. The difficulty of distinguishing between many different versions of events is also an urgent issue for Anna. Psychoanalysis, for example, is considered to be another possible way of explaining her problems. She undergoes regular therapeutic sessions with an analyst she nicknames 'Mother Sugar', whose real name (ironically enough) is Mrs Marks, and many of the diary entries concentrate on retelling and interpreting Anna's dreams. Lessing makes little attempt to reconcile psychoanalytic interpretations with Marxist, or feminist, ones. Instead, it could be argued that the novel offers each of them as rival narratives with equal ability to explain Anna's situation. This 'incredulity towards metanarratives'[20] or the sense that there is little point in searching for one all-powerful framework with which to explain the world, is perhaps the most obvious criticism of Barrett and Rowbotham's Marxist idea that the material, or economic basis of our society is the most important factor in determining an individual's life and a society's way of organising itself.

Related to this issue is the novel's greater flexibility in discussing issues of race in connection with class and gender. Barrett acknowledges in the new introduction to the revised edition of *Women's Oppression Today* (1988) its weaknesses in this and other similar respects. She admits that her own analysis was insufficiently attentive to the ways in which black women's experiences of the workplace and the home differ from those of white women. She suggests that the family may not necessarily be a site of oppression for all black women when compared with the workplace. Even the title of the book suggests that all women are equally oppressed, regardless of other variables like class, race and sexuality, whereas Lessing's novel makes particularly clear the ways in which white middle-class women are sometimes in positions of power over black women, and black men. The 'Mashopi Hotel' sequences set in wartime South Africa culminate in Jackson, the black cook, being sacked by his white mistress because a drunk and sentimental white man puts his arms round him, and says '"You love me Jackson, don't you"' (p. 145). Issues of class, race, gender and sexuality are here seen as a troubling mixture rather than in terms which demand the prioritisation of one over the other as methods used to explain the world.

The novel tackles issues related to the body and biology in ways which suggest the limitations of the idea that our physical experiences are purely socially constructed. Barrett herself admits that the issue of essentialism has become a vexed one for feminism because of the fear that acknowledging the importance of physical differences between men and women necessarily leads to endorsing women's social inferiority. She also questions the usefulness of the sex/gender distinction which many feminists have found to be important, on the grounds that it is very difficult to distinguish conceptually between those aspects of physical experience and gender identity which are biological and those which are socially produced. Instead she suggests that we must examine these issues in historically specific ways. Lessing does not provide neat explanations for her characters' sense that their physical experiences are profound and important in distinguishing them from men; rather she lets the reader debate several answers to the question of why this should be so. As we saw earlier, she considers the purely social constructionist position in the idea that women's subservient status makes them dependent on emotional security in order to achieve sexual pleasure. She also considers the radical feminist argument that basic biological differences like childbirth have crucial (and positive) effects on women's psyche. Tommy, Molly's son, resents the fact that women see people as going through phases rather than as completed individuals. Anna replies:

'That's how women see – people. Certainly their own children. In the first place, there's always been nine months of not knowing whether the baby would be a girl or a boy ... And then babies go through one stage after another, and then they are children. When a woman looks at a child she sees all the things he's been at the same time. When I look at Janet sometimes I see her as a small baby and I *feel* her inside my belly and I see her as various sizes of small girl, all at the same time ... That's how women see things. Everything in a sort of continuous creative stream – well, isn't it natural we should?'   (p. 243)

The passage explains women's mental processes in terms of their physical experience and uses images of fluidity, process and sensation to align the two. However, it ends with a question, 'Isn't it natural we should?', which Tommy and the reader do not necessarily answer in the affirmative. Thus the novel encourages the reader to debate issues relating to women's experiences of their bodies and biology rather than attempting to suggest a coherent answer to questions such as whether or not our physical experience is socially constructed.

Conclusion

The Golden Notebook can be read as an important Marxist feminist text. It makes many points about the necessity of analysing our society in terms of the intersections of class and gender, capitalism and patriarchy. It demonstrates the relevance of understanding women's subordination in terms of their interlocking roles in the home and the workplace, and it also acknowledges the profound ways in which ideology affects sexuality, the body and fantasy, and thus gender identity. However, the ways in which the text moves beyond Marxist feminist analysis also suggest some of the limitations of this body of work. The unwillingness to break entirely from a materialist analysis means that the importance of language, discourse and the unconscious in constructing gender identity is not always sufficiently stressed. Similarly, the ultimate adherence to class, in intersection with gender, as the most important systems of oppression makes it very difficult to do more than merely 'add on' issues like race and sexuality as an afterthought. It remains very problematic to see a way for individuals out of the impasse of capitalist patriarchy when Marxist feminists tend to be unclear about the extent of the individual's freedom to resist their ideological and material positioning. The unambiguously social constructionist position on the body and women's physical experience has been another area of disagreement with other feminist theorists. However, unlike some other feminist theories, Marxist feminism has been capable of being rigorously self-critical on just these issues, even if this has meant, in some cases, moving entirely outside a Marxist theoretical framework.

4

Psychoanalytic Feminism

Introduction

Although it is the relationship between Marxism and feminism which has been described as an 'unhappy marriage',[1] the metaphor is perhaps even more appropriate for that between psychoanalysis and feminism. Rachel Bowlby uses a similar analogy in the following remarks:

> Psychoanalysis and feminism, it seems, have been together for a long time now, fixed into what seems to have become a virtually interminable relationship, marked repeatedly by expressions of violent feeling on both sides. Passionate declarations are followed by calm periods and then by the breaking out or resurgence of desperate denunciations and pleas once again ... Vehement denials and vehement advocacy characterize the proposals of both parties. 'We were made for each other', says one partner in the first flush of rapture; only to be followed at a later, more bitter stage by a transformed insistence that 'the relationship was doomed from the start'.[2]

The metaphor of a troubled yet exciting sexual and emotional relationship is particularly apposite given the stress in psychoanalytic theory on the importance of sexuality, the unconscious and family structures in shaping identity. Psychoanalysis marks a turn inward into the individual psyche to explain human behaviour, although it also acknowledges that individual identity is formed in relationship to others. Sigmund Freud, the 'father' of psychoanalysis, developed its main tenets as a 'talking cure' for the hysterical and neurotic symptoms of his patients in turn-of-the-century Vienna which could not be explained in physiological ways. As a thera-peutic practice, psychoanalysis involves listening to, and, most crucially, *interpreting* patients' own accounts of themselves and their problems, paying particular attention to such apparently unimportant matters as dreams, fantasies, jokes and slips of the tongue. Although these may appear to be trivial they are actually important because it is only in such ways that troubling desires repressed in the unconscious reveal themselves. Freud's 'discovery' of the unconscious is most important for psychoanalysis. Only by speculating that there must be a region of the human psyche where unacceptable desires and fantasies are contained, a region rarely accessible to the conscious mind, was he able to explain the bizarre details of even the most apparently 'normal' adult's dreams, day-dreams and parapraxes (jokes, slips of the tongue, temporary forgetfulness). The concept of the unconscious thus goes hand in hand with that of repression: repression of disturbing material and wishes is what creates the unconscious in the first place, and repres-sion is the main process which protects the conscious mind from this material. However, it is not always entirely successful, hence the reappearance of repressed desires from the unconscious in the distorted symptoms of the neurotic, or our strange and initially inexplicable dreams. Only through the process of analysis can such condensed and displaced versions of our unconscious desires be made comprehensible to us; by becoming conscious, such wishes cease to disturb and the therapeutic 'cure' is effected.

The most significant reason for the unnacceptability of uncon-scious material to the conscious mind is its sexual nature. Freud argues that the human being is a sexual being from birth, dominated initially by the pleasure principle (the desire to satisfy instinctual libidinal drives). Only through the process of associating pleasure with different regions of the body, and then from interacting with others in the family, does infantile sexuality come to be organised and contained in a way which subjects the pleasure principle to the reality principle. Initially, the child gets pleasure from sucking at the breast in the oral stage, then from controlling defecation in the anal stage, and finally from the genitalia in the genital stage. Most important of all, however, is the passage through the Oedipal stage. Freud's model of the Oedipus complex starts with the understand-ing that children of both sexes are primarily identified with the mother, who is the first love-object, and perceive the father as a rival for their affections. The little boy must learn that he cannot possess his mother and give her up, in order to identify with his father and enter successfully into 'normal' sexual and psychic life. This process occurs as a result of the castration complex, where the boy fears that the father will punish him for his desire of the mother by robbing him of his penis so that he will become castrated like his mother and other women. Resolving the castration and Oedipus complexes means that the little boy learns to identify with his father and with the patriarchal power he possesses, and to accept the dictates of social convention, which are internalised in the form of the super-ego or conscience. For little girls, the process is more complicated, and it is Freud's reliance on a normative masculine model of child development which has been problematic for many feminists. According to Freud, the girl's recognition of her own and her moth-er's inferior, castrated status provokes a rejection of the mother as love object and the transference of desire to the father. The girl's envy of the penis can only be satisfied by the prospect of one day giving birth to a male child. Because the girl does not pass through the castration complex in the same way as the boy (she does not fear castration as much, being castrated 'already', and has no investment in paternal law, having no prospect of exercising it), she does not develop a similarly strong superego or conscience. Instead she is forced to accept her passive feminine role.

Freud's most influential concepts are thus those of the uncon-scious and of infantile sexuality. His accounts of their regulation by the processes of repression and the Oedipus complex, which create 'normal' adult gendered identity, form the cornerstone of psychoan-alytic theory. Equally, however, Freud acknowledged that this process was fraught with difficulties which could result in various types of deviation from a 'norm' which is often, therefore, shifting and illusory. His emphasis on the Oedipal stage has been questioned by subsequent object-relations theorists, who have studied the child's relationship with 'objects', particularly the mother as object, in the pre-Oedipal stage. Object-relations theory has proved to be important for feminist theory, particularly in the USA, as will become apparent in the following discussion of Nancy Chodorow's *The Reproduction of Mothering* (1978). Other important psychoanalyt-ic theories (although they have been of less significance for feminism) are those of Carl Jung, who examined the function of archetypal dream images as evidence of a cross-cultural collective unconscious, and saw analysis as serving to encourage the individ-uation of the person from shadow personalities and compulsions.

Perhaps the most influential psychoanalyst for feminism after Freud, however, was Jacques Lacan, whose theories will be discussed in the next chapter on poststructuralist feminism, because they mark a very clear conceptual break with previous work for both feminism and psychoanalysis. Some important women psychoanalysts of the 1920s and 1930s reacted against Freud's theories in significant ways. Analysts like Karen Horney and Melanie Klein re-emphasised the pre-Oedipal stage, the infant's relationship with the mother and the importance of women's ability to reproduce. They thus countered the Freudian stress on the role of the penis, castration and the Oedipus complex in developing adult gendered identity. Feminist reaction against Freud at the start of the second wave attacked what was perceived as his biological determinism, his ahistoricism, his reliance on masculine models as normative, and his stress on sexuality as *the* determining factor in human identity and culture. More recently, however, feminist theory has effected a serious return to Freudian concepts. Perhaps the most significant early work of this kind is Juliet Mitchell's *Psychoanalysis and Feminism* (1974).[3]

Juliet Mitchell, *Psychoanalysis and Feminism* (1974)

Mitchell's book argues that rejecting, or ignoring, Freudian psychoanalysis is 'fatal for feminism', and that, crucially, 'psychoanalysis is not a recommendation *for* a patriarchal society, but an analysis *of* one'.[4] Freud was not a biological determinist; rather, he saw that the body functions within culture and society, and that its meanings are socially produced in specific, patriarchal circumstances. For the individual, acquiring gender identity is a complex negotiation of the meaning of biology in a society which does assume the inferiority of women:

> Freud says that though the presence of two sexes is a fact of biology, the mental experience of this is a matter for psychology: it does not *cause* our mental life, but our mental life has to take it into account ... In taking into account the biological 'great antithesis' between the sexes, we are psychologically bisexual; each of our psychologies contains the antithesis ... the concept of bisexuality has moved from being a simple notion, a postulate of

a sort of infantile unisex, to being a complex notion of the oscilla-
tions and imbalance of the person's mental androgyny.   (p. 51)

While Marxist theory can explain 'the historical and economic situation' in which we live, psychoanalysis, Mitchell suggests, can help
us understand the workings of ideology and sexuality in the unconscious (p. xxii).

Psychoanalysis and Feminism opens with careful accounts of those
of Freud's psychoanalytic theories which have been most important for women, demonstrating how they can be 'rescued' for
feminism if seen in relation to the above points. Part 2 of the book
engages with the writings of Wilhelm Reich and R. D. Laing, radical psychotherapists who were more popular with early
second-wave feminists than Freud. Mitchell is concerned to show
that this popularity is undeserved when the implications of this
body of work are examined. Although their stress on sexuality and
the family as areas where women are oppressed has influenced
radical feminist politics, many of their ideas actually return to the
biological determinism and depersonalising methodology of
which others have accused Freudian psychoanalysis. Mitchell goes
on to discuss the ways in which popularised American versions of
Freudian theory have 'increasingly been used to preserve the status quo' (p. 297), and suggests that the dominance of much of this
work (at the expense of Freud's own) can explain early second-
wave feminist hostility to his ideas. A large section of
Psychoanalysis and Feminism is then devoted to a consideration of
some examples of this hostility in the writing of Simone de
Beauvoir, Betty Friedan, Eva Figes, Germaine Greer, Shulamith
Firestone, and Kate Millett. Mitchell argues that much of this work
does not set Freud's studies of women in the context of his theory
as a whole. It wrongly rejects the importance of the unconscious
and the primacy of sexuality at the expense of 'social actuality and
conscious choice' (p. 356) in explaining identity. In the concluding
part of the book, Mitchell discusses how and why the oppression
of women takes place in our society. She discusses how the
Oedipus complex institutes and upholds patriarchal systems such
as the exchange of women by men and the prohibition of incest.
She considers whether these systems are specific to capitalism or
are universal and concludes that although the Oedipus complex
cannot be limited to capitalism, it assumes different forms in
different economic and social contexts.

Nancy Chodorow, *The Reproduction of Mothering* (1978)

Whereas *Psychoanalysis and Feminism* effects a feminist return to Freud on the grounds that Freud was descriptive rather than prescriptive of patriarchy, Nancy Chodorow's *The Reproduction of Mothering* reveals in its subtitle – *Psychoanalysis and the Sociology of Gender* – a rather different approach. Unlike Mitchell, Chodorow argues that Freudian theories *are* guilty of 'unexamined patriarchal cultural assumptions'.[5] According to Chodorow, Freud defined gender as 'presence or absence of masculinity and the male genital rather than as two different presences' (p. 157). She also finds his work guilty of biological determinism in that it assumes that differences in male and female psychic development are ultimately caused by the biological necessity that humankind reproduce itself. In contrast, Chodorow's use of object-relations theory stresses the importance of the interaction of the child with objects in a social context in explaining the acquisition of gender identity.

Chodorow's book seeks to answer the question: why do women mother? She rejects arguments that explain motherhood in terms of biological instinct or role training. Biological theories cannot explain why women nurture beyond pregnancy and lactation and role-training arguments are vulnerable to the criticism that they are overly functionalist or determinist, allowing little room for individual agency or the evident differences apparent in family structures historically. Chodorow argues that only a psychoanalytic account of the acquisition of gender identity which situates it in the specific social context of the nuclear family in capitalism can answer this question properly. She points out that 'the structure of the family and family practices create certain differential relational needs and capacities in men and women that contribute to the reproduction of women as mothers' (p. 51). For Chodorow, the pre-Oedipal and Oedipal periods, and the different ways in which boys and girls experience them, are crucial in reproducing the status of women as the primary nurturers. Because girls are parented by someone of the same gender, they have a longer pre-Oedipal stage which is less efficiently resolved than it is in boys. As a result women develop a more fluid, relational and permeable sense of their connection with others than men. In being forced to give up the mother and identify with the father during the Oedipal stage, the boy develops instead qualities of separation and individuation, and firmer ego boundaries. These psychic differences are exactly those which enable women to find satisfaction in the experience of mothering, which recapitulates desires and needs that a heterosexual relationship alone cannot. They also explain why women's relationships with other women are of more importance to them than a man's with other male friends. Chodorow suggests that only with a change in parenting arrangements will these psychic structures be challenged. The sharing of primary parenting between women and men will overcome the sexual division of labour which oppresses women, because it will allow children to be

> dependent from the outset on people of both genders and estab-lish an individuated sense of self in relation to both. In this way, masculinity would not become tied to denial of dependence and devaluation of women. Feminine personality would be less pre-occupied with individuation, and children would not develop fears of *maternal* omnipotence and expectations of *women*'s unique self-sacrificing qualities. This would reduce men's needs to guard their masculinity and their control of social and cultural spheres which treat and define women as secondary and power-less, and would help women to develop the autonomy which too much embeddedness in relationship has taken from them.
>
> (p. 218)

Margaret Atwood, *Lady Oracle* (1976)

A central theme in Margaret Atwood's novels is the formation of gender identity; she writes about women's childhood experiences, their interaction with male partners and other women, and the pre-cariousness of feminine subjectivity in a male-dominated society. Her heroines are often creative, exploring such issues in their writ-ing or painting. Atwood is particularly interested in literary and fictional conventions, generic boundaries, and narrative methods. She has written science fiction (*The Handmaid's Tale*), and frequently makes intertextual use of genres such as the romance, the gothic novel and the fairy-tale to create self-conscious parodies of those fic-tional techniques and motifs which have been particularly important for women readers. Atwood's Canadian background is also apparent in her novels; the complex history of negotiation of relationships with the USA and Europe creates in her texts a hybrid Canadian social and cultural heritage which resembles women's split or multiple identity. The heroine of *Lady Oracle*, Joan Foster, recognises this link when, as a child, she creates a fantasy image of a fat lady from a freak show at the Canadian National Exhibition walking across a high wire over a map of Canada.

This fantasy is central to the issue of feminine identity in *Lady Oracle*. Joan Foster is a woman who has faked her own death in order to escape the difficulties created by her compulsive creation of multiple personalities for herself. In her lifetime she has been both fat and ugly and thin and glamorous, a writer of historical romances (or 'costume gothics' as she terms them) and widely admired poetry (extracts from which are contained in the text), the lover of various different men, a political revolutionary, and an advocate of spiritualism, automatic writing and the paranormal. The novel opens with Joan in exile in disguise in a villa in Terremoto in Italy, and proceeds by a series of first-person flashbacks or retrospectives to explain the circumstances of her faked death and disappearance. Joan is a classically unreliable narrator, whose accounts of events are contradictory and illusory just like her identity. Indeed, this is one of the most obvious ways in which the novel can be read in psychoanalytic terms. Joan's narrative, addressed to no one in particular except herself and the reader, and perhaps, in a less significant sense, to her husband Arthur, closely resembles the 'talking cure' of psychoanalysis. The therapeutic method works from the apparently superficial or trivial manifestation of symptoms, dreams and fantasies to release the hidden significance of this material in the unconscious. Similarly, Freud's own method in devising his theories was, as Mitchell stresses, to work backwards from the adult to the childhood experience: 'you can only read a person, as you can only read history, backwards, you start from last things first' (p. 27). Thus the novel's shape and the narrative technique employed resemble both a case history and a Freudian theoretical discourse in their analeptic (backward-looking) structure.

Theory into Practice

In becoming Joan's analysts, readers of *Lady Oracle* are made aware of the significance of the unconscious, sexuality, and the pre-Oedipal and Oedipal stages in Joan's life. However, we also encounter their existence in relation to a specific social and cultural context, a context which is clearly patriarchal. Joan's fantasies and day-dreams demonstrate all the devices of condensation and displacement which Freud discovered were crucial for psychic protection. The fat lady fantasy, for example, is clearly a self-image, related to Joan's concerns about her body image. She is a condensation or amalgamation of the visit to the Canadian National Exhibition, where Joan is never actually allowed to see the fat lady in the freak show, and a childhood incident where Joan is forced to act the part of a mothball rather than a butterfly in her dancing-class recital because of her weight. The laughter of the watching crowd in the dream as she wire-walks across Canada is slowly replaced by an awed respect. Thus Joan blends a masochistic pleasure in her own victimisation with a narcissistic (self-loving) image of her own success and triumph over others' derision. In case this interpretation should be too clear to her conscious mind, various key elements are displaced. Joan gives the fat lady the face of another fat girl at her school, whom she terms 'my despised fellow sufferer',[6] and makes her carry 'a diminutive pink umbrella; this was a substitute for the wings which I longed to pin on her' (p. 102). Patriarchal ideologies of femininity centred around dress, weight and appropriate behaviour, and self-congratulatory nationalist 'flag waving', have clearly influenced Joan's unconscious 'dream work' and are affecting her psychic life.

Sexually, Joan initially appears to be fixed in the oral stage: as a child she is overweight and eats continuously. This fact is, as she recognises, intimately connected with her relationship with her mother:

> this is one of the many things for which my mother never quite forgave me. At first I was merely plump; in the earliest snapshots in my mother's album I was a healthy baby, not much heftier than most, and the only peculiar thing is that I was never looking at the camera; instead I was trying to get something into my mouth: a toy, a hand, a bottle. The photos went on in an orderly series; though I didn't exactly become rounder, I failed to lose what is usually referred to as baby fat. When I reached the age of six the pictures stopped abruptly. This must have been when my mother gave up on me, for it was she who used to take them; perhaps she no longer wanted my growth recorded. She had decided I would not do. (p. 43)

Joan's oral fixation is maintained, and her entry into and resolution of the Oedipus complex prevented, by her intense relationship with her mother and the ineffectual personality of her father. As Mitchell comments, Freud came to acknowledge the significance of the pre-Oedipal mother–daughter relationship for women: 'More important, however, than all the innumerable reasons a girl might have, or might later conceive of (as rationalizations), for her hostility to her mother, is the general tendency towards ambivalence: the very primacy and intensity of this relationship makes it liable to contain hate as well as love' (p. 57). The novel suggests that Joan's mother's concerns about her daughter's appearance and behaviour – her urge that she should be the appropriate daughter in a patriarchal society which values a feminine (thin) appearance and compliant behaviour – create a resistance in Joan which manifests itself in the intense orality of overeating. Joan's dream about her mother, in which she realises while watching her apply make-up in a three-way dressing-table mirror that she has three heads, is a manifestation of her ambivalent feelings about her. In one sense, Joan wants her mother to be the 'phallic', or all-powerful, mother of the pre-Oedipal stage, able to satisfy all demands and desires. This is apparent in her early version of the dream, where she tries to prevent a nameless man waiting outside the door from seeing her mother's self-division, or three heads. In the other sense, Joan realises as she grows older that her dependence on her mother needs to be resolved by the transfer of maternal to paternal omnipotence in the Oedipal stage, hence the dream changes to encompass the desire that the man (clearly a father-figure) would enter and uncover her mother's secret.

Joan's father is literally, and then metaphorically, absent from her childhood. During his absence in the war, Joan discovers that he worked in Intelligence and killed people; now, as a surgeon, he brings suicidal patients who have overdosed back to life. This ambiguity, coupled with his ineffectual role as a parent (normal according to the twentieth-century capitalist gendered division of labour) suggests that he is never a sufficient authority figure to wrench Joan through the Oedipal stage:

> I wanted him to tell me the truth about life, which my mother would not tell me and which he must have known something about, as he was a doctor and had been in the war; he'd killed people and raised the dead. I kept waiting for him to give me some advice, warn me, instruct me, but he never did any of these things. (p. 77)

As a result, Joan never adequately resolves her relationship with her mother, a situation which, according to Mitchell, creates potential psychosis: 'In psychosis there is evidence that the girl never really entered into her Oedipal relationship with her father, the father is in an important sense "absent" from her world ... the father's absence is not literal, but symbolic' (p. 288).

Thus, one way of interpreting Joan's compulsive creation of multiple personalities, her contradictory narratives about her life, and her difficulty in distinguishing reality and fantasy, is as the behaviour of a psychotic. By the end of the novel, when Joan is at her most confused, she becomes obsessed with the idea that she is being followed and will be forced to return from the dead and confront reality. At this point a narrative insert involving the characters in Joan's latest costume gothic, which she has been finishing in Terremoto, obtrudes into the text. The fictional status of this extract from 'Stalked by Love' is confused by the presence of various characters from Joan's 'real-life' existence. These include her Aunt Lou, the fat lady from the freak show (dressed this time in butterfly wings, demonstrating a deterioration in Joan's ability to displace self-images), her father, the Polish count, the Royal Porcupine, and Arthur, her husband. The protagonist of the piece is no longer Charlotte, the irritating, conventional heroine of 'Stalked by Love', but the villainess, Felicia, who is modelled throughout on Joan herself. The extract is a persecution fantasy in which Redmond, the hero, reveals himself to be the real villain of the piece who has incarcerated several wives in the maze at his gothic mansion. It demonstrates Joan's complete breakdown, her inability to distinguish reality and fantasy, and the fracturing of her identity, and shows how both relate to the pressure Joan has experienced to be a 'normal' 'feminine' woman in a patriarchal society.

Even if we see Joan as finally attaining 'normal' adult femininity, however, she can be seen to bear what Mitchell terms the 'marks of womanhood', which are, according to Freud, masochism, passivity, vanity, jealousy and a limited sense of justice. Mitchell argues that, for Freud, masochism, or pleasure in pain, 'typifies the feminine predicament' (p. 114). Passivity is the outcome of the ineffectual resolution of the Oedipus complex in women. Vanity and jealousy result as compensations for penis envy and the castration complex, and a limited sense of justice is created by women's inferior internalisation of the prohibitive Oedipal father-figure and consequent creation of a weaker superego, or moral sense. Joan seems to be reluctant to take active decisions to change those things in her life which give her pain: for example, unsatisfactory love affairs or family relationships. Instead, she tends to use passive strategies of avoidance or diversion, including faking her death, and creating new identities to substitute for inferior ones. She is at different times both jealous, for example of Marlene, who bullied her as a child, and vain of her appearance after her weight loss (seen in her love of dressing up in glamorous, unusual clothes). Her 'limited sense of justice' is apparent in her lies, evasions and deceit, even when faced with the prospect of Sam and Marlene's arrest for her murder. However, as Mitchell states, Freud 'refers all these qualities to the influence of "social custom", "social conditions", "matters of convention" and so on. The demands of human culture as such (which to Freud is patriarchal) and the particular patriarchal society interlock' (p. 117). It is not surprising that Joan struggles to reconcile herself with an ideology where the ideal woman is thin, pretty and passive.

Mitchell's discussion of the more populist appropriations of radical psychotherapy in feminism suggests that such explanations for women's oppression are often too simple, and rely on biologistic arguments about gender and a false objectivity which are not, despite what many commentators have believed, present in Freud's work. *Lady Oracle* is similarly sceptical about radical politics, as is apparent in the treatment of Joan's husband Arthur, whose political enthusiasms are satirised for their impermanence and pat theorising of complex issues:

> I soon discovered there were as many of Arthur as there were of me. The difference was that I was simultaneous, whereas Arthur was a sequence. At the height of his involvement with any of these causes, Arthur would have the electricity of six, he'd scarcely sleep at all, he'd rush about stapling things and making speeches and carrying signs. But at the low points he'd barely be able to make it out of bed.   (pp. 211–12)

Arthur's multiple identity is 'sequential', linear and teleological (believing in progress towards fulfilling an end purpose). Joan's is 'simultaneous', circular and regressive. Atwood associates each type with masculinity and femininity, but she also demonstrates that these are primarily cultural norms, by explaining the splitting and multiplication of Joan's identity in terms of understandable (if not always conscious) responses to family expectations, high-school pressures and male attitudes rather than as an innate tendency towards madness. The weakness of Arthur's radical politics when it comes to explaining the oppression of women is obvious when Joan imagines his interpretation of her fat lady fantasy:

> What a shame, he'd say, how destructive to me were the attitudes of society, forcing me into a mold of femininity that I could never fit, stuffing me into those ridiculous pink tights, those spangles, those outmoded, cramping ballet slippers. How much better for me if I'd been accepted for what I was and had learned to accept myself, too. Very true, very right, very pious. But it's still not so simple. I wanted those things, that fluffy skirt, that glittering tiara. I liked them.   (p. 103)

Arthur's view of women's oppression seems to involve the 'layering' of an enforced, inauthentic femininity over an essentially authentic femaleness which it should be possible to discover beneath the superficiality of such things as clothes. However, Joan acknowledges (and Mitchell's point is that Freud does too) that it is impossible to discover 'what you are' without accepting that your most intimate understanding of your body, your sexuality and your identity have been shaped and formed in relation to the society in which you live.

Mitchell's concluding arguments about the particular significance and stresses of the Oedipus complex in the nuclear family in twentieth-century capitalist society are made more central in Nancy Chodorow's *The Reproduction of Mothering*, and are also important in *Lady Oracle*. Apart from her Aunt Lou, Joan has no extended family, and her mother has sole responsibility for her physical and emotional care. Joan sees that her mother is not satisfied by a role which only encompasses the home and childcare, but any job she can get outside the home (for example, travel agent, interior decorator) is insufficiently challenging precisely because it is segregated by sex: appropriate to prescribed notions of femininity. As a result, Joan's mother makes Joan her project: 'she was to be the manager, the creator, the agent; I was to be the product' (p. 67). This situation, coupled with her father's absence working outside the home, and lack of interest or responsibility for Joan in it, creates the characteristic fluidity, merging and permeability which Chodorow sees as typical of the pre-Oedipal mother–daughter relationship:

Because they are the same gender as their daughters and have been girls, mothers of daughters tend not to experience these infant daughters as separate from them in the same way as do mothers of infant sons ... the resurfacing and prevalence of pre-oedipal mother–daughter issues in adolescence (anxiety, intense and exclusive attachment, orality and food, maternal control of a daughter's body, primary identification) provide clinical verification of the claim that elements of the preoedipal mother–daughter relationship are maintained and prolonged in both maternal and filial psyche. (pp. 109–10)

Joan's and her mother's problems with merging and separating from each other are never resolved in *Lady Oracle*. When Joan starts to lose weight in order to fulfil the terms of her aunt's legacy we believe that she will be able to satisfy her mother's desired image of her and finally separate from her. However, Joan's sudden and stunning weight loss infuriates her mother to the extent that she stabs her in the arm with a paring knife. This bizarre incident can only be explained in terms of her mother's fear that by losing weight, collecting her legacy and leaving home, Joan will cease to be under her control. As Joan suggests: 'making me thin was her last available project ... there was nothing left for her to do, and she had counted on me to last her forever' (p. 123). Just before she learns of her mother's death, Joan experiences a vision of her. In an earlier childhood experience a medium at the spiritualist church she attends with her Aunt Lou receives a message from her mother, even though she is still alive. The medium explains this phenomenon as the appearance of Joan's mother's astral body, which 'could float around by itself, attached to you by something like a long rubber band' (p. 111). This 'umbilical' metaphor is a striking and appropriate one for the intensity of the mother–daughter bond.

According to Chodorow, the psychic differences between men and women which result from contemporary parenting arrangements have certain consequences, for example the failure of heterosexual sexual relationships to satisfy women as much as men, and the greater importance for women of relationships with those of the same sex. In *Lady Oracle*, Joan finds that her romantic relationships with men are unsatisfactory, both sexually and emotionally. She believes that:

> Love was merely a tool, smiles were another tool, they were both
> just tools for accomplishing certain ends. No magic, merely chem-
> icals. I felt I'd never really loved anyone ... I'd polished them with
> my love and expected them to shine, brightly enough to return
> my own reflection, enhanced and sparkling.   (p. 282)

Joan recognises that loving another involves a splitting of the self
which attaches emotion to the love object, but also retains a narcissistic (self-loving) element. She also acknowledges the failure of any
of her male partners to be 'deserving enough' objects of more than
this narcissistic love. One possible reason for this is these men's
inability to provide the primary intensity she experienced with her
mother, but because Joan is unable to resolve this relationship, she
continually seeks out new lovers in a doomed attempt to recreate
and resolve it through a different male partner. Similarly, Joan's
relationships with other women retain some of the anxieties about
dependence, splitting and identification which Joan experienced
with her mother. As a child, Joan feels she cannot tell her mother
about her bullying by Elizabeth, Marlene and Lynn 'because I felt
that whatever she would say, underneath it her sympathies would
lie with them. "Stand up for yourself," she would exhort. How
could a daughter of hers have turned out to be such a limp balloon?'
(p. 59). When Joan meets Marlene again as an adult, she feels as
though her 'dormant past burst into rank life' (p. 229), although
Marlene does not recognise her. Joan is unable to separate from the
anxieties of childhood.

Practice into Theory

Atwood's *Lady Oracle* suggests some of the problems in Mitchell's
and Chodorow's different appropriations of psychoanalysis for
feminism. Mitchell provides a very selective reading of Freud, de-
emphasising, for example, those aspects of his work which do
suggest a determinist view of biology. An emphasis on different
Freudian theories would produce very different results, as is apparent if we choose to consider *Lady Oracle* as a text which is primarily
about what Freud termed the 'death drive'. Mitchell mentions the
death drive infrequently, but its significance in Freud's later work is
great. The idea that the unconscious wish for the stability and

wholeness of a pre-animate state appears in an impulse towards death is of obvious relevance in *Lady Oracle*. Joan's narrative begins as follows:

> I planned my death carefully, unlike my life, which meandered along from one thing to another, despite my feeble attempts to control it. My life had a tendency to spread, to get flabby, to scroll and festoon like the frame of a baroque mirror, which came from following the line of least resistance. I wanted my death, by contrast, to be neat and simple, understated, even a little severe, like a Quaker church or the basic black dress with a single strand of pearls much praised by fashion magazines when I was fifteen.
>
> (p. 7)

The similes of clothing, architecture and furnishings suggest that death is attractive to Joan because it offers her images of simplicity, regularity and self-control which life does not. Although Joan is only faking her death, the novel is preoccupied with the subject in other ways. During the progress of the text, Aunt Lou dies, leaving Joan the legacy which allows her to leave home, her mother dies (in rather mysterious circumstances which potentially implicate her father), and she has a recurring connection with spiritualism and the paranormal. Although much of the material concerning the spiritualist church is comic, there is a serious undercurrent in Joan's vision of her mother before learning of her death, and her production of the 'Lady Oracle' poems by automatic writing. To state the obvious, death plays a big part in Joan's life, and this fact is only a paradox when not considered in terms of Freud's theory of the death drive in *Beyond the Pleasure Principle* (1920).

The fact that Mitchell's appropriation of Freud is selective is inevitable. It only becomes problematic if we want to argue that Freudian psychoanalysis is a science with principles about which there can be no disagreement. On the contrary, we may want to suggest that Freud's theories are best understood as a discourse, or an interpretation like any other. Related to this issue is the question of how universal we consider Freudian theory to be. Is it applicable in all contexts, or is it culturally and historically specific? Mitchell does not seem to be clear on these points:

> Certainly, then, psychoanalysis ... was formed and developed within a particular time and place; that does not invalidate its

claim to universal laws, it only means that these laws have to be extracted from their specific problematic – the particular material conditions of their formation. In this connection we need to know of the historical circumstances of their development mainly in order *not* to limit them thereto ... Though they seem to be universal, different societies, either contemporary or historical, different classes at the same or different times or situations, will not acquire these laws in an identical manner.   (pp. xx–xxi)

This rather contradictory double emphasis on 'extracting' the kernel of objective psychoanalytic truth from a specific social context, only in order subsequently to replace it within such a context, is rather confusing. Mitchell claims at the end of her book that psychoanalysis explains the universal acquisition and internalisation of the patriarchal laws prohibiting incest and instituting the exchange of women, although she states that these operate in rather different ways in different societies. This argument is also vulnerable to the same criticism. Is patriarchy *necessary* for, or inevitable in, society, and if so, how can we imagine a culture in which men do not exercise power over women? How can feminist political activism work to change such a situation?[7]

Some of the same ambiguities attach to Mitchell's reliance on Marxist theory, characteristic of her British socialist feminist background.[8] *Psychoanalysis and Feminism* proffers a 'dual systems' theory which uses historical materialism to explain the economic and social oppression of women, and psychoanalysis to explain their experience of internalising patriarchal ideology in the unconscious. Mitchell thus relies on the same conception of ideology as relatively independent from the economic which informed Michèle Barrett's *Women's Oppression Today* (see previous chapter). Her ideas are therefore vulnerable to the same criticisms. Possibly she undervalues the role of economic factors in constituting women's oppression, at the expense of the overly 'privatised' (Wilson, p. 68) psychoanalytic explanation, and is thus insufficiently historically specific.[9] Alternatively, she is unwilling to free ideology entirely from the economic and see it as just as material and important a factor in explaining the position of women. A psychoanalytic reading of *Lady Oracle* is appropriate and interesting, then, but if different aspects of psychoanalytic theory are emphasised, different interpretations result; the same would be true if another theory entirely, for example Marxism, was used. Equally, the problem of explaining the exact nature of the intersection between psychoanalysis and Marxism as theories, or between unconscious ideology and economic and social circumstances as 'objects' of those theories, bedevils *Psychoanalysis and Feminism.*

One of the most noticeable things about *Lady Oracle* is the extent of its intertextuality and self-consciousness about different types of writing. Atwood's references to other novels, plays, poems and fairy-tales (as well as, for that matter, to films, television programmes and advertisements) are many and various. Her comments about the type of literature which women often read, for example gothic novels and romantic fiction of various sorts, are of importance in relation to a central theme in the text: the distinction between popular fiction and canonical literature. Joan writes both costume gothics and widely admired poetry, but she cannot see much to differentiate the two: 'On re-reading, the book [her prose poem 'Lady Oracle'] seemed quite peculiar. In fact, except for the diction, it seemed a lot like one of my standard Costume Gothics, but a Gothic gone wrong. It was upside down somehow' (p. 232). The point, of course, is that both romance and poem are *texts*, and can be interpreted as *discourses* with particular motifs, character types, plot trajectories and diction. The significance of their similarity lies not in their sameness, but in the fact that one is an inversion of the other, in the same way that *Lady Oracle* is a parodic rewriting of the popular romance, which functions by disrupting romantic conventions such as the characterisation of the heroine (who should be slim, vulnerable yet feisty but who is, in fact, overweight, and vulnerable to the point of breakdown). Atwood's novel thus emphasises the significance of language in constructing identity. Joan's multiple personalities begin to proliferate when she starts publishing historical romances and corresponding with her publishers and accountants under the *nom de plume* of her aunt, Louisa K. Delacourt. In this sense, the novel's poststructuralist (see next chapter) conception of identity as discursive (constructed in relation to language) suggests that Mitchell's conception of Freudian theory is weakest precisely where it resists interpreting his own writing as text or discourse. As Jane Gallop comments, without the inclusion of such a conception of language (which she associates particularly with the work of Jacques Lacan) Mitchell 'falls back into that kind of common sense which underlies her interlocutors' [i.e. her early second-wave feminist critics'] belief in a rational, utility-based explanation for human behaviour'.[10] For Gallop, the attractions of psychoanalytic theory for feminism lie precisely in its articulation of a human subject discursively constructed, and thus open to disruption, subversion and change.

Ambiguities surround *Lady Oracle*'s conception of identity. Does the novel offer the conventionally 'normalised' and adjusted version of the self which Mitchell at times suggests patriarchal ideology creates, and psychoanalytic theory explains? Does Joan's 'self-analysis' effect any therapeutic 'cure'? Has she achieved a resolution of her problems or come to understand herself by the end of the novel? Is this possible, or even desirable? One interpretation would point to the fact that by the end of the text Joan appears to have decided to return from the dead, face up to her actions, and admit the existence of her multiple personalities. However, the concluding two paragraphs also show her beginning to repeat compulsively some of the behaviour she has exhibited before. She remarks: 'there is something about a man in a bandage ... Also I've begun to feel he's the only person who knows anything about me' (p. 345). Joan is possibly beginning to attach romantically to the reporter who has discovered her, in exactly the same way in which she has attempted to solve problems and create new selves by falling in love before. In one sense, then, Joan is an example of the failure of the 'talking cure'; like Dora, one of Freud's women patients, she breaks off the analysis and resists readers' attempts to adjust her to normality.[11] The novel offers us a much more disturbed and radical conception of the feminine subject as fractured by desire and language, which may be incompatible with the rational, conscious feminist project for destroying the tyranny of patriarchal structures and ideologies in the unconscious which Mitchell's conclusion envisages. As we have seen, *Lady Oracle* is highly cynical about the value and purpose of revolutionary political activism.

The novel can be used to highlight the similar problems with some of the arguments in Nancy Chodorow's *The Reproduction of Mothering*. Chodorow also neglects to take account of the role of language in creating identity. Her version of the self explains how it is constituted according to object relations in the pre-Oedipal period which vary for men and women as a consequence of parenting structures. This theory is vulnerable to the criticisms that it is empiricist, functionalist and determinist. Chodorow does not allow for failure, disruption and subversion of the 'norm' that women mother. As Toril Moi comments: 'Chodorow simply abandons the question of women who choose *not* to "reproduce mothering"'.[12]

Lady Oracle never suggests that Joan wants to have a baby, nor does she achieve the sort of normal, stable, maternal identity which Chodorow argues is an *inevitable* result of the combination of social arrangements and psychic structures of gender differentiation. Exactly how the psychic and social intermesh to reproduce mothering is another vexed issue. Chodorow's vagueness here resembles Mitchell's confusion over the relationship between ideology and the economic. Do social arrangements and norms (such as the norm that all women mother) come into existence independently of their psychic internalisation and then insinuate themselves into the individual unconscious, or do universal psychic laws create supporting social arrangements? How and where is it possible for feminist activism to intervene in this situation in order to change it? It is clear that, as Elizabeth Grosz points out, 'the relevant issue here is not simply who parents', because 'the meanings of their actions will remain different'.[13] In other words, social change independent of changes in language, signification and meaning is ineffectual.

Conclusion

In *Lady Oracle* we see the failure, disruption and subversion of any specific psychoanalytic models of the acquisition of gender identity. These failures suggest a crucial weakness in Mitchell's and Chodorow's use of psychoanalytic theory: their reliance on conceptions of normality and adjustment which do reproduce patriarchal structures. What happens to homosexuality and lesbianism in psychoanalytic models of 'normal' gender development, and how are they inflected by racial and ethnic difference? One obvious, but buried, implication of Chodorow's argument is that a woman's primary sexual orientation is lesbian because her first, never satisfactorily resolved, love relationship is with someone of the same sex. Only with a lesbian feminist reappraisal of *The Reproduction of Mothering* (see Chapter 7) is the significance of this absence made clear. Atwood's novel shows that any normative conceptions of gender identity are inevitably subject to failure. She pokes fun at psychoanalysis while using it. *Lady Oracle* encourages its readers to embrace multiple forms of desire and language and consider whether any of these could form the basis for a new feminist political project for emancipation.

5

Poststructuralist Feminism

Introduction

This chapter might easily have been called 'French feminism', because many early commentators have used this umbrella term when analysing the work of Hélène Cixous, Luce Irigaray and Julia Kristeva.[1] However, there are a number of difficulties with this categorisation which make 'poststructuralist feminism' a more appropriate one. First, none of the three is French by birth: Cixous was born in Algeria, Irigaray in Belgium and Kristeva in Bulgaria. They exhibit more hybrid and tangential relationships with the country where they now live and work than might seem appropriate in writers categorised unproblematically as 'French'. Secondly, their work is not in any way representative of mainstream feminist political activity or thinking in France, which they argue is flawed by its reformist agenda, which merely echoes masculine, bourgeois political conventions and structures. Thirdly, the category 'French feminism' has arguably been created to serve certain US and UK political and intellectual agendas: in an imperialist move, ideas which would seem unpalatable if ascribed to UK or US authors are categorised as 'French' in order to make them seem exotic and 'other', but thus paradoxically acceptable.[2] If there are problems with the 'Frenchness' of French feminism it is equally difficult to describe Cixous, Irigaray and Kristeva as 'feminist'. All three have expressed (to varying degrees) their discomfort with the term. Partly their objections are made as judgements about its specific meaning in the French context, as is suggested above, but they also imply a wider suspicion about the usefulness of categories which they believe to be part of masculine thinking.

This chapter has opened defensively by describing why a particular way of defining certain theorists has *not* been used. This strategy suggests some of the reasons why characterising these writers' work as 'poststructuralist' may be more appropriate than describing them as 'French'. If Cixous, Irigaray and Kristeva share anything it is their sense of the potential instability of concepts like nation, gender and identity. This sceptical approach is distinct from a structuralist one which explains concepts in terms of fundamentally stable structures. Structuralists such as Ferdinand de Saussure, Claude Lévi-Strauss and Jacques Lacan, who examined the way that structures determine meaning in language, kinship relations and the psyche respectively, assumed that it is possible to uncover the underlying patterns which explain the way that something works. In their different disciplines of linguistics, anthropology and psychoanalysis, Saussure, Lévi-Strauss and Lacan examined the binary oppositions which provide the foundations for human behaviour and language use. A binary opposition consists of a pair of terms which are dependent on each other to make sense. These terms exist in a hierarchy, where one is more valued than the other. Immediately accessible examples are 'masculine' and 'feminine' and 'young' and 'old'. It is important to recognise that structuralism looks beneath the apparent diversity of surface phenomena to find those structures which explain the actual function of such phenomena. Structuralism explains that function in terms of relationships between oppositions, rather than in terms of any intrinsic meaning which can be found in any one thing. So, to return to my example, the concept 'masculinity' is unthinkable without the concept 'femininity', because it can only be thought in opposition to that concept, and vice versa. It should be obvious that in the opposition masculine/feminine the term 'masculine' is the more valued one and thus comes first in the hierarchy.

Cixous, Irigaray and Kristeva began writing in the 1960s in Europe when structuralism came to prominence. It had the greatest impact on precisely those disciplines which have most influenced these three writers: linguistics, philosophy and psychoanalysis.[3] As writers and theorists Cixous, Irigaray and Kristeva all share an inheritance which includes respect for, and divergence from, their structuralist forebears. Along with writers like Jacques Derrida, they are suspicious of the totalising claims of structuralist linguistics to explain the diversity and plurality of language. Derrida's thinking has been hugely influential in literary studies, and many

commentators on Cixous's, Irigaray's and Kristeva have argued
their indebtedness to his work.[4] I would prefer to situate all four as
part of a turn away from structuralism which embraces the notion
of language as inherently unstable. Thus, whereas structuralist linguistics proposes a theory of language as explicable in terms of
underlying governing oppositions between terms, poststructuralism suggests that language always eludes final, fixed meanings.
Cixous's, Irigaray's and Kristeva's work uses a number of devices
such as punning, allusion, quotation, neologism, compound words,
and what we may think of as 'poetic' language. Their writing forces
us to recognise that the meaning of a word or concept is not merely 'constructed' in relation to another opposing word or concept,
but is always open to deconstruction. The meaning of a word can
never be defined finally or absolutely because meanings generate
other meanings endlessly. Similarly, binary oppositions are inherently unstable because there will always be occasions when the
hierarchy of terms inverts itself (moments when, to return to our
example of masculinity and femininity, femininity becomes the
more privileged term, as in certain sorts of religious or mystical discourses). There will also be points where a third term exceeds and
destabilises the distinction between opposed terms, as in the case
of transgressive or queer sexualities of various kinds (see Chapter
7), which disturb the masculine/feminine binary by parodying elements of both or bringing them into sharp juxtaposition in the same
context. Cixous's, Irigaray's and Kristeva's work also necessitates a
reappraisal of the distinction between creative and critical writing,
pointing in fact to the collapse of this binary distinction as a useful
way of categorising different kinds of writing. For poststructural-
ists all writing is important because we can only really know
anything through language: language, if it does not always actually *construct* our perceptions and experiences, always *mediates*
them.[5]

In applying the insights of structuralist linguistics to the practice
and theory of psychoanalysis Jacques Lacan provided a model for
Cixous's, Irigaray's and Kristeva's writing practice. In this case it is
justifiable to claim an influence which is more direct than that of
Derrida.[6] Lacan's argument that 'the unconscious is structured like
a language'[7] suggests that we acquire identity, or consciousness, at
the same time as we learn to speak, also the same point at which we
acquire an unconscious. In order to understand this point, we need
to relate his ideas to Freud's discussion of the Oedipal stage, men-

tioned in the previous chapter. For Freud, the Oedipal stage marks the moment at which the child gives up the mother as love object and attaches to the father. Lacan argues that this is a crucial point which marks the child's exit from what he terms the 'Imaginary' and entrance into the 'Symbolic Order'. For Lacan, the Symbolic Order connotes the adult, normative, patriarchal, rational world, dominated by the phallus, which symbolises what he terms the Law of the Father. It is marked by division of the self from the other (and specifically the mother), the acquisition of language and the creation of desire. The Imaginary can be equated with the pre-Oedipal stage, in which the child is less aware of any consistent distinctions between himself and others, has no language, has no sense of loss, and thus has no sense of desire. It is only through acquiring language and passing into the Symbolic Order that identity can be assumed, and this process goes hand in hand with the creation of the unconscious through the repression of those experiences, such as a sense of oneness with the mother, which form part of the Imaginary. The Imaginary is not a stage which is completely outgrown once entry into the Symbolic Order occurs; rather than perceiving them as linear sequences it is important to understand that, like other binary oppositions, they only acquire meaning in relation to each other.[8]

The crucial intervention of our triumvirate of poststructuralist feminists into this debate is first to foreground and secondly to question its basis in gendered assumptions. For both Derrida and Lacan the feminine is simultaneously excluded and essential. Derrida makes femininity into the figure of linguistic undecidability;[9] Lacan makes woman something which does not exist in the Symbolic Order, but which, through repression of desire for the (m)other, founds the creation of that order in the first place. In other words, it is the rejection of the maternal which allows the masculine subject to assume his privileged place in patriarchy, and the refusal of the awareness of linguistic play (equated metaphorically with femininity) which, however temporarily, allows the creation of apparently fixed meanings. Cixous, Irigaray and Kristeva ask, in different ways, what women readers, thinkers and writers do when faced with their essential exclusion from language and the Symbolic. The following analysis will consider Cixous's 'The Laugh of the Medusa' first, followed by Irigaray's 'When Our Lips Speak Together' and Kristeva's 'From One Identity to An Other'. The reasons for this choice will become apparent *en route*.

Hélène Cixous, 'The Laugh of the Medusa' (first published in French in 1975; in English in 1976)

The first thing a reader of Hélène Cixous's 'The Laugh of the Medusa' might notice is its poetic, lyrical style. The text does not read like most of the theory we have already examined: it seems 'literary' and creative rather than formal and structured. This 'literariness' is part of Cixous's pleasure in language, in the playful, wayward capacity of a word to mean more than any single inter-pretation of it might suggest. Some of this is admittedly lost in translation (see for example footnotes 7 and 8 to the essay, which explain the double meanings of certain words in French). Other examples, such as the play on the slippage between 'sex' and 'sects' in the sentence 'Let the priests tremble, we're going to show them our sects!',[10] still work in English. Cixous emphasises linguistic ambivalence for two purposes: to undermine the phallocentric (lit-erally, centred on the phallus) foundations of culture and writing, which attempt to deny such playfulness, and to suggest ways of writing which might provide different and authentic versions of femininity for women readers. In her analysis of existing culture and writing she suggests that woman has always functioned as the 'other': as whatever is excluded in order to create culture in the first place. Like de Beauvoir, Cixous's analysis of western culture sug-gests that femininity is never allowed to be anything but the opposite of masculinity: 'writing has been run by a libidinal and cultural – hence political, typically masculine – economy ... this locus has grossly exaggerated all the signs of sexual opposition (and not sexual difference), where woman has never *her* turn to speak' (p. 249).

The distinction between opposition and difference is crucial: in psychoanalytic terms women merely lack the phallus; the real dif-ferences in their bodies are not acknowledged. It is those positive differences that Cixous argues must be brought into feminine writ-ing to disturb and alter the functioning of the patriarchal machinery: 'Woman must write her self: must write about women and bring women to writing, from which they have been driven away as violently as from their bodies – for the same reasons, by the same law, with the same fatal goal. Woman must put herself into the text' (p. 244). Cixous rejects liberal or reformist agendas which seek to give women access to those rights and privileges which patriarchy offers to men because they ultimately fail to acknowledge women's difference. Her analogy between the female body and women's writing is designed to point out the paradox that the physical, material facts of sexed bodies are seen, explicitly, as irrelevant to writing and culture, but implicitly function (in the case of the female body) as the rejected basis for the creation of that culture in the first place.

In calling for the writing of a feminine difference based on women's bodies Cixous takes a deliberate risk. The essay relies on a feminine imagery which consists of fluency, liquidity, softness, monstrosity, sickness, darkness, exclusion, song, hysteria, pregnancy, maternity and sexuality. She risks aligning femininity with the physical, emotional and irrational in ways which merely echo patriarchal stereotyping. For Cixous, however, it is only by taking this risk that real change can be effected in the patriarchal status quo: this imagery has to be revalorised before it can be abandoned at some future point. Her strategy is to deploy stereotypically feminine imagery repetitiously and with humour so that it acquires subversive qualities: the subversive qualities inherent in the instability of language itself. She thus hopes to point beyond the existing order: 'At times it is in the fissure caused by an earthquake, through that radical mutation of things brought on by a material upheaval when every structure is for a moment thrown off balance and an ephemeral wildness sweeps order away, that the poet slips something by, for a brief span, of woman' (p. 249).

'The Laugh of the Medusa' forces together the physical and the linguistic, which are normally held to be opposites. In doing so the essay points out two things: first, that bodies, and their gendered qualities, are discursively constructed and secondly, that language is marked by traces of a physicality which cannot be eradicated. The body is textual and the text is physical; it is at the site of this conundrum that, for Cixous, feminine writing and new forms of femininity can precariously exist. The essay's concentration on maternity, bisexuality, love and the gift as points where culture and nature collide is particularly important. If normative masculinity and entry into the Symbolic Order are founded on a repression of the relation with the mother, then women's resurrection of that relation in writing can inscribe new forms of femininity in culture. The closeness of the relationship between mother and daughter is never effectually abandoned by women. As we saw in the last chapter, they have little inducement to renounce it and identify with the father, unlike the boy who has the prospect of one day wielding his father's power, if he gives up the mother. Releasing the unconscious force of the maternal relation into language is thus an essential part of writing women's difference. This 'maternal return' also explains Cixous's interest in bisexuality: a woman's first love relationship is with someone of her own sex, and she never entirely represses this fact: 'at present, for historico-cultural reasons, it is women who are opening up to and benefiting from this vatic bisexuality which doesn't annul differences but stirs them up, pursues them, increases their number' (p. 254). Cixous's bisexuality is not the idea of 'having it both ways', which would invalidate feminine difference by containing it within a sexuality still ultimately governed by the phallus. Rather it is a plural and inclusive conception of desire which genuinely acknowledges difference. Desire and love on such terms become potentially liberating: 'Woman of course has a desire for a "loving desire" and not a jealous one. But not because she is gelded; not because she's deprived and needs to be filled out, like some wounded person who wants to console herself or seek vengeance. I don't want a penis to decorate my body with. But I do desire the other for the other, whole and entire, male or female' (p. 262). Cixous demonstrates that desire and love function in a patriarchal society in economic terms, where systems of exchange dominate. Men expect something in return for an emotional or sexual investment, because the Symbolic Order relies on entry into the rights and privileges of patriarchy as a reward for giving up the desire for the mother. Abandoning this desire also avoids the feared punishment of castration: the fate of the mother and all women. Cixous argues that women's ability to give without thought of return distinguishes their relationships from those of men. This giving eludes and disturbs the masculine libidinal economy which organises desire and emotion around concepts like profit, loss and IOU.

To appreciate Cixous's aims in 'The Laugh of the Medusa' means to agree with her alignment of writing with the body, and politics. Ultimately, she refuses a representational theory of language, one which sees language as a separate system from society which can only attempt to mirror that society accurately. Instead, she argues that both language and society are interpenetrating discourses, consisting of text open to reading, interpretation and rewriting. Interventions in writing and culture will inevitably change society, since to separate the two is a false opposition. To take the Medusa, whose face, in legend, turned men to stone, who became, for Freud, a metaphor for castration anxiety in men,[11] and write the following does make a difference: 'You only have to look at the Medusa straight on to see her. And she's not deadly. She's beautiful and she's laughing' (p. 255).

Luce Irigaray, 'When Our Lips Speak Together' (first published in French in 1977; in English in 1980)

Luce Irigaray's 'When Our Lips Speak Together' is in some ways very like 'The Laugh of the Medusa'. A reader who begins with Cixous's essay and follows it with Irigaray's is likely to note the similar lyrical and polemical style. Compare the openings: 'I shall speak about women's writing: about *what it will do*' (Cixous, p. 245); 'If we keep on speaking the same language together, we're going to reproduce the same history'.[12] Irigaray's analysis also resembles Cixous's in its discussion of the 'othering' of woman in western patriarchal culture. However, Irigaray emphasises that in positioning woman as man's opposite or inferior copy (through emphasising her lack of a penis instead of, for example, the presence of a vagina) patriarchy actually constructs femininity as the 'same' as masculinity – the same because still centred on the presence or absence of the phallus: 'Listen: all round us, men and women sound just the same. The same discussions, the same arguments, the same scenes. The same attractions and separations. The same difficulties, the same impossibility of making connections. The same … Same … Always the same' (p. 205). Whereas for Cixous it is otherness and difference that must be distinguished, for Irigaray otherness *conceals* sameness, so woman's difference must be written into culture and into the Symbolic Order to challenge what is, in effect, woman's absence as woman.

Irigaray embraces imagery of fluidity, proximity, touch and blood to create a language of feminine difference. This strategy resembles Cixous's in its deliberately risky tactical adoption of patriarchy's essentialist stereotyping of women: 'I love you: body shared, undivided. Neither you nor I severed. There is no need for blood shed, between us. No need for a wound to remind us that blood exists. It flows within us, from us. Blood is familiar, close. You are all red. And so very white. Both at once' (pp. 206–7). She also works with a very similar conception of the gift to Cixous's. By virtue of the absence of expectation of a return, the gift of one woman to another disrupts the masculine libidinal economy which tries to prevent the free circulation and exchange of desire.

The main difference between Cixous's and Irigaray's essays that readers are likely to notice is the evocation of lesbian love in 'When Our Lips Speak Together'. The speaking voice in Irigaray's essay addresses an unspecified 'you', a 'you' who shares desire, pleasure and emotional contact with the speaker. Although the sex of both is never explicitly specified, Irigaray uses the resonant image of the two lips to suggest not merely the lips of the mouth but also the lips of the vagina: her own and another woman's:

> Open your lips; don't open them simply. I don't open them simply. We – you/I – are neither open nor closed. We never separate simply: *a single word* cannot be pronounced, produced, uttered by our mouths. Between our lips, yours and mine, several voices, several ways of speaking resound endlessly, back and forth. One is never separable from the other ... You touch me all over at the same time. In all senses. Why only one song, one speech, one text at a time? To seduce, to satisfy, to fill one of my 'holes'? With you, I don't have any. We are not lacks, voids awaiting sustenance, plenitude, fulfillment from the other. By our lips we are women.
>
> (pp. 209–10)

The suggestiveness of this language forces us as readers to confront the proximity, even interweaving, of the body and discourse; the sexuality of textuality and vice versa. Irigaray's performance of this textual sexuality effectively writes woman as presence and difference precisely because, in evoking lesbian sexuality she speaks the unspeakable within phallocentric culture. Her writing practice in this instance is arguably more effective than Cixous's because she avoids some of the risks of recuperation involved in associating femininity with maternity and bisexuality. In creating what one critic has termed a 'lipeccentric' text,[13] Irigaray raises an important issue: the extent to which writing and culture function metaphorically. Both she and Cixous are concerned with the implications for women of the fact that femininity in patriarchy stands metaphorically for what is outside culture. Indeed, Irigaray suggests that metaphor itself works by virtue of similarity, identity, sameness – the denial of difference: it functions according to patriarchal rules. Irigaray's text forces us to ask whether its lips are literal, metaphorical, or something in between. Her 'lipeccentrism' particularly responds to, and questions, Lacan's privileging of the phallus in the Symbolic order. In bringing together anatomical and cultural meanings in new configurations she questions the conventional metaphorical, or representational, relation between text and body. For Irigaray the body is always textual but the text is also physical, a point spoken forcefully by the essay's 'two lips'. This is why, if we return for a moment to the opening sentences of Cixous's and Irigaray's essays (quoted at the start of this section on Irigaray) it is worth noting the emphasis on speech, as well as writing, in both.

Julia Kristeva, 'From One Identity to An Other' (first published in French in 1975; in English in 1980)

The dense and difficult style of Julia Kristeva's 'From One Identity to An Other' contrasts markedly with the evocative lyricism of Cixous's and Irigaray's pieces. Readers are confronted with a wide range of reference to other philosophers and linguists and extensive use of theoretical terminology (which is not always explained). Rather than anxiously trace the precise meaning of words like 'noesis' and 'noemis', it seems more appropriate in this context to grasp the central ideas in the essay in relation to those of Cixous and Irigaray. Like them, Kristeva is interested in questioning the dominance of representational theories of language, but she is also interested in what kind of *speaking or writing subject* such ideas imply. Structuralist linguistics was the most influential theory of language in 1975 when the essay was written, and part of Kristeva's purpose is to demonstrate that it has more in common with earlier theories of language than might at first be apparent. This commonality exists, for Kristeva, because structuralist linguistics still implies a conventional idea of the 'thetic' subject and language. The thetic subject, or self, is one that fails to acknowledge difference within itself. It assumes it has unity, identity and ability to act, or, in linguistic terms, to predicate (the ability to affirm, deny or assert): to make a thesis or statement. Such a conception of subjectivity and language is important, because it is this aspect of language that creates its socially enforcing power. However, Kristeva goes on to discuss language which embraces heterogeneity or difference. In the language of poetry she finds evidence of what she calls a 'semiotic disposition':

> There is within poetic language ... a *heterogeneousness* to meaning and signification. This *heterogeneousness*, detected genetically in the first echolalias of infants ... which is later reactivated ... in psychotic discourse ... produces in poetic language 'musical' but also nonsense effects that destroy not only accepted beliefs and significations, but, in radical experiments, syntax itself, that guarantee of thetic consciousness.[14]

Before infants learn to speak they 'babble'; psychotic episodes produce similar linguistic effects in those who experience them. The speaking subject in both these examples is, for Kristeva, outside the symbolic order, which guarantees logical meaning in both language and subjectivity. The child has not yet entered the symbolic and accepted/learnt its rules; the psychotic has (perhaps temporarily) abandoned them. These examples are interesting to Kristeva because they provide evidence of a disposition which she argues exists in any language (p. 101), but which is admitted more obviously in poetic language. Poetic language demonstrates an 'undecidable process between sense and nonsense, between *language* and *rhythm* ... between the symbolic and the semiotic' (p. 103). She finds the semiotic in poetry in its sentential rhythms, which allow a sentence to acquire multiple meanings and connotations, and obscene words, which mark the eruption of desire into the text. The semiotic disposition of poetry encourages the reader 'to shatter his own judging consciousness in order to grant passage through it to this rhythmic drive ... experienced as jouissance' (p. 110). Jouissance is an almost untranslatable term embracing many meanings including intense pleasure. Poetic language must therefore create a different type of subjectivity in the writer and reader from the thetic subject of conventional language. Kristeva terms this the '*subject-in-process*' (p. 103) because it is fractured, diffuse and open to change.

Kristeva's essay argues that the semiotic disposition in language is intrinsically disruptive to the social order. Like Cixous and Irigaray she thus makes moves to imbricate (overlap) the political and the textual. The most important distinction between her ideas and theirs is the extent to which she is prepared to align the semiotic and difference with femininity and the body. She does link the semiotic with the unconscious and the physical, but she only provisionally suggests that the semiotic could be maternal or feminine. She borrows Plato's image of the 'chora' to describe the semiotic as a 'receptacle ... unnameable, improbable, hybrid, anterior to naming, to the One, to the father, and consequently, maternally connoted to such an extent that it merits "not even the rank of syllable"' (p. 102). Later in the essay she describes symbolic language as marking the repression of the relation with the mother and identifies the semiotic with 'reactivating this repressed instinctual, maternal element'. Poetic language is thus the *'equivalent of incest'* because it resists the linguistic and social exchange of women which founds patriarchy (p. 104). These ideas seem to resemble Cixous's and Irigaray's views about woman's exclusion from language and the symbolic and the necessity of provisionally writing her back into it as presence and difference, but there is an important distinction. For Kristeva, the semiotic is not something which can be accessed or made present in any simple or straightforward fashion, even as a tactical move. It only comes into existence in language *in tension with* the symbolic because it is only through such an antagonistic oscillation that either term acquires meaning: 'It goes without saying that, concerning a *signifying practice*, that is, a socially communicable discourse like poetic language, this semiotic heterogeneity posited by theory is inseparable from ... the *symbolic* function of significance' (p. 102). Similarly, the semiotic only comes to have maternal 'connotations' in tense relation with the paternal connotations of symbolic language. Towards the end of the essay Kristeva remarks:

> It is probably necessary to be a woman (ultimate guarantee of sociality beyond the wreckage of the paternal symbolic function, as well as the inexhaustible generator of its renewal, of its expansion) not to renounce theoretical reason but to compel it to increase its power by giving it an object beyond its limits. Such a position, it seems to me, provides a possible basis for a theory of signification, which, confronted with poetic language, could not in any way account for it, but would rather use it as an indication of what is heterogeneous to meaning (to sign and predication): instinctual economies, always and at the same time open to bio-physiological socio-historical constraints. (p. 113)

Kristeva offers readers a version of femininity as a position which provides an example of what exceeds the symbolic order, even if that excess is always at the same time marked and defined by the symbolic. For Kristeva, woman is a space or place which makes clear how the entire system functions by showing, paradoxically, what is theoretically absent from it. Thus femininity is on the edge of the semiotic and the symbolic, an extremely important and necessary position to be in. Trying to move woman from margin or limit to centre-stage, using the tactic of writing her physical difference into language, is a strategy that will not change the symbolic order, but will merely be recuperated by it. However, there is an ambiguity remaining in the above quotation, which centres on the word 'probably' in the opening phrase. This probability troublingly refers us back to biophysiology – to the sexed body. Even if it is *probable* that those sexed female occupy the position of femininity more easily than those sexed male then Kristeva retains a definition of femininity which, like Cixous's and Irigaray's, hints at biologically essentialist notions of woman.

Virginia Woolf, *Orlando* (1928)

Virginia Woolf's work is often placed in two contexts: those of modernism and feminism. She is permitted entry into the high modernist literary canon (dominated by male writers such as T. S. Eliot, W. B. Yeats, James Joyce and Ezra Pound) because of her critique of those aspects of the nineteenth-century and Edwardian realist novel which failed to give a truthful impression of people's inner lives.[15] She experimented with conventions of character portrayal, plotting and narration, creating different ways of presenting thoughts and feelings by using devices like interior monologue, shifting narrative perspectives, unconventional chronology and subjective portrayals of the passing of time. Her novels use lyrical, poetic, sometimes playful and ironic styles. To interpret her writing in this fashion is to see it as part of a wider cultural shift that occurred in the first part of the twentieth century. In part a reaction to the shocking events of the early decades of the century such as world war, the General Strike, economic depression, unemployment and the Wall Street Crash, the movement in the arts known as modernism sought to question the assumptions of earlier writers, thinkers, artists and musicians that it was possible to create the truth about the world in any simple, objective or exterior way. This version of Woolf's oeuvre emphasises novels like *To the Lighthouse, Mrs Dalloway* and *The Waves* and sees them as contributing to the break-up of the 'nineteenth-century consensus'.[16]

Those who wish to situate Woolf in a feminist context discuss her in very different terms. Instead of analysing what might appear to be the purely formalist, deconstructive and potentially nihilist aspects of her work, feminist critics have concerned themselves with Woolf's practical suggestions for improving the inferior position of women in early twentieth-century society. As we saw in chapter one, Woolf's views in essays like *A Room of One's Own* and *Three Guineas* can be aligned with other first-wave feminists' insistence that material changes are needed to enable women to become men's equals. Many critics have focused on the non-fiction, and on the images of women characters such as Lily Briscoe and Mrs Ramsay in *To the Lighthouse*, as evidence of Woolf's commitment to a feminist politics. It is clear that these versions of Woolf's writing are potentially conflicting. Scepticism about the ability to write an objective, truthful version of reality does not happily accompany a confident ability to diagnose accurately the problems in society's treatment of women. However, this apparent conflict may say more about criticism of Woolf's work than it does about the work itself. For Woolf, the stylistic experiments associated with modernism are inseparable from the political aims of feminism. More recent criticism has demonstrated that the construction of the traditional patriarchal modernist canon is interwoven with gender issues.[17] It has sought to include other women modernists in the canon and redefine modernism in ways which account for gender differences. The First World War, for example, may have had very different effects on the lives and writing of men and women. For some women, it may even have had an emancipatory effect, offering the opportunity to work outside the home for the first time. Many women modernists, including Woolf, saw their avant-garde styles as ways of attacking the patriarchal status quo.

Theory into Practice

What could be called a simultaneously deconstructive and reconstructive strategy is present in Woolf's *Orlando* (1928). This is one of the ways in which it can most obviously be interpreted using feminist poststructuralist theory. The opening sentence of the novel is immediately suggestive of the ambivalent, playfully deconstructive style of Cixous's and Irigaray's essays: 'He – for there could be no doubt of his sex, though the fashion of the time did something to disguise it – was in the act of slicing at the head of a Moor which swung from the rafters.'[18] Orlando is performing the typically aggressive action of a young Renaissance nobleman, yet his masculinity is cast in doubt by the parenthetical statement which apparently seeks to confirm it. This ostentatious digression, or 'aside', thus anticipates the central ambiguous event half-way through the novel, where the protagonist inexplicably changes sex from male to female. Woolf's style throughout *Orlando* seeks to foreground and, by implication, to question many conventions and rules: rules of biography (the text purports to be a biography), fiction, sexuality, gender and identity. *Orlando* continually points out the rigid, turgid conventions of the biography in Woolf's era: the 'plodding' through from birth to death, the deliberate omission of unpleasant or inappropriate material, the hagiographic style. This was in part, no doubt, a joking reference to the fact that her father had been the editor of the *Dictionary of National Biography*, which was in her day a dry tome recording the lives of great men in exactly such terms. The narrator jokes about the insufficiency of manuscript evidence at crucial points in Orlando's life, and ironically bemoans the moments when Orlando does nothing worth recording except think. Serious points are being made about the version of a life contemporary biographical conventions necessarily created.

Orlando also brings a deconstructive strategy to bear on questions of gender. The change of sex enables the narrator to play with many different interpretations of gender identity and sexual difference, yet Woolf particularly wishes to suggest that throughout the historical sweep of the text, woman remains 'other to' yet 'same as' man (to use Cixous's and Irigaray's terms respectively). She demonstrates how necessary woman is to man's self-definition, and how he struggles to resist this knowledge by continual attempts to exclude and dominate women. As she travels home to England after becoming a woman, Orlando is in an odd transitional state where she is learning the rules of femininity while not forgetting those of masculinity. Initially she enjoys the lazy passivity of being a wealthy woman on board ship, the decorative display of feminine clothing and the ability to refuse or yield flirtatiously to male demands. The

prospect of being rescued by a brave sailor in an emergency is exciting, as is the sexual power she can exert merely by showing her
ankle. However, she gradually comes to realise that these qualities
are instituted in women in order that men can define themselves as
the opposite: as active, independent, rational, functional and self-
controlled creatures. She also realises that those defined according
to these masculine attributes exert a power and control which she
loses now she is a woman. The othering of woman has real social
effects, but it also poorly conceals the fact that if men's self-definition is so dependent on positioning women as their other then they
are potentially vulnerable. This vulnerability arises from the threat
of women's real difference asserting itself in a way which disrupts
what Irigaray terms the economy of the Same: a sexual economy
centred on the phallus.

In the essays discussed earlier in this chapter Cixous and Irigaray
deliberately write a stereotypically physical language of feminine
difference as a tactical move in order to insert woman into the symbolic order. Kristeva is sceptical about this, arguing instead that
poetic language embodies semiotic forces which can have feminine
connotations, but which exist in inescapable tension with the symbolic, patriarchal aspects of language. *Orlando*'s use of multiple and
conflicting explanations for the protagonist's change of sex suggests
several answers to the question of what constitutes gender identity.
Exactly similar ambiguities around biology, textuality and sexuality
are created. Immediately after her change of sex, the narrator
remarks: 'We may take advantage of this pause in the narrative to
make certain statements. Orlando had become a woman – there is
no denying it. But in every other respect, Orlando remained precisely as he had been' (p. 133). The narrator appears to suggest that
at the most profound level there is some aspect of Orlando which
remains fundamentally the same throughout the experience, and
implies that this is essentially ungendered. The indeterminacy centres on the phrase 'in every other respect': by implication, it could
be argued that becoming a woman is such a significant experience
that in no 'respect' can Orlando remain unaffected. Later in the
novel the narrator reconsiders what was already an ambivalent
account of the effects of the sex change: 'what was said a short time
ago about there being no change in Orlando the man and Orlando
the woman was ceasing to be altogether true' (p. 179). Orlando is
becoming more modest about her intelligence and more concerned
with her appearance. The narrator then offers several explanations

for this shift. Initially she seems to support the idea that social conditioning is all important in creating one's personal experience of gender: 'the change of clothes had, some philosophers will say, much to do with it. Vain trifles as they seem, clothes have, they say, more important offices than merely to keep us warm. They change our view of the world and the world's view of us ... it is clothes that wear us and not we them' (pp. 179–80). This startling inversion of our conventional idea that we *choose* our clothes to express or reflect certain aspects of our selves makes the social constructionist argument forcefully. Immediately, however, the narrator does an about-face: 'That is the view of some philosophers and wise ones, but on the whole, we incline to another. The difference between the sexes is happily one of great profundity. Clothes are but a symbol of something hid deep beneath. It was a change in Orlando herself that dictated her choice of a woman's dress and of a woman's sex' (pp. 180–1). The metaphors of depth and surface here suggest that one's biological sex is all-important, and is simply mirrored in our gender identity. This biologically essentialist argument is immediately complicated, however: 'Different though the sexes are, they intermix. In every human being a vacillation from one sex to the other takes place, and often it is only the clothes that keep the male or female likeness, while underneath the sex is the very opposite of what it is above' (p. 181). Here we encounter the idea that human nature is basically androgynous, an argument with which we are familiar from *A Room of One's Own*, discussed in Chapter 1. Carefully tracing some of the shifts in opinions about Orlando's change of sex and its effects demonstrates that the text demands close reading, and that often the ambiguities in the treatment of this issue are generated at the level of the sentence. *Orlando* resists what Kristeva would term 'thetic' language and allows the semiotic to erupt in the text in its digressions, contradictions, interruptions, ellipses and hiatuses. After all, what else is Orlando but a 'subject-in-process'? The text also creates a reading subject who is 'in process'. One is forced to abandon any desire for consistency, unity and conclusive argument and instead accept deferral, indeterminacy and ambiguity.

It would appear that Woolf is only willing to link this experience with Orlando's body on occasions, but the physicality of the female body persists as a deliberately troubling remnant in the text, as it does in Kristeva's 'From One Identity to An Other'. The actual effects of the change of sex on Orlando's body are never alluded to;

this creates an 'unsaid' in the novel, an 'unsaid' which is actually very important. It is also obvious that the confusion about gender only really begins when Orlando becomes a woman. Possessing a body sexed female is what causes proliferating interpretations rather than the sex change itself – it is doubtful whether the same sorts of anxieties would come into play if Orlando had changed from a woman into a man. At points Woolf does consider the implications of writing the female body as difference. Throughout the text Orlando has ambitions to become a writer, but her long poem, 'The Oak Tree', is only published after she has become a woman, which strongly suggests that the experience of becoming female is creatively necessary for her to succeed as a writer. Writing well is linked in the text with experiences of bisexuality, love and maternity, a link also made in Cixous's 'The Laugh of the Medusa'. It is after Orlando marries Marmaduke Bonthrop Shelmerdine and just before her son is born that she completes her manuscript and Nick Greene arranges to publish it. Both Shelmerdine and Orlando are intensely aware of, and attracted by, the qualities of the other sex each possesses: '"Are you positive you aren't a man?" he would ask anxiously, and she would echo, "Can it be possible you're not a woman?" and then they must put it to the proof without more ado' (p. 246). Yet these qualities of manliness in Orlando and womanliness in Shelmerdine paradoxically 'prove' their essential difference: '"I am a woman," she thought, "a real woman, at last." She thanked Bonthrop from the bottom of her heart for this rare and unexpected delight' (p. 241). Orlando and Shelmerdine take pleasure in the desire this difference and plurality create. Their love and marriage allows Orlando to write well for the first time, and the agreement to publish her manuscript is closely followed by the birth of her son. The narrator's hint that something of significance is about to happen is followed by a lengthy digression which tries to conceal, in typically Victorian fashion, the embarrassment of the pregnancy and labour. The birth itself is announced as follows: '"It's a very fine boy, M'Lady," said Mrs Banting, the midwife, putting her first-born child into Orlando's arms. In other words Orlando was safely delivered of a son on Thursday, March the 20th, at three o'clock in the morning' (p. 282). The experience of maternity is never referred to again. This absence, like the absence of reference to the physical facts of Orlando's becoming female, is indicative both of its official exclusion from the symbolic order, and its importance as the foundation of that order.

Like Irigaray, Woolf also aligns writing the female body, albeit implicitly, with lesbianism. The novel was written as a tribute to her lover Vita Sackville-West, whose life, history and country seat were the models for Orlando's; it is full of in-jokes which Vita and her family would have understood. It has been persuasively argued that Woolf concealed the lesbian aspects of the text to avoid the opprobrium attendant on the appearance of Radclyffe Hall's *The Well of Loneliness*, which deals explicitly with lesbian issues, three months before *Orlando* was published.[19] Suggestions of same-sex love exist as ironic traces throughout the novel. As a young nobleman at the court of King James, Orlando is intensely attracted to a person whom he at first assumes to be a boy because she is such a good skater. He is 'ready to tear his hair with vexation that the person was of his own sex, and thus all embraces were out of the question' (p. 36). The ostensible relief on his (and the text's) part when Sasha turns out to be a woman (albeit one who posseses distinctly masculine qualities) does not invalidate the erotic thrill attached to the prospect of a homosexual liaison. A very similar episode occurs much later on, when Orlando has become a woman, but chooses to dress as a man to go for an evening walk. She is accosted by a prostitute, and does not reveal her sex until the last possible moment. The erotic potential of the scene is considerable and persists as a disturbing supplement in the text. Immediately after her change of sex, Orlando finds that her deepest feelings are still for women. Although this is explained as 'the culpable laggardry of the human frame to adapt itself to convention' (p. 154), Orlando is still greatly affected by suddenly seeing Sasha again at the very end of the novel, when one might assume that such an adaptation would have taken place. To read the lesbian subtext of the novel carefully may mean acknowledging the possibility that Orlando's change of sex is motivated by the desire to experience *same-sex* love with other women.

Orlando debates the same central question which puzzles Cixous, Irigaray and Kristeva: how to deal with women's difference while simultaneously acknowledging that that difference cannot really exist in the patriarchal symbolic order. When Orlando reveals the fact that she is a woman to the prostitute, Nell gathers together her friends and all the women share an enjoyable evening of gossip, chat and rumination on their situations. What they actually say is not told to the reader, indeed the idea that such an evening of companionship among women is possible is doubted by the narrator who, instead, ironically repeats a series of men's opinions of women:

> 'It is well known', says Mr S. W., 'that when they lack the stimulus of the other sex, women can find nothing to say to each other. When they are alone, they do not talk, they scratch.' And since they cannot talk together and scratching cannot continue without interruption and it is well known (Mr T. R. has proved it) 'that women are incapable of any feeling of affection for their own sex and hold each other in the greatest aversion', what can we suppose that women do when they seek out each other's society?
>
> As that is not a question that can engage the attention of a sensible man, let us, who enjoy the immunity of all biographers and historians from any sex whatever, pass it over, and merely state that Orlando professed great enjoyment in the society of her own sex, and leave it to the gentlemen to prove, as they are very fond of doing, that this is impossible.   (p. 210)

In this clever passage, the narrator assumes a sexless voice merely to demonstrate that this apparent 'neutrality' can easily conceal masculine prejudice. In quoting examples of such prejudice about women Woolf mimics it so that it begins to seem ridiculous. The possibility that women enjoy each other's company then emerges by implication from the gaps in the text. This exactly resembles poststructuralist feminism's insistence on deconstructing the category 'woman' as it exists in patriarchy, but simultaneously reconstructing it tactically and strategically using the flawed language available. Woolf suggests, like Cixous, Irigaray and Kristeva, that the body and language are mired together and that language is thus a political weapon and has more than a merely representational or metaphorical function. The fact that Orlando is a woman is finally confirmed linguistically, through the thetic language of the Law: 'my sex is pronouned indisputably female' (p. 243). Immediately after her change of sex the shifts in the pronouns used to describe Orlando ('we must for convention's sake say "her" for "his", and "she" for "he"' – p. 133) also demonstrate the importance of language in creating a binary gender system. Orlando particularly ponders the relation between life and art, and finds the conventional metaphorical or representational way of perceiving this relationship deeply unsatisfactory. He notes his own propensity to use elaborate figurative language, and finally deems it pointless, recognising that perceiving the relation between life and poetry, or masculinity and femininity, as metaphorical fails to account for difference. In each case, the latter is not a similar copy of the former because both are discursively constructed in multiple ways.

Practice into Theory

The reception of Woolf's *Orlando* suggests one important problem with feminist poststructuralist theory: the possibility that the risk attached to using essentialist language to define woman's difference – however strategically – is too great to make it worth taking. Isn't emphasising the importance of women's bodies and suggesting that they are the source of innate differences between men and women exactly what patriarchy has always believed, and is quite happy to hear? In the Victorian period the ideology of separate spheres for women and men, which confined middle-class women in the home, was based on beliefs about the intrinsic differences of women's physical natures from men's. Many early feminist readers of Cixous, Irigaray and Kristeva found their arguments to be essentialist, and failed to see this essentialism as a tactical move.[20] If this interpretation can be suggested by other *feminists* it is more than likely to be made by readers unsympathetic to feminism of any kind. Jacqueline Rose discusses Kristeva's work as encountering a dilemma: 'the hideous moment when a theory arms itself with a concept of femininity as different, a something other to the culture as it is known, only to find itself face to face with, or even entrenched within, the most grotesque and fully cultural stereotypes of femininity itself'.[21] This risk of incorporation is well demonstrated by the way that contemporary readers and reviewers perceived *Orlando*: as a humorous, light-hearted 'romp' which was not to be taken too seriously. Indeed, this view was shared by Woolf herself during the novel's composition.[22] Treating *Orlando* in this way meant that it had to wait for feminist criticism to take it seriously; the novel is very rarely given any lengthy discussion in early studies of Woolf's work.

This point suggests that what Rose calls the 'fully cultural' nature of femininity is, like the fully cultural nature of a text's reception, inescapable. The idea that somehow femininity exists outside of or before culture, language or the symbolic, and can therefore be the source of a disruptive language of difference, cannot, according to this argument, be the case, even in the very provisional sense which Cixous, Irigaray and Kristeva may imply. Similarly, the transgressive aspects of *Orlando* can only be perceived by those looking for them: irony is in the eye of the beholder. The text itself suggests that the exact difference in Orlando once she becomes a woman is almost impossible to locate outside what are perceived as its 'effects' in society. The experience of being both a man and a woman and the fact that Orlando lives from the Elizabethan age until 1928 without aging much make her uniquely placed to understand how 'woman' means something very different in different historical periods. In the Victorian era, for example, Orlando notes with distaste the new emphasis on life-long companionate marriage, but is unable to resist its manifestation in an irritating tingling in her wedding-ring finger, an irritation that persists until she finds a husband to appease it. The fact that the desire for marriage precedes meeting a likely suitor is an ironic comment on the Victorian idealisation of romantic love, which concealed a ruthlessly economic marriage market. The physical effects of these ideologies on Orlando suggest that the body cannot be the source of pre-cultural meanings because it is entirely culturally produced.

Orlando retains an emphasis on economic and social forces in constructing identity, which is not surprising for the author of *A Room of One's Own*. It is important that Orlando is a wealthy property owner, and one of the significant ways in which her femininity creates problems is when her ownership of this property is questioned. The lack of emphasis on such material factors in poststructuralist feminist analyses is grounded in the argument that the economic and social are discursively constructed anyway. It is this breaking-up of an apparently false opposition between language and reality that explains the political significance Cixous, Irigaray and Kristeva accord to writing. However, it is certainly not the case that poetic language, or writing the body, necessarily has a socially subversive function: that function is, as we have seen in relation to the reception of *Orlando*, context-dependent. Decisions about what gets published are often made on commercial grounds. Virginia Woolf and her husband ran their own press, but the publication of Orlando's 'The Oak Tree' suggests some of the fortuitous chances involved for those less fortunate. Her meeting with Nicholas Greene and the fact that he is now in a position powerful enough to help her, by contacting publishers and reviewers, are matters of chance. More importantly, the text suggests that one reason why Orlando makes a success of 'The Oak Tree' is because it is now in keeping with 'the spirit of the age' (p. 253), not because she is finally able to write her female body. In other words, it is because 'The Oak Tree' fits with Victorian ideologies that it is published, which suggests the exact opposite of the anarchic effects Kristeva perceives in poetic language. Breaking down the distinction between such language and the economic and social by demonstrating that both are discourses does not mean that they are the *same* discourse with *identical* effects, which are *equally* significant in shaping our lives.

There is also a problem with the idea that ambiguous, ironic and complex language generates productive questioning in the reader. Many readers of both Woolf's *Orlando* and Kristeva's work, in particular, find it impossibly abstruse, experiencing nothing but frustration and resentment. All four of the writers discussed here use such language particularly when making extensive reference to their literary, philosophical and cultural heritage, which is usually male. Even though such allusions are very rarely respectful, it is often difficult to 'get the joke' if one does not know the source. The treatment of their psychoanalytical forefathers is a case in point. Without a knowledge of Freud and Lacan (as a bare minimum) it is difficult to understand the vocabulary of Cixous, Irigaray and Kristeva, and to comprehend how this playfully and inventively innovates on previous orthodoxies. If we pause to consider *Orlando* as a commentary on Freudian psychoanalysis a similar point can be made. The Hogarth Press, owned and run by the Woolfs, published the English translation of all of Freud and work by other contemporary psychoanalysts such as Melanie Klein and Ernest Jones. Although Woolf claimed not to have read Freud until 1939, the year she met him, many of her friends and relations were training as analysts and invited them as speakers. She was thus part of a circle in which psychoanalysis was influential,[23] and we could read *Orlando* as a travesty of Freud's account of the acquisition of gender identity. Freud's story arguably creates a straightforwardly narrative and even teleological (designed to serve a particular purpose) version of normative masculine development. Woolf institutes an incredible, deliberately excessive example of such a development (the change of sex). She asks whether this change can be understood in any way as part of a progressive sequence or whether it is in fact profoundly anti-narrative, because totally random. She also makes Orlando, who began life biologically male, reach an 'end-point' (if she has one) of being female; a joke at the expense of Freud's theory of the

Oedipus complex, which ultimately seeks to align gender identity and sexual object choice with genital sexuality. All of these allusions are lost on the reader who has no acquaintance with Freud. If Woolf, Cixous, Irigaray and Kristeva are so concerned to disrupt the patriarchal symbolic order then why do they make so much reference to their male forebears anyway? Is the risk of being perceived as 'dutiful daughters' worth taking?

Of related concern is the fact that many of the examples of subversive feminine writing that Kristeva and Cixous discuss are by men. Kristeva mentions Mayakovsky, Artaud, Lautréamont, Mallarmé, Beckett, the Marquis de Sade and Céline. Cixous mentions in a footnote Colette, Marguerite Duras and Jean Genet. Irigaray's essay does not explicitly apply her ideas to any writer's work. This discovery of femininity as a trace in the most canonical male texts certainly breaks down any assumption of a naive, or automatic, link between anatomy and style, but an equally significant part of the trio's argument concerns the ways in which this link must be reconstructed, admittedly in more sophisticated ways. It would seem necessary to demonstrate this in relation to writing by women authors. Woolf's *Orlando*, as has been suggested, provides a good case in point, which is why it has been included here, especially since it is also, like many of the male examples, a modernist text.

Another significant accusation levelled at Cixous, Irigaray and Kristeva concerns the way they downplay differences *between* women. This is apparent in the number of occasions when they tend to discuss 'woman' rather than 'women'. Their analyses don't always acknowledge the fact that class, race and sexuality can fracture and complicate such a simple categorisation. By placing their work in the context of the practice of clitoridectomy Gayatri Spivak suggestively complicates ideas about the female body as source for a subversive writing: 'I see no way to avoid insisting that there has to be a simultaneous other focus: not merely who am I? But who is the other woman? How am I naming her? How does she name me?'[24] It could be argued that *Orlando*'s narrowness in class terms has similarly reductive effects. The text takes great pleasure in the aristocratic, luxurious life of its protagonist and relishes the manifestations of wealth and property that surround him/her. Orlando's love of land and his country house stays with him when he becomes a 'she' – this is one of the ways in which a continuity of identity is suggested. The most significant effect of the change of sex is to call into question Orlando's rights to her estate, and the novel takes pains to restore these by the end. Undoubtedly, very different effects would be prominent in the life of a man of a lower class who underwent a similar change. The pleasure the novel takes in class privilege is one of its least enjoyable aspects, unless we see *Orlando* as satirising that pleasure as well as celebrating it. The episode where Orlando lives with the gypsies for a short while immediately after becoming a woman is an interesting case in point. The gypsies react to her proud descriptions of her house and lineage with polite embarrassment: they 'thought a descent of four or five hundred years only the meanest possible ... there was nothing specially memorable or desirable in ancient birth; vagabonds and beggars all shared it ... there was no more vulgar ambition than to possess bedrooms by the hundred ...when the whole earth is ours' (p. 142). The narrator is certainly using this episode to jibe at upperclass assumptions. Part of Woolf's complex attitude is bound up with her feelings for Vita, whose background was significantly different from Woolf's own, but the text does at times suggest that women of different classes share more than they realise. When Orlando spends an evening with Nell and her prostitute friends the differences between them are merely superficial, and are lost beneath the key experience of exploitation by men.

The implicit nature of the lesbian subtext in *Orlando* also suggests some of the difficulties in Irigaray's evocation of lesbianism in 'When Our Lips Speak Together'. Woman is the underside and the mainstay of the symbolic order for Irigaray; lesbianism, in evoking the initial same-sex love relation with the mother, inserts woman as positive difference into that order. This performs what one critic has termed a '*provisional* maneuver, one whose function is tactical and temporary, remedial – one step in a long series of struggles necessary to establish an autonomous identity for women'.[25] Lesbianism thus becomes subordinate to a narrative which seeks to empower all women. This exactly resembles the place accorded lesbianism in *Orlando*, where it is hidden beneath a more overt narrative about androgyny and the emancipation of women. The association between lesbianism and maternity, and the emphasis on maternity in the writing of Cixous, Irigaray and Kristeva, has also been severely challenged. Judith Butler argues that the maternal body is not 'the hidden ground of all signification, the tacit cause of all culture'. Rather, it is 'an effect or consequence of a system of sexuality in which the female body is required to assume maternity as the essence of its self and the law of its desire'.[26] Elsewhere, she argues that it is the lesbian who is culturally constructed as 'other' yet essential to those distinctions which are crucial to the patriarchal symbolic order such as mind/matter and gender/sex: not the woman.[27] Therefore lesbianism cannot be easily abandoned once its tactical effectiveness appears to have served its purpose (a position some have found Irigaray taking in her more recent interest in heterosexual love relationships).[28] The maternal metaphor for lesbian sexuality has been questioned by more recent interest in lesbian s/m practices as subversive rewritings or redeployments of gay male and male heterosexual sexual practices.[29] The heterosexism of patriarchal culture will not be effectively challenged until the difference of lesbianism, as well as differences of class and race, is genuinely acknowledged within it. These debates will be discussed in more depth in Chapters 7 and 8.

Conclusion

What becomes clear when we read Virginia Woolf's *Orlando* alongside Hélène Cixous's 'The Laugh of the Medusa', Luce Irigaray's 'When Our Lips Speak Together' and Julia Kristeva's 'From One Identity to An Other' is the sheer variety of interpretations they all produce, and the fact that many of these are totally contradictory. Most of these contradictions centre, as we have seen, around the position of the sexed body in relation to culture, writing and politics, and the questioning of that very phrase 'in relation to' (metaphorical, and thus problematic!). In raising these issues and generating debate about them, all four of these texts perform a vital function: in Kristevan terms they are poetic texts which embody the 'undecidable process ... between the symbolic and the semiotic' (p. 103). They forcibly generate productive uncertainty in the reading subject. In their simultaneous use of deconstructive and reconstructive linguistic strategies, they are all (even *Orlando*) distinctly poststructuralist feminist texts.

6

Postmodernism
and Feminism

Introduction

To write a book with one chapter on poststructuralist feminism and one on postmodernism and feminism suggests certain things. First, it implies that poststructuralism and postmodernism are different and, secondly, it puts one before the other. A particular narrative trajectory is created for the reader, which might go something like this: poststructuralist feminism exists in crucial relation to psychoanalysis and linguistics, so the chapter discussing it immediately follows the one on psychoanalysis. It is, however, part of a broader range of philosophical and cultural investigations which can be termed postmodernist, so this chapter situates its exemplary texts in a wider field of inquiry, while referring back to the work of the previous chapter. Using spatial rather than linear metaphors, Best and Kellner make a similar point: 'poststructuralism forms part of the matrix of postmodern theory ... we shall interpret poststructuralism as a subset of a broader range of theoretical, cultural, and social tendencies which constitute postmodern discourses'.[1] Why, though, is the chapter called 'Postmodernism and Feminism' and not 'Postmodernist Feminism'? The 'post' of postmodernism also begs questions. Does it imply merely a succession, a respectful continuation, or a rejection of modernism? What is the difference between postmodernity and postmodernism? Possible answers to these questions should become apparent in the rest of the chapter.

We might begin by saying that we are now in the postmodern era, or the historical period which follows the modern period. If we wanted to risk dating the modern period, we could do worse than place it as occupying the years from 1750 to 1950.[2] However, the 'post' prefix also suggests significant differences from the modern period: differences which have more to do with a significant shift in those philosophies, ideologies and social and economic structures which characterise an era. The shifts which allow us to distinguish one period from another are also those which enable the use of terms like modernity and postmodernity to define and explain those beliefs (whether implicit or explicit) and ways of organising the economy and society which are representative of a particular period. One such shift becomes apparent if we consider the argument that modernity was characterised by its belief in metanarratives: accounts of the world which sought to explain a huge variety of phenomena in terms of one overarching and all-inclusive story. Examples of metanarratives are provided by religions such as Christianity, scientific theories of progress such as Darwin's evolution theory, economic and social theories such as Marxism and psychological theories such as Freudian psychoanalysis. In postmodernity most people no longer believe in the explanatory power of any one of these narratives, or in the way of looking at the world they imply. We doubt that it is possible to find any single way of accounting for everything that happens around us, greeting the arrival of yet another metanarrative with weary scepticism, or what Jean-François Lyotard, one of the most significant exponents of this theory of postmodernity, terms 'incredulity'.[3] This feeling results partly from the fact that in a postmodern world we know that our perceptions are continually mediated by sophisticated media and computer technology. It therefore becomes increasingly difficult to distinguish between reality and representations of reality, and thus make meaningful judgements. In fact such a distinction becomes meaningless; we exist in what Jean Baudrillard has termed a state of 'hyperreality' where all that surrounds us is a series of texts.[4] In such a situation we begin to lose faith in traditional ways of understanding identity and the self. Humans no longer seem to be the rational, unified creatures, capable of sound judgement and ethical behaviour that we believed them to be in the modern period. Instead, they become fractured, inconsistent and irrational beings who are forced to turn to a multiplicity of small-scale, local explanations to account for the various phenomena they encounter.

If postmodernity is the period in which we now live, characterised by the distinct cultural differences from modernity briefly discussed above, what has caused such a shift to take place? Some have argued that these changes can best be understood in the context of 'late capitalism', which can be distinguished from industrial capitalism, characteristic of modernity, by its emphasis on consumption of products rather than their production.[5] Consumption of increasingly numerous and various commodities now dominates people's lives in a global market economy. Others point to different causes of the general malaise as we reach the beginning of the twenty-first century: the sheer number of atrocities and disasters in the twentieth; the amount of 'information' we have about them; the manifest corruption and domination by image of the political sphere.

Whatever the causes of the turn from modernity to postmodernity, many critics have still worked with the rough distinction between postmoder*nity* as a description of the social and economic factors that characterise the period in which we live and postmodern*ism* as that period's cultural products.[6] To describe postmodern*ism* merely as a cultural response, whether critical or otherwise, to social changes might appear to be naïve, because it retains a distinction between reality and representations of reality which is becoming increasingly redundant. While accepting that point, if we use the distinction very provisionally for the purposes of elucidation we can begin to discuss some of the distinguishing features of postmodernism in culture. First we could point to the breakdown of the distinction between high and popular art forms and the mixing of elements of both in the same text. After all, if it has become increasingly difficult to make value-laden aesthetic judgements then the only appropriate response is to treat everything equally as a discourse or text. Secondly we might note the ironic use of the past and history. In architecture, for example, postmodernist buildings can be recognised by the use of elements of different architectural styles from different historical periods in the same building. Thirdly, of great importance is an increasing self-consciousness about the methods used to create a text; in fiction this might mean explicitly exposing the conventions used, for example a particular narrative method, to the reader's scrutiny. Fourthly, postmodernist art tends to make intertextual use of other texts in a humorous, playful way. Some of these simplified descriptions might well remind us of *Orlando*, the supposedly modernist text discussed in the previous chapter, and here we come to another important issue: the relationship between modernism and postmodernism in the arts, culture and literature. Although much has been written about this,[7] it could be argued that although some of the methods of modernism and postmodernism are similar, what distinguishes the two is, first, the anti-elitism of postmodernist when compared with modernist texts, and secondly the loss of belief in any possibility of representing reality truthfully. Thus, if the modernist text is often difficult, even abstruse, in its allusions to canonical art forms, the postmodernist text can be more easily accessible because it also takes pleasure in reference to the popular. Whereas the critical relation of a modernist literary text to its forebears suggests an attempt to improve or advance on those ways of depicting life, the pleasurable scavenging of the postmodernist text in a wide range of other sources implies a laid-back enjoyment of a variety of ideas and methodologies which are all perceived to be equal in value (or lack of value). Most discussion of the relationship between feminism and postmodernism in the late 1980s concentrated on the similarities, differences, alliances and antipathies between postmodernism and feminism rather than on synthesising a new theory from both.[8] We cannot describe the features of a postmodernist feminism in the same way as we can (however provisionally) describe those of psychoanalytic feminism and Marxist feminism.

Alice Jardine, *Gynesis* (1985)

Alice Jardine's book *Gynesis: Configurations of Woman and Modernity* makes cautious links between feminism and postmodernism, but also acknowledges the tensions between the two. The book explicitly situates itself in relation to American and French culture, attempting to interpret the latter for the former. Jardine thus takes pains to ask 'whom are we writing to and for?'[9] in a way which suggests some awareness of the kinds of questions about location that Gayatri Spivak asks of Cixous, Irigaray and Kristeva in her article 'French Feminism in an International Frame' (quoted at the end of the previous chapter). Rather confusingly for us, Jardine uses the term 'modernity' to characterise the kinds of thinking we are terming 'postmodernist', arguing that 'modernity' is the word used in France while 'postmodernity' is favoured in the USA. In the discussion that follows, particularly when reading quotations from

Gynesis, this difference should be kept in mind. This difficulty is indicative of the issues raised in the book about comparativism and translation in the context of postmodernist thinking. Jardine's point is that traditional ways of comparing ideas from different disciplines, or translating one language into another, both rely on a modernist, representational model where a perfect idea or ideal text is merely copied in a different context. One of the most significant interventions of postmodernist thought has been to argue against the reflective or synthetic views involved in this way of thinking. Thus 'postmodernism' in Anglo-American culture does not mean the same as 'modernity' does in French culture and we cannot extract, or synthesise, the basic similarities between feminism and postmodernism from their contexts to prove their identity. For Jardine, French and Anglo-American culture and French and Anglo-American feminism are different and feminism and postmodernism are different, but her book tries to force these discourses together in a productive encounter.

Jardine defines postmodernism as a crisis in nineteenth-century narratives or ways of perceiving subjectivity, representation and truth. She emphasises that feminism is one of the narratives that has been questioned by postmodernism because of its reliance on straightforward categorisations of female identity, experience, representation and liberation. American feminism is criticised for retaining an emphasis on this definition of feminism in the face of its deconstruction by French exponents of postmodernist theory. However, Jardine also recognises that feminism has in common with postmodernism an emphasis on the exclusive and dominating aspects of those narratives which were characteristic of Enlightenment thinking. What she is fascinated by is the process for which she coins the 'believable neologism: *gynesis* – the putting into discourse of "woman" as that *process* diagnosed as intrinsic to the condition of modernity; indeed the valorization of the feminine, woman ... as somehow intrinsic to new and necessary modes of thinking, writing, speaking' (p. 25). The book thus enacts a twofold process: first it elucidates the explicit absence (yet necessary presence) of femininity in those conceptual and methodological systems and distinctions which upheld modern history, religion and philosophy. Jardine demonstrates that the feminine has always acted as metaphor for the inferior term in dichotomies which have been central in the dialectical thinking which founded such disciplines, for example form and matter, self and other, and truth and fiction.

Secondly she points out the curious fact that femininity also provides the more or less explicit metaphor for the destabilisation or deconstruction of those binaries in the work of male theorists of postmodernism.

This fact is both interesting and disturbing to Jardine, and she stresses that it should be both these things for feminist readers, writers and critics also. She traces the appearance of the feminine in the writing of male French theorists of postmodernity such as Lacan, Derrida and Deleuze and Guattari, focusing particularly on those of their texts which interpret contemporary French fiction. In each case, her analysis suggests that where they use femininity to evoke things like difference, jouissance and linguistic undecidability they simultaneously create 'some very traditional, recognizable images and destinies of women' (p. 207), which may be problematic for feminists. American postmodernist fiction has equally disturbing, but very different tendencies. Jardine argues that what happens at the level of language or discourse in the French texts occurs at the level of representation or theme in American fiction. This distinction can be explained by American resistance to the most radical anti-representational implications of French postmodernist thought about language and reality. To distinguish these different types of gynesis she uses the images of painting and sculpture. The American novelist 'adds more and more images, more narrative, more "characters," more words – however random – to cover up the emptiness at the foundations of his construction'. French writing 'constantly moves around the material to be formed, never staying in one position very long, removing more and more material in order to create a shape' (p. 235).

For Jardine, the gynesis of French and American postmodernist thought and writing offers challenges to the feminist reader, whether 'Anglo-American' or 'French'. French postmodernism presents feminists with a valuable critique of those modernist assumptions that feminism has historically shared; American postmodernism reminds us of the political importance of issues of representation for women, however covertly they reappear in the writing of male French theoreticians of postmodernity like Derrida and Lacan. *Gynesis* is to some extent a hybrid text, as Jardine admits: 'I am neither "above it all" nor somewhere in the middle of the Atlantic. But then neither is my reader' (p. 18). Instead she points to various spaces for further work in this area for feminists: 'the theories and practices of modernity, *when taken up by female voices,* become strangely and irresistibly subversive' (p. 258). One example she suggests is research into the possibility of a link between historical periods of instability or shift in conceptual and ideological systems and periods when feminist issues are to the fore. More generally, Jardine points to the work of those feminist theorists who were studied in the previous chapter of this book as examples of thinkers who have tried to work within and move beyond gynesis. In one sense then, her book, like this one, takes Cixous, Irigaray and Kristeva and returns them to the wider intellectual, cultural and *patriarchal* context of postmodernism in order to situate their thinking, and explain their innovation more precisely. Jardine believes that it is essential for feminism to engage with postmodernism and take part in the debates it has created if only to ensure that women themselves contribute to what she terms 'gynesis'.

Seyla Benhabib, 'Feminism and the Question of Postmodernism' (1992)

Seyla Benhabib's 'Feminism and the Question of Postmodernism' is the seventh chapter in her book *Situating the Self: Gender, Community and Postmodernism in Contemporary Ethics*. The book as a whole contributes to the discussion about the future and purpose of philosophy in the context of current debates about postmodernism; in this chapter Benhabib particularly addresses the implications of a possible alignment of feminism with postmodernism. She argues that only what she categorises as a 'weak' version of postmodernism is compatible with a feminist agenda. According to Benhabib, postmodernism has precipitated a crisis in modern conceptions of representation. It is no longer possible to represent reality accurately because of postmodernism's critique of the modern subject, object and sign, each of the three axes conventionally involved in representing something. The modern conception of the subject, or perceiving consciousness able to make objective distinctions and accurate judgements about reality, has been undermined by the understanding that the self (and therefore its judgements) is shaped by historical and unconscious forces of which it is not always aware. How we define the object or what is out there to be represented has been shown to be dependent on ideas of power: we externalise things in order to dominate and control them. The signs, or words, we use to represent things are not naturally and automatically related to those things but are attached to them arbitrarily, by convention and agreement. It thus becomes almost impossible to describe reality accurately. Benhabib suggests that postmodernity can be distinguished from modernity by the consequent shift in emphasis from consciousness to language. The consequences of this shift are important: some critics, like Lyotard, suggest that all that remains in the postmodern world are multiple language games which lead to the proliferation of local, context-specific judgements and values. It is this 'strong' version of postmodernism which Benhabib feels has little to offer feminists.

Instead, the remainder of the chapter argues that 'weak' versions of the three most significant theses of postmodernist theory allow more scope for feminist philosophy and criticism. Benhabib borrows these three theses, the death of man, the death of history and the death of metaphysics, from Jane Flax's *Thinking Fragments: Psychoanalysis, Feminism and Postmodernism in the Contemporary West*. She demonstrates that feminism has created three very similar theses, which she defines as the 'demystification of the male subject of reason', the 'engendering of historical narrative' and 'feminist skepticism towards the claims of transcendent reason'.[10] In other words, for a feminist critic or philosopher it is gender issues and inequalities which have particularly deconstructed and made fallible modern conceptions of identity, history and reason. Yet to agree with 'strong' versions of postmodernist theses is possible for feminists 'only at the risk of incoherence and self-contradictoriness' (p. 213). While Benhabib is happy to endorse a 'weak' version of the *situatedness* of the subject, claims that it is *dead*, she argues, leave us with no concept of agency at all:

> a subjectivity that would not be structured by language, by narrative and by the symbolic codes of narrative available in a culture is unthinkable ... we can concede all that, but nevertheless we must still argue that we are not merely extensions of our histories, that vis-a-vis our own stories we are in the position of author and character at once ... I want to ask how in fact the very project of female emancipation would be thinkable without such a regulative ideal of enhancing the agency, autonomy and selfhood of women. (p. 214)

Benhabib makes similar points about the death of history and metaphysics. It is easy to agree that history can no longer provide access to a grand narrative or absolute truth about the past and understand that the idea of historical progress is fundamentally flawed. It is more difficult to abandon the impulse to use history to recover the interests of oppressed groups. What would the purpose of historical research be for feminist historians if it were not to account for women's experiences in some narrative way? Benhabib concludes that 'postmodernist historiography ... poses difficult alternatives for feminists which challenge any hasty or enthusiastic alliance between their positions' (p. 223). Benhabib also suggests that philosophy has to retain some sort of metadiscursive function. Even if we accept that it is extremely difficult to define any ultimate abstract philosophical principles that do not in the end reveal themselves to be context-dependent, philosophers cannot self-consciously retreat to local, situated criticism. If they do so they ignore the fact that it is sometimes necessary for us to project beyond our own situation, either because our own context is hostile to our thinking or because any narrative account, even a local or situated one, inevitably generalises. A 'weak' version of the postmodernist thesis of the end of metaphysics would allow feminists to retain what Benhabib terms the 'ethical impulse of utopia' (p. 229) or what we might describe as a desire to project, to generalise and to narrate 'grandly', even while we acknowledge and address the risks involved.

Angela Carter, *Nights at the Circus* (1984)

Angela Carter's novels concern themselves with precisely the kinds of debates about postmodernism and feminism that we are discussing here. Throughout her career, prematurely cut short by her death at the age of 51 in 1992, Carter's writing was preoccupied with sexuality, desire and identity (particularly gender identity). This preoccupation manifests itself in ways that some critics have identified as distinctly postmodernist. Carter 'raids' literary history, both popular and canonical, for intertextual allusions, she uses an eclectic mixture of styles, genres and forms, her fiction is non-realist and highly self-conscious, and embraces marginality, perversity and the fantastic. These are all features which align her with a postmodernist critique of modern distinctions such as those between good and bad literature, canonical and popular genres and mainstream and marginal themes and styles. Yet her commitment to feminism has always chafed against the implications of what Benhabib would define as the 'strong' postmodernist position. In an extremely controversial piece, which appeared shortly after her death, John Bayley associated Carter's work with 'political correctness' and commented that Carter 'always comes to rest in the right ideological position'.[11] What Bayley means is that Carter's writing is unapologetically feminist, and that for him the best literature should 'rise above' such issues and assume the greater objectivity of perfect art. He does not accept the fact that all writing has a political agenda, even if some of those agendas, like his own liberal humanist one, are inconspicuous because they are acceptable and familiar. In pointing out a contradiction between feminism and an ideal of apolitical art, Bayley does, however, suggest to us some of the similar problems involved in yoking together Carter's feminism and postmodernism. As Benhabib argues, in making the postmodernist gesture of abandoning grand narratives we may also abandon what is a necessarily political commitment to reconstructing the stories of those, like women, who have historically been oppressed.

If Carter is potentially 'too feminist' to be a postmodernist writer, she does not sit entirely comfortably in the feminist 'camp' either. Some critics have expressed concerns about her depiction of violence against women and the way she constructs female desire as passive and responsive to men. These issues are most apparent in *The Sadeian Woman: An Exercise in Cultural History* (1979) in which she argued in favour of the liberating potential for women of the non-reproductive erotics contained in the Marquis de Sade's work. This pro-pornography stance was particularly controversial in the late 1970s context of contemporary radical feminist concerns with pornography as committing actual violence against women.[12] If anything this debate serves to reveal the fact that Bayley's construction of a polemical, politically correct feminism in monolithic opposition to the greatest (because purely apolitical) literature hugely oversimplifies feminism. It demonstrates that our categorisations of feminism and postmodernism in relation to Carter's work are of necessity provisional and specific and it also suggests that Carter's work exceeds both.

Theory into Practice

Carter's *Nights at the Circus* (1984) is an exuberant embodiment of excess: interpretative excess, physical and sexual excess and stylistic excess. In *Gynesis* Alice Jardine defines postmodernity in terms of its dismantling of key nineteenth-century narratives of truth, subjectivity and representation. The surpluses of *Nights at the Circus* spill over boundaries and confuse categorical distinctions, precipitating playful crisis in all three narratives, and demonstrating in the process, as Jardine does, that they were built on patriarchal foundations. What initially appears to be the central question in the text is whether or not Fevvers, the famous trapeze-artist heroine, has real wings. The novel opens with Fevvers being interviewed by Jack Walser, a young American journalist, whose aim is to reveal her to be a fake. As the plot unfolds, Walser, initially disguised as a clown, follows Fevvers on her travels with Colonel Kearney's circus through Russia and Siberia, falls in love with her, and experiences a process of self-discovery. These experiences severely question his rationalist assumptions. By the end of the text we have been brought to a point where the question – are Fevvers' wings real? – itself seems odd, framed in the wrong way, even pointless. It begins to seem like the question of a naïve empiricist, who believes that observation of and experiment on external reality will provide verifiable answers. The text demonstrates, in multiple ways, the problems with this approach, which is purposefully associated with the young male American, Walser, and with a distinctly nineteenth-century mindset. Walser finds, for example, that Fevvers and Lizzie, her elderly companion, seem to be able to intervene in the passing of time: while he interviews Fevvers the clock strikes midnight on several occasions. His disorientating experiences as a clown in the circus and later, when he is trained as an apprentice shaman, suggest the possibility that external 'reality' is merely a manipulable construct.

Most important, however, in the process of undermining Walser's assumptions about truth and falsity is the sheer power of Fevvers' narrative ability. A large proportion of the first 'London' section of the novel consists of Fevvers' account of her life thus far, an account which is exotic, rumbustious and totally gripping. Walser finds himself powerless to resist the sheer gusto of this story and the version of Fevvers it contains. This is emphasised by the violent imagery with which the telling of the tale is associated. A short interpolation by Lizzie is introduced thus: 'Lizzie fixed Walser with her glittering eye and seized the narrative between her teeth';[13] a later interjection by Fevvers 'lassooed him with her narrative and dragged him along with her' (p. 60). Clearly Carter wishes to suggest not merely that with narrative ability goes power, but that stories create their own truths. Any externally verifiable 'facts' of Fevvers' autobiography tend to be scandalous and involve people in important positions, so that it would be difficult for Walser to check them. The 'grand narrative' of Walser's nineteenth-century masculine rationalism is thus pitted against the twentieth-century feminine pleasure in storytelling of Fevvers and Lizzie and the multiple embedded narratives of women that the text contains, such as those of the Sleeping Beauty, the Wiltshire Wonder, Mignon and the Russian woman who murdered her husband. It is not a particularly equal contest, but the text battles it out in a deliberately *fin de siècle* (end of the century) context where late-Victorian ideologies and certainties are being questioned anyway by the dawn of a new century.

If the nineteenth-century narrative of truth is severely undermined in *Nights at the Circus* so is that of conventional masculine subjectivity. The rational, independent, unified notion of the modern self is again associated with Walser, but it is continually questioned by a very different understanding of identity. Carter demonstrates that identity is constructed in narrative and is to a great extent context-dependent. Walser's rational sceptical self, which has 'not felt so much as one single quiver of introspection' (p. 10) is plunged into confusion by the experience of extreme erotic attraction and romantic attachment to Fevvers, an experience generated just as much by the frissons of her narrative as her physical presence. When he injures his arm rescuing Mignon from a tiger he can no longer write or type and is unable to send dispatches home to his newspaper. As Carter comments, 'he is no longer a journalist masquerading as a clown; willy-nilly, force of circumstance has turned him into a *real* clown, for all practical purposes' (p. 145).

The deliberate artifice of Fevvers' advertising slogan, 'Is she fact or is she fiction?', creates an important distinction between this form of words and something like 'Is she real or fake?' This distinction suggests that the issue of how to interpret Fevvers becomes important at a symbolic rather than literal level for those around her and for us as readers. The question of whether or not Fevvers 'really' has wings is revealed as unanswerable and irrelevant, and trying to pin down her 'essential' self is equally impossible. Therefore we have to turn to what she *represents*. Yet Carter flummoxes us here as well.

Nights at the Circus also rejects nineteenth-century conceptions of representation: if we cannot know the truth about the world around us how can we meaningfully represent it? We see the potential dangers of symbolic interpretations in the episode when Christian Rosencreutz abducts Fevvers from Madame Schreck's museum of women monsters and almost succeeds in sacrificing her as 'Queen of ambiguities, goddess of in-between states, being on the borderline of species' (p. 81) in the belief that her death will bring him eternal life. A similar situation occurs when the Grand Duke almost manages to imprison Fevvers in a jewelled cage in a Fabergé egg. The potentially 'deadly' effects of symbolic representation for women lie in the fact that the power to create symbols has clearly belonged to men and not women themselves, who have merely been the objects of representation. Carter acknowledges her own ambivalence about allegorical readings of the novel: 'using the word allegory may make it all too concrete. Certainly I was using straightforward allegorical ideas in parts of *Nights at the Circus* ... But it does seem a bit of an imposition to say to readers that if you read this book you have got to be thinking all the time; so it's there only if you want it.'[14] Carter thus accepts and encourages readings of the novel which differ from her own. The stultifying masculine urge to fix representation is resisted by the proliferation of interpretations in the text. Fevvers is all and none of the symbols used to represent her. She escapes from the Grand Duke by grabbing a toy train from another of his collection of eggs, jumping aboard and joining the rest of the circus on its journey away from St Petersburg and into Siberia. This narrative sleight of hand alerts us to the fictionality of the text by breaking the current fictional frame and effortlessly substituting it with another one. There are many postmodernist literary devices in the text, for example multiple embedding of narratives, self-conscious literary allusions, the inclusion of real people as characters in the text, the intrusion of the implied author into the text to comment on her choices and devices and the use of questionably reliable narrative. All emphasise the impossibility of representing anything, least of all Fevvers. The purpose of fiction is no longer to represent reality, but to play what Colonel Kearney calls 'the ludic game': the playful, excessive generation of meaning and significance.

Nights at the Circus, like Jardine's *Gynesis*, makes apparent the fact that femininity is always the inferior term in those binaries which are essential to modern conceptions of truth, subjectivity and representation. Fevvers must be revealed to be a fake in order for Walser to retain his sceptical, rationalist stance; the 'inauthentic' superficial elements of her personality must eventually reveal her essential self; the fictive aspects of her story, life and performance must be replaced by the authentic version. Of course Walser fails in this masculinist modern project because fakery, inauthenticity and fiction are all that remain in the postmodern world of the novel. Yet is there a potential difficulty in associating femininity with the cultural shift created by postmodernism? Alice Jardine uses the term 'gynesis' to suggest exactly this association, and she is disturbed by its implications in the work of male writers and theorists. Is Fevvers really nothing more than a patriarchal cliché: the tart with a heart; the Mae West figure (Haffenden, p. 88); cheerful survivor of abuse and degradation because really she asked for, even enjoyed it all? If this caricature is manifestly inaccurate in detail (Fevvers claims to be the 'only fully-feathered intacta' and tends to escape or avoid abuse rather than spiritedly endure it), this is because Carter evokes the stereotype only to disturb subtle (and sometimes not so subtle) aspects of it. Fevvers is a tart, or perhaps a virgin, with wings as well as a heart, and a head for figures! This shifting quality is perhaps what Jardine characterises as part of the 'strangely and irresistibly subversive' quality in gynesis *'when taken up by female voices'* (p. 258). She suggests that feminist writers should explore the possibility that those historical periods where conceptual and ideological shifts take place are identical with those periods when feminist issues are at the forefront of public consciousness. This suggestion is echoed in Carter's fictional exploration of the dying spirit of the end of the nineteenth century where it is possible that 'in a secular age, an authentic miracle must purport to be a hoax, in order to gain credit in the world' (p. 17).

Like Jardine, Seyla Benhabib describes postmodernity as a crisis in modern ideas about representation. She also remarks on the shift in emphasis from consciousness to language in postmodernism. As one of the greatest of stylists, Carter exhibits a lipsmacking pleasure in language throughout *Nights at the Circus*. Her vocabulary is wide and varied and she frequently juxtaposes the vernacular with the (quasi-) scientific: 'bums aloft, you might say; up she goes, in a steatopygous perspective' (p. 7). She loves neologisms: Fevvers' dressing room is described as a 'mistresspiece of exquisitely feminine squalor' (p. 9) and her attitude as one of 'bonhomerie' deliberately adjusted to 'bonnefemmerie?' (p. 11). She often uses multi-syllabic, sometimes onamatopoeic, words like 'crepuscular', 'meretricious', 'voluptuous', 'vertiginous'. Some of this pleasure arises from the mere sounds of the words, what Kristeva would call their semiotic quality (see previous chapter); on other occasions the enjoyment comes from knowing reference to the importance of linguistic theories in contemporary literary and cultural criticism. Thus not only does Carter refer frequently to her literary predecessors and genres such as the picaresque and magic realism but also to the sign and the signifier (p. 29), the simulacra (p. 39) and deconstruction (p. 117). Yet she stops short of taking what Benhabib calls the 'strong' postmodernist position that reality is entirely inaccessible outside language. After the disappearance of the clowns in a snowstorm the Escapee tries to discuss the event's significance with Fevvers:

> 'Look, love,' I says to him, eventually, because I'm not in the mood for literary criticism. 'If I hadn't bust a wing in the trainwreck, I could *fly* us all to Vladivostock in two shakes, so I'm not the right one to ask questions of when it comes to what is real and what is not, because, like the duck-billed platypus, half the people who clap eyes on me don't believe what they see and the other half thinks they're seeing things.' That shut him up.   (p. 244)

Fevvers' frustration arises from her knowledge that her wings could make a real difference – they could effect an escape – but they are only perceived symbolically: in terms of what they could be made to mean in language.

Carter is as sceptical as Benhabib about the value for feminists of 'strong' versions of postmodernist theses of the death of the subject, history and metaphysics. *Nights at the Circus* demonstrates the necessity for feminist politics of substituting weak notions of all three. The episodes with the clowns, particularly Buffo, most obviously allude to the dangerous consequences of perceiving subjectivity as entirely constructed and performed. The performance is all there is for Buffo: '"What am I without my Buffo's face? Why, nobody at all. Take away my make-up and underneath is merely not-Buffo. An absence. A vacancy"' (p. 122). The total erasure of Buffo's agency or capacity for self-determination results in the nihilism of his final drunken performance and descent into madness. This version of the 'strong' postmodernist position on the 'death' of the subject is contrasted with the new identities

Fevvers and Walser achieve at the end of the novel. Like Buffo, both have experienced total self-loss, but unlike him, each emerges with a situated sense of subjectivity which allows them a degree of agency. After the train crash, the injury to her wing, the loss of Lizzie's magical handbag, her hair-dye and, indeed, Walser himself, Fevvers feels dowdy and freakish rather than wondrous. The final straw is Walser's sudden reappearance. He too has been near the edge of insanity: his previous scepticism and all but traces of his memory have disappeared and he is being trained as an apprentice shaman in an obscure tribe. Fevvers sees that he looks at her as if 'she was perfectly natural – natural, but abominable' and has the same deadly plans to 'turn her from a woman into an idea' (p. 289) as had Rosencreutz and the Grand Duke. The only fit response, as Lizzie suggests, is to show him her wings and in her pleasure in being looked at, admired and amazing, Fevvers recovers a sense of identity. The sort of subjectivity she gains is a situated, reciprocal and mutual one: it is part of a context of display, performance and theatricality; it is responsive to others, including Lizzie, whose suggestion again saves Fevvers from destruction; it is created in a relationship with Walser. Thus it is neither controlled nor controlling.

In *Nights at the Circus* history is certainly not dead: the novel is determinedly historical in a number of ways. The turn-of-the-century environment is important not just to provide an exotic background or setting. It allows comment on the gendering of historical narrative, an exploration of the nature of history itself and suggestions for ways of revising patriarchal history. Fevvers' personal history is obviously a *herstory* which reveals the feminine underside of stuffy late nineteenth-century respectability. Fevvers brings to light the 'other' Victorian culture of prostitution, exploitation, poverty, monstrosity and crime and makes clear how it is gendered female. In doing so she creates an almost Foucauldian history which suggests that the construction of deviancy and normality are interdependent and that the process of repression is necessary to generate desire.[15] Yet Fevvers does more than merely make this machinery obvious. She also offers a revisionary feminist account of the past where women can, by cooperation and cleverness, jam this machinery and either use it to their own advantage or sometimes escape it. The women who work in Ma Nelson's brothel all have schemes ready to put into practice which make them economically self-sufficient after her sudden death. Louisa and Emily run a boarding-house in

Brighton; Annie and Grace set up a clerical agency; Jenny marries and then, with Lizzie's help, engineers the death of her wealthy husband; Esmerelda joins the theatre. These choices suggest the widening options for women at the beginning of the twentieth century.

If Fevvers can be said to stand for anything it is 'the pure child of the century that just now is waiting in the wings, the New Age in which no women will be bound down to the ground' (p. 25). In this sense Fevvers is, as many critics have recognised,[16] a figure who determinedly echoes what Benhabib terms the 'ethical impulse of utopia' (p. 229). The strength of this impulse suggests that *Nights at the Circus* never endorses the 'strong' version of the death of metaphysics. Finally, it seems, we must be able to tell a story that makes 'grand' philosophical claims, even if we are aware of all the problems in so doing. Aidan Day makes the point that Carter doesn't just 'settle for hybridity and fragmentation' but instead reinvents traditional forms like that of the picaresque: the eighteenth-century novel genre where the lovable rogue hero travels on a series of random adventures before finally coming to terms with his place in the world.[17] The utopian narrative in *Nights at the Circus* centres on cooperation and love, the primary example obviously being the relationship between Fevvers and Walser. Yet what we might almost call an 'ethic of care'[18] also develops within and without sexual and romantic attachments, and in heterosexual and homosexual relationships. Consider for a moment the different examples provided by Fevvers and Lizzie, the surrogate mother and daughter, Fevvers and Mignon, where Fevvers generously helps Mignon despite believing her to be Walser's lover, Mignon and the Princess of Abyssinia, and the female inmates and guards of the Siberian prison. Perhaps the most interesting example is seen in the relationship that develops between Mignon, the Princess and the Strong Man. The Strong Man is initially nothing more than a cowardly exploiter of women. He abandons Mignon to the clutches of the escaped tiger after having casual sex with her leaving Walser and Fevvers to help when her husband beats her to a pulp afterwards. However, a combination of jealousy and sentimentality create in the Strong Man genuine emotion, and he is transformed:

All my life I have been strong and simple and – a coward, concealing the frailty of my spirit behind the strength of my body. I abused women and spoke ill of them, thinking myself superior to the entire sex on account of my muscle, although in reality I was too weak to bear the burden of any woman's love. I am not vain enough to think that, one day, either Mignon or the Princess might learn to love me as a man; perhaps, some day, they will cherish me as a brother. This hope casts out fear from my heart and I will learn to live among the tigers. I grow stronger in spirit the more I serve.   (p. 276)

Just in case this seems hectoring, Carter gives Lizzie a somewhat rebarbative retort: ""'Out of the strong comes forth sweetness,' as it says on the Golden Syrup tins," said Lizzie. "Samson turns up trumps. Well, I never"' (p. 276). Yet the self-consciousness about Samson's metamorphosis into a sensitive, supportive, brotherly figure only partially detracts from the claims Carter is making here about the possibilities for cooperation between women and men.

Practice into Theory

One of the most significant problems in many of the debates about feminism and postmodernism is their first-world emphasis. Postmodernist accounts of the death of the subject, history and metaphysics may make even less sense to those who don't live in western capitalist economies than they do to white middle-class women who do. A certain 'blindness' to this issue is apparent in Alice Jardine's *Gynesis*, which couches its discussion of postmodernism and feminism solely in terms of Anglo-American versus European thought. Although Jardine is to a degree self-conscious about this position, she does not relate it to any other location. Thus we retain a considerably limited perspective. If Jardine does succeed in demonstrating the patriarchal aspects of those modern narratives which postmodernism has dismantled, Carter is attentive to many of their colonialist implications as well. The circus is managed by the ridiculous but powerful 'Uncle Sam' figure of Colonel Kearney, whose greedy consumerism prefigures the twentieth-century world domination of US culture. However, the novel progressively undermines this impulse as the circus moves further east; at its conclusion it has been derailed, the tigers and elephants are dead and several of the Colonel's best acts have left his employ. Similarly, Walser's American background is significant in creating his scepticism and blank, unfinished quality, all modern traits which are severely questioned by the end of the novel. It is the case, however, that *Nights at the Circus* ultimately relies on a similar European versus Anglo-American structural binary to that employed in Jardine's *Gynesis*.

However, the text does raise race issues in ways that remind us of their absence in some accounts of postmodernism and feminism. The most striking example is provided by Toussaint, Madame Schreck's black servant. Toussaint's missing mouth clearly symbolises both his lack of agency and his powerlessness. After an operation to create a mouth (performed by a white surgeon) Toussaint becomes widely known for his eloquence and rhetorical ability. The successful operation initially suggests the necessity for racial and ethnic minorities to access those privileges which white men possess. Thus a rather different idea of subjectivity is created from that contained elsewhere in the text, where the emphasis is on postmodernist deconstruction of traditional masculinist forms of identity and construction of new ones. The point seems to be that you can't deconstruct what was never there in the first place: for those, symbolised by Toussaint, who have traditionally been denied access to modern subjectivity, gaining it can be an important first step. *Nights at the Circus* sets up multiple and complex comparisons between the appropriately named Toussaint,[19] Fevvers and Walser. Toussaint and Fevvers are both initially seen as creatures of economic necessity in their enforced servitude in Madame Schreck's museum. Like Fevvers, Toussaint acquires some power by narrating: his written version of Fevvers' abduction by Rosencreutz and the escape from Madame Schreck is admired by Lizzie for its 'lovely way with words' (p. 85). It is shown to Walser as evidence of the truthfulness of Fevvers' spoken narrative; the account of his operation in the *Lancet* is intended to provide evidence of her story's validity. Thus, while acquiring a speaking voice finally gives Toussaint a degree of rational self-determination, paradoxically it is the persuasive rhetorical quality in these *written* accounts that begins to suspend Walser's empiricist, sceptical impulses and thus his confident, rational self: 'Walser read this document, noted the scholarly handwriting, the firm signature, the all too checkable address. He handed it back to Lizzie humbly' (p. 85). Carter is ambiguous here about the value in different contexts of a model of empowerment through access to rhetorical ability. The text thus creates complex relationships between oral and written persuasiveness, conventional modern accounts of identity and postmodernist versions of the death of the subject. It also demonstrates how race and gender issues interact in multiple ways to complicate notions of autonomy and agency.

If Jardine's creation of an Anglo-American versus European binary is problematic, even more so is the way in which she creates a similar dichotomy between postmodernism and feminism and then puts both terms in a hierarchy. Although the book is framed as an equal encounter between the two, postmodernism is actually seen as the more significant cultural movement: for Jardine the important issue is really the challenge that it offers to feminism. An accompanying tendency genders postmodernism male and feminism female: consideration of women postmodernists like Cixous, Irigaray and Kristeva is left to a short afterword. Benhabib's piece also works with similar gendered dichotomies between postmodernism and feminism and strong (macho) and weak (emasculated?) versions of postmodernism. In contrast, in *Nights at the Circus* it is Fevvers who is, from beginning to end, the central vehicle for the exploration of these issues in the text. Feminist issues are seen as entirely relevant to the lives and experiences of men as well as women, as the examples of Walser and Samson the Strong Man suggest. Thus, the novel provides an example of a text where the postmodernism has a distinctly 'feminine' orientation and, if anything, arises out of new thinking about gender and feminism rather than the other way around.

Jardine describes the ways in which feminism has utilised blanket notions of women's shared identity, experience, representation and liberation which have some of the problematic qualities of modern accounts of subjectivity, representation and truth. In their universalising tendencies both modernity and feminism have been guilty of ignoring specificity and difference. *Nights at the Circus* is particularly sensitive to this issue, as we have already seen in the example of Toussaint and the relationship between racial and gender difference, but Carter is equally interested in exploring the similarities and differences between women and the types of alignment and relationship that are created between them as a result. When Walser takes Mignon to Fevvers' hotel after she has been thrown out by the ape man we see from Mignon's eyes the differences that can separate women from each other:

the girl ... was quite overcome by the drawing-room and turned
round and round in one spot on the carpet drinking everything in
– the beautiful pictures on the walls; spindly-legged tables holding onyx ashtrays and chalcedony cigarette boxes; the merry log
fire; plush, glitter and high-piled rugs. Ooooooh!

As she watched the starveling girl's delight, Fevvers' good
nature fought with her resentment.   (p. 128)

The luxury Mignon observes initially creates a rift between the
women, as does competition over a man (Fevvers wrongly believes
Mignon to be Walser's mistress). Carter thus highlights two of the
most significant potential differences and causes of conflict between
women and shows both to be fundamentally economic. If Fevvers
has earnt her 'own' money why should she share it with a waif? and
if Mignon is Walser's 'property' why should she provide for her?
The rest of the chapter shows Fevvers' generosity overcoming these
feelings. Carter's argument here is that many of the real differences
between women are generated by patriarchal, capitalist economies
to obscure the fact that all women have shared to some extent in the
experience of oppression, although such oppression may manifest
itself in different ways. Until women recognise this fact and collec-
tively support each other their situation will not change.

Nights at the Circus thus asks a central question for feminist theory in postmodernity: how can it embrace difference and specificity
while retaining broad categories of women's identity and experience which are politically useful? This is the question which both
Jardine and Benhabib also ask, but the insistent materialism apparent in much of Carter's text provides an answer which is rather
different from Jardine's concept of a subversive woman-authored
gynesis, and Benhabib's argument in favour of the 'ethical impulse
of utopia'. Indeed, the utopian aspects of the novel are either
grounded in the materiality of the body or ironically juxtaposed
with Lizzie's Marxist feminist analysis. Fevvers' physical presence
is emphasised throughout the text, but particularly so in the first
chapter, where Walser is perhaps at his most sceptical. Fevvers
assaults all Walser's senses with her larger-than-life appearance, a
voice that 'clanged like dustbin lids' (p. 7), her 'highly personal
aroma' (p. 9), the slithering touch of her stockings and other 'elabo-
rately intimate garments' (p. 9) and continually refilled champagne
glasses. The emphasis is on the slow revelation of the 'real' Fevvers

from beneath her stage costume as she takes off her false eyelashes and make-up and has her hair brushed out. It is this pungent physical intimacy that begins to suspend Walser's disbelief and make her credible, and from this credibility, paradoxically enough, her efficacy as a utopian symbol springs. Later in the novel we find another example of a feminist utopia based on women's bodies: the story of the women murderers' escape from their prison. Modelled on Jeremy Bentham's design for a panopticon, which institutes a system of self-surveillance in its inmates based on the internalised gaze, the prison should be a completely effective means of punishment.[20] Yet the inmates and the guards forge an alliance based on touch and the exchange of love-notes written in whatever female bodily fluids are available. The desire that is created leads to the women's rebellion and escape.

This emphasis on the importance of physical materiality is accompanied by a recurring economic materialism, most obviously present in Lizzie's analyses. She terms marriage 'prostitution to one man instead of many' (p. 21), compares the purely 'symbolic exchange' of Fevvers' trapeze act unfavourably with 'productive labour' (p. 185) and enjoys *The Marriage of Figaro* 'for the class analysis' (p. 53). To Fevvers' peroration on the utopian possibilities of her alliance with Walser she sourly replies: '"It's going to be more complicated than that ... improve your analysis, girl, and *then* we'll discuss it"' (p. 286). Throughout the St Petersburg and Siberia sections of the novel Lizzie sends 'news of the struggle in Russia' back to 'a spry little gent with a 'tache she met in the reading-room of the British Museum' (p. 292). These communications with Karl Marx himself, it is implied, significantly further the cause of the Bolsheviks and are instrumental in aiding the revolution of 1917. The incipient danger for Fevvers, from Lizzie's materialist feminist point of view, lies in her potential commodification: all the shops sell multitudinous Fevvers products, including a brand of baking powder. Fevvers even 'dreamed, at nights, of bank accounts' (p. 12). In the twentieth century, postmodernity is at the service of late capitalism: merely another fetish to be marketed, packaged, sold and consumed.

Perhaps Jardine, Benhabib and even this chapter commodify both postmodernism and feminism in the sense that we try to define, characterise and list the features of it in a way that makes it accessible, but also uniform. Isn't this a distinctly modern gesture? As

Judith Butler comments: 'to the extent that the postmodern functions as such a unifying sign, then it is a decidedly "modern" sign, which is why there is some question whether one can debate for or against this postmodernism'.[21] Both postmodernism and feminism are as variable as the people writing about them. Benhabib does not recognise that it is precisely this diversity and plurality in postmodernism that can make it politically efficacious. The death of the subject, for example, can be enabling for feminists if it means the death of the unchanging, reasonable and autonomous masculine subject, which is constructed by ruthless expulsion of the 'feminine' qualities of mutability, emotion and dependency. Only through recognising the constructed nature of concepts such as the self and the body does the possibility of altering that construction emerge. In *Nights at the Circus* the single most important extended metaphor for identity is of the act or performance, a metaphor which combines a sense of creative freedom and self-expression with one of following a pre-determined script. As Buffo the clown sourly remarks:

> The code of the circus permits of no copying, no change ... It is given to few to shape themselves, as I have done, as we have done, as you have done young man, and, in that moment of choice – lingering deliciously among the crayons; what eyes shall I have, what mouth ... exists a perfect freedom. But, once the choice is made, I am condemned therefore, to be 'Buffo' in perpetuity. (p. 122)

A similar paradox extends to Fevvers herself. By her own account, as a freak of nature from birth, Fevvers 'served my apprenticeship in *being looked at* – at being the object of the eye of the beholder' (p. 23). Of course that beholder is usually male, and so Fevvers could be seen as a victim of the male gaze from the start, which shapes and constructs her as Cupid, the Winged Victory, Sophia (or wisdom) or the 'dark angel of many names' (p. 75). Yet Fevvers does not seem like a victim. Unlike Buffo, who becomes trapped in a singular identity, she plays around with patriarchal definitions of herself. It is this multiplicity and variability that allows her some kind of control. Recognising that all notions of identity, even chauvinist ones, are fluid and shifting is precisely what gives her the leverage to exert pressure on the conceptual systems that generate them.

Conclusion

The first paragraph of this chapter asked why it is called 'Postmodernism *and* Feminism' rather than 'Postmodern*ist* Feminism'. Later, I suggested that one answer to this question is that we are unable to describe, even provisionally, the features of a postmodernist feminism. In debating whether or not the two can be aligned, we are inevitably engaged in a modern narrative of large-scale definition and categorisation. In a world where such paradigmatic thinking has been severely questioned, novelists and critics have deliberately avoided the dangers of grand theory and turned instead to the local, specific narratives in black, postcolonial, lesbian and gay writing. In this sense, the next two chapters are those where a postmodernist feminist writing is discussed, although the term is superseded there. Carter's *Nights at the Circus* lies precisely on the cusp where it is possible to discuss issues like these at some level of abstraction. The publication of the novel in 1984 is not insignificant: the debate about feminism and postmodernism is precisely a late 1980s, early 1990s debate. In both its *fin de siècle* setting and its conceptual and stylistic apparatus the novel points backward to the grand nineteenth-century narratives of modernity and forward to the local late twentieth-century narratives of postmodernity.

7

Lesbian Feminism and Queer Theory

Introduction

Lesbianism is already present in various places in this book: it is an implicit trace which lies behind the more explicit theme of androgyny in Virginia Woolf's *A Room of One's Own* and *Orlando*; in Luce Irigaray's 'When Our Lips Speak Together' it appears in evocative imagery used to insert woman as positive difference into the symbolic order and suggest the sexuality of textuality and vice versa. Elsewhere, however, it functions as a noticeable absence: as something that could be a logical consequence of a particular argument, but is ignored, as in Nancy Chodorow's *The Reproduction of Mothering*. Thus lesbianism is either implicit in, tangential to, absent from or problematic for much feminist theory. It has occupied these positions because it has most obviously, with the exception of racial and ethnic difference, questioned the assumption, dear to many (though not all) feminist theorists, that we can define a shared identity for women and thus agree on a feminist politics. Relations between feminism and lesbianism have thus been problematic for the reason that feminism has too often relied on heterosexual norms in its theories and politics. For example, Julia Kristeva (see Chapter 5) arguably constructs a governing opposition between the (feminine) semiotic and the (masculine) symbolic which is implicitly heterosexual. Such heterosexism has failed to account adequately for lesbianism as difference and paid little attention to analysing the ways in which lesbians can be oppressed on the grounds of both gender *and* sexuality. Early lesbian feminists were thus concerned to theorise a specific lesbian feminist identity which took account of the intersections between patriarchy and heterosexism. Increasingly, however, lesbian theorists began to question the usefulness of positioning lesbianism in relation to feminist theory. In a homophobic society which tends to categorise all homosexual sexual behaviour as deviant, lesbians may have more in common with gay men than they have with straight women. Therefore, if feminist theory tends to focus on gender identity and define it in heterosexual terms, then diverse sexualities demand a new discipline – gay and lesbian studies – and a new theory – queer theory.

The title of this chapter seeks to echo the shift from lesbian feminism to queer theory as a way of demonstrating the diversity of responses to a complex question, namely, how the divide occasioned by the gender difference between men and women and the divide occasioned by heterosexuality and homosexuality relate to each other. In the introduction to a special issue of the journal *differences* called 'Queer Theory: Lesbian and Gay Sexualities', Teresa de Lauretis suggests using the term 'queer' to emphasise 'differences between and within lesbians, and between and within gay men, in relation to race and its attendant differences of class or ethnic culture, generational, geographical, and socio-political location'.[1] In this coinage, it is noticeable that queer theory has moved beyond the difference of gender, recognising that sexuality can be explained in terms other than those framed by gender difference. Clearly, defining queer theory and lesbian and gay studies as separate from feminist theory and women's studies is necessary politically to achieve recognition in the academy. Such recognition, which brings with it all-too-necessary funding and academic prestige is still dependent on acquiring status as a 'discipline'. However, completely separating issues of sexuality and gender is as problematic as assuming them to be entirely commensurate: sexuality and gender are imbricated (overlap) in complex and subtle ways. Thus, some have questioned the political usefulness of 'divorcing' queer from feminist theory.

Indeed, the extrication of queer from feminist theory whereby sexuality is defined solely in terms of sexual practices or behaviours and gender is defined solely in terms of masculine or feminine identity is demonstrably unsustainable.[2] If such a manoeuvre suggests anything, it reminds us of the mobility and permeability of issues of biological sex, sexual ascription, gender identity, sexual orientation and sexual practice. A historical examination of such interconnections suggests two things: first, that this mobility is nothing new and secondly, the extent to which attempting and failing to fix such mobility takes place in language. Same-sex sexual practices have always existed and have been variously condemned, tolerated or admired depending on the context. (Compare, for example, biblical injunctions against male homosexuality with its elevated place in Ancient Greek and Roman texts.) Defining or categorising groups or types of people on the basis of such behaviour is comparatively recent. The creation of the category of homosexual has been variously placed in the seventeenth, eighteenth and nineteenth centuries, but is usually perceived to be a distinctly modern phenomenon.[3] The category of the heterosexual arrived contemporaneously; as Alan Sinfield puts it: 'Shakespeare couldn't have been gay. However, that need not stem the panic, because, by the same token, he couldn't have been straight either'.[4] Michel Foucault argues that late nineteenth-century 'scientific' studies of sexuality were crucial in defining homosexual typologies associated not just with certain sexual practices, but also with particular inherited personality traits and congenital dispositions, orientations and desires.[5] The turn-of-the-century work of writers such as Carl von Westphal, Richard von Krafft-Ebing and Henry Havelock Ellis subsumed lesbianism in the category of 'inversion' or the 'third sex', which also included neurosis, insanity, criminality, feminist sympathies and transvestism. Both Victorian sexual scientists and more contemporary historians of the social construction of homosexuality, such as Foucault, were usually male and focused on the construction of male homosexuality, implicitly assuming that lesbianism can be understood within the same frames of reference. The category of the homosexual was thus a male-defined one, as is evidenced by the fact that anti-homosexual legislation usually criminalises male rather than female homosexuality. In 1921 the Director of Public Prosecutions advised the British parliament against legislating against lesbianism on the grounds that this might 'bring it to the notice of women who have never heard of it, never thought of it, never dreamed of it' (Sinfield, p. 49). If the category of homosexual was a male one, then the category of lesbian was always associated with feminism. Havelock Ellis claimed that 'the women's movement has involved an increase in feminine criminality and in feminine insanity ... in connection with these we can scarcely be surprised to find an increase in homosexuality, which has always been regarded as belonging to an allied, if not the same, group of phenomena'.[6]

The mutability of definitions of same-sex desire, behaviours and identities and their fluid relations with concepts of biological sex, gender ascription, gender identity and sexual orientation is most obvious if we examine the shifts that have taken place in queer politics. Activists working on gay and lesbian issues have deliberately used the definitions created by others and redeployed them. If homosexuality is innate or congenital, for example, any moral opprobrium attached to it is necessarily misplaced since the homosexual has no choice in the matter of whether or not to be homosexual and thus cannot be blamed for perversity. This is the (risky) choice taken in Radclyffe Hall's version of lesbianism in her novel *The Well of Loneliness* (1928) (see Chapter 5) which deliberately echoes contemporary sexological interpretations of inversion and makes a plea for compassionate treatment of other 'sufferers'. Although the novel was banned in November 1928, in more recent years it has been reclaimed as vital for lesbian readers who want to utilise masculine imagery to define themselves as butch.[7] That the redeployment of unsympathetic definitions has often taken place linguistically is suggestive: words that were originally terms of abuse have acquired ironic, or positive connotations, as in the cases of 'dyke', 'queer' and 'fag'. Other examples, like that of 'gay' itself, suggest that positive words have been annexed and have replaced more negative ones. The sophisticated understanding of the discursive construction of meaning is one of the greatest strengths seen in campaigns by groups like Queer Nation and ACT-UP.

Adrienne Rich, 'Compulsory Heterosexuality and Lesbian Existence' (1980)

As the title suggests, this crucial early lesbian feminist text argues that heterosexuality is neither a freely chosen sexual preference nor an innate orientation but a system, or institution, that oppresses women. By demonstrating the absence of lesbianism in feminist scholarship, where one might expect to find it, Rich persuades us of the pervasiveness of the 'bias of compulsory heterosexuality, through which lesbian experience is perceived on a scale ranging from deviant to abhorrent'.[8] Recent feminist studies which point to the importance of the early relationship between mother and daughter (such as Nancy Chodorow's *The Reproduction of Mothering*, discussed in Chapter 4) ignore the possibility, implied by their own work, that women's orientation may be originally lesbian. Rich goes on to explain the means by which the institution of compulsory heterosexuality encourages women to deny their primary affiliation with other women. They include marriage, the ideology of romantic love, prostitution, pornography and job segregation as well as practices like clitoridectomy, control of reproduction and rape. These methods enforce heterosexuality as normative and institute a process of 'double-think' whereby women abandon their identification with other women. This insight allows Rich to redefine lesbianism:

> I have chosen to use the terms *lesbian existence* and *lesbian continuum* because the word *lesbianism* has a clinical and limiting ring. *Lesbian existence* suggests both the fact of the historical presence of lesbians and our continuing creation of the meaning of that existence. I mean the term *lesbian continuum* to include a range – through each woman's life and throughout history – of woman-identified experience; not simply the fact that a woman has had or consciously desired genital sexual experience with another woman. If we expand it to embrace many more forms of primary intensity between and among women, including the sharing of a rich inner life, the bonding against male tyranny, the giving and receiving of practical and political support ... we begin to grasp breadths of female history and psychology which have lain out of reach as a consequence of limited, mostly clinical, definitions of 'lesbianism'.   (pp. 648–9)

Rich resists an interpretation of lesbianism which focuses on sexual practice or desire and instead positions it as a woman-centred, politically conscious stance. This involves emphasising the links between lesbians and heterosexual women as victims of compulsory heterosexuality, rather than aligning lesbian with gay male experience. Rich claims that 'all women ... exist on a lesbian continuum ... whether we identify ourselves as lesbian or not' (pp. 650–1) and suggests that women's erotic choices 'must deepen and expand into conscious woman-identification – into lesbian/feminism' (p. 659). For Rich, it seems that all women can be defined as lesbians and that lesbianism is the genuine feminist response to the interlocking systems of compulsory heterosexuality and patriarchy.

Monique Wittig, 'One is Not Born a Woman' (1981)

If Rich suggests that all women can be defined as lesbians, Monique Wittig explicitly states that the lesbian 'is *not* a woman'.[9] The explanation for this statement, which may at first seem startling, forms the basis of her essay. The title of her article borrows Simone de Beauvoir's famous claim in *The Second Sex* that 'one is not born a woman' (discussed in Chapter 1). Wittig uses this quotation to support her argument against the commonly held view that women form a group because they share the same natural, biological characteristics. She claims that this interpretation, shared by men and by some feminists, is not a 'physical and direct perception' (p. 11) but is created by heterosexist economics and ideology. She demonstrates that both the first- and second-wave feminist movements have been damaged where they have adhered to this view. As a materialist, Wittig argues against the idealist assumption that anything precedes material factors in determining identity. She redefines women as an oppressed class rather than a natural group. Yet her ultimate aim is to destroy the classes of 'man' and 'woman' and fight for a new sense of individual subjectivity which escapes class definitions. Until this aim is achieved, the only way of escaping one's position as a woman is to be a lesbian. Wittig claims that:

> Lesbian is the only concept I know of which is beyond the categories of sex (woman and man), because the designated subject (lesbian) is *not* a woman, either economically, or politically, or ideologically. For what makes a woman is a specific social relation to a man, a relation that we have previously called servitude … a relation which lesbians escape by refusing to become or to stay heterosexual. We are escapees from our class in the same way as the American runaway slaves were when escaping slavery and becoming free.   (p. 20)

If the concept 'woman' is dependent for its meaningful definition on heterosexist social systems, then for Wittig the lesbian is not a woman precisely because she resists and subverts those systems.

Judith Butler, *Gender Trouble: Feminism and the Subversion of Identity* (1990)

Rich's essentialist account of lesbian identity may initially appear to be the binary opposite of Wittig's materialist, social constructionist version. Judith Butler's *Gender Trouble* complicates this assumption by suggesting that any account of sexual orientation or gender identity which sees essentialism as the opposite of social constructionism is a consequence of heterosexism itself. She demonstrates how diverse sexual practices and identities are mapped onto a binary framework based on what is perceived to be the original distinction between male and female. The purpose of the book is to examine the consequences for feminist theory and politics if the binary by which we regulate our understanding of sexual orientation and gender identity is questioned or 'troubled'. Butler shows that the distinction between sex and gender is not watertight. This is a controversial move, because separating gender from biological sex has been politically useful for feminists. The insight that gender is socially constructed and historically variable has allowed feminists to resist those arguments about woman's 'natural' or 'proper' place or role which are based on biological definitions. However, Butler fails to find any aspect of sex which can be seen to pre-exist gender or remain uncontaminated by it: 'gender is not to culture as sex is to nature; gender is also the discursive/cultural means by which "sexed nature" or "a natural sex" is produced and established as "prediscursive", prior to culture, a politically neutral surface *on which* culture acts'.[10] If we abandon the sex/gender distinction as a way of theorising identity with what should it be replaced? If there is nothing that pre-exists or post-dates the social construction of gender identity then how can we find a space for resistance to all-pervasive gender ideologies? After all, the subversive possibilities generated by positing the existence of a pre-Oedipal (pre-cultural) female-oriented space are great, as we have seen in Chapter 5.

Butler finds such a space in her conception of gender as performance. Gender identity is less a question of 'being' a gender than of 'doing' a gender repeatedly, a series of acts which give 'the appearance of substance, of a natural sort of being' (p. 33). All gender identities are performances, some of which appear to be more natural than others because they are closer to those binary models of gender and sexual desire (male/female; heterosexual/homosexual) which are socially enforced. Yet it is impossible to give a perfect performance, precisely because the performance is never over and exists in relation to continually varying contexts. The necessity of repeating and adjusting one's performance is what creates the possibility of subverting dominant models of gender identity, offering opportunities to exercise a new kind of agency, one which does not rely on a conventional version of pre-discursive or pre-social subjectivity. As Butler puts it: 'only when the mechanism of gender construction implies the *contingency* of that construction does "constructedness" per se prove useful to the political project to enlarge the scope of possible gender configurations' (p. 38). Butler finds in the sexual practices of lesbian and gay subculture precisely those resignifications of normative versions of desire and gender identity that trouble the dominant heterosexist, masculinist culture. What appears to be the fakery and inauthenticity of lesbian and gay sexual behaviour and identity is troubling because it suggests, not the originality and authenticity of straight behaviour and identity, but rather that both straight and gay are equally artificial, constructed sexualities and identities. In her discussion of drag, cross-dressing and butch/femme lesbian identities Butler sees revealed *'the imitative structure of gender itself – as well as its contingency'* (p. 137). Also crucially revealed is the interdependence of heterosexuality and homosexuality, masculinity and femininity. If homosexuality and femininity are not inferior copies of heterosexuality and masculinity, neither can they be uncontaminated by them and thus serve as (pre-cultural) sources of a revolutionary politics. Amongst others, Butler takes Julia Kristeva and Monique Wittig to task for suggesting that they can. Instead, Butler demonstrates that masculinity and femininity are actually founded on an incomplete repudiation of homosexual desire, a desire which is thus retained as a mournful loss or grief in the subject. As such, homosexuality is intrinsic to the creation of heterosexuality and deeply entwined in the construction of gender identity: 'fully within culture, but fully excluded from *dominant* culture' (p. 77).

Jeanette Winterson, *Sexing the Cherry* (1990)

Controversy has surrounded the writer Jeanette Winterson: controversy which has always focused on sexuality. Scurrilous gossip about her private life and alarm over the staging of lesbian sex scenes in the television adaptation of her first novel, *Oranges Are Not the Only Fruit* (1985), suggest that lesbianism has been inseparable from the interpretation and evaluation of her work. Yet attempts have been made to neutralise its perceived 'threat', as has been suggested in a perceptive discussion of reviews of the novel *Oranges* and its television adaptation, which tell the story of the heroine's repressive childhood and adolescent discovery of her attraction to other women. The lesbian aspects in both were either downplayed or made more acceptable through their juxtaposition with religious fundamentalism and association with a liberal, 'high art' agenda.[11] The need for this strategy of displacement only suggests the importance of lesbianism in the first place. For Winterson, lesbianism is inseparable from feminism. One reviewer remarked that her novels 'feel like pretexts' for a 'vengeful hostility to men and marriage, her fascination with androgyny, and her compensatory vision of women as the stronger, more sane, and even physically dominating sex'.[12] Although these comments do not use the terms feminism or lesbianism both are present implicitly in confused stereotypes of the irrational man-hater who seeks both to collapse and to reverse sexual distinctions. Winterson does use both the latter devices at different times in her texts; the problem in this review is that these strategies are perceived negatively as purely political interventions in an art form where politics is inappropriate. As we saw in the last chapter in the discussion of the reception of Angela Carter's work, politics is only visible in fiction and art if it is the politics of a minority or disadvantaged group which questions the dominant liberal-humanist perception of the purpose of art and culture. Like Carter, Winterson also uses postmodernist literary strategies in the service of her particular politics. In doing so, it has been argued that she 'envisions the contours and logic of a lesbian postmodern'.[13]

Set for the most part in the time of the English Civil War and Restoration, *Sexing the Cherry* is the story of the gigantic Dog-Woman who finds a baby in the river Thames and names him Jordan. After being taken as a child to view a banana, a 'great rarity' at that time, Jordan becomes obsessed with travel and grows up to be an explorer, returning from one voyage with the first pineapple England has seen. The majority of the novel is made up of the Dog-Woman and Jordan's juxtaposed first-person narratives, indicated in the text by the symbol of the banana for the Dog-Woman and the pineapple for Jordan. These symbols are unconventional in gender terms: the phallic banana, for example, is associated with the woman. Jordan's exploration of the globe functions throughout the novel as an extended metaphor for self-discovery, enabling Winterson to discuss the subjective nature of identity, time and language: all distinctly postmodernist concerns. However, *Sexing the Cherry* is equally preoccupied with love, desire, sexuality and gender: Jordan's voyages throughout the novel are provoked just as much by his search for Fortunata, the dancer with whom he falls in love, as his urge to travel the globe. Indeed the two aims are seen as integral parts of a masculine impulse to dominate and control. On Jordan's travels he encounters many diverse and speculative conceptions of love, desire, sexual practice and gender identity, which re-educate him in these matters, from the city where love is (unsuccessfully) forbidden to the secret alliance between the inmates of a brothel and a nunnery. If Jordan's narrative is figurative, analytical and emotional the Dog-Woman's is empirical, intuitive and physical. Her account is more securely anchored in a specific time, place and space and her approach to life apparently more literal: John Tradescant, the King's Chief Gardener and explorer, tells Jordan that 'the sea is so vast no one will ever finish sailing it. That every mapped-out journey contains another journey hidden in its lines'. The Dog-Woman 'pooh-poohed this, for the earth is surely a manageable place made of blood and stone and entirely flat'.[14] However, as we read the novel our (gendered) binary perceptions of the two central characters are questioned and revised. The end of the novel brings us into the twentieth century by introducing us to two 'new' characters, a young boy named Nicholas Jordan and a woman activist who protests against environmental pollution. Their narrating voices are represented by a severed banana and a split pineapple. Only if we read attentively do we recognise them to be contemporary echoes or reincarnations of Jordan and the Dog-Woman.

Theory into Practice

The setting of *Sexing the Cherry* in the time of the Civil War and Restoration allows Winterson to juxtapose the forces of Parliamentarianism with those of Royalism:

They said that the King was a wanton spendthrift, that the bishops were corrupt, that our Book of Common Prayer was full of Popish ways, that the Queen herself, being French, was bound to be full of Popish ways. Oh they hated everything that was grand and fine and full of life, and they went about in their flat grey suits with their flat grey faces poking out the top. The only thing fancy about them was their handkerchiefs, which they liked to be trimmed with lace and kept as white as they reckoned their souls to be. I've seen Puritans going past a theatre where all was merriment and pleasure and holding their starched linen to their noses for fear they might smell pleasure and be infected by it.

(pp. 26–7)

In the Dog-Woman's eyes the Roundheads are Puritan, oppressive, hypocritical, intolerant and dull whereas the Cavaliers are Catholic, libertarian, open, tolerant and glamorous. The Puritans are particularly concerned to police sexual behaviour and institute what Rich terms 'compulsory heterosexuality'. Preacher Scroggs condemns all but heterosexual sexual acts and makes love to his wife through a hole in a sheet to avoid the sin of lust. Same-sex sexual acts are particularly singled out in the carvings in church representing the consequences of sin. The story of the twelve dancing princesses, which Winterson adapts from a Grimms' fairy-tale, is also used to suggest the institutional nature of heterosexuality and demonstrate how it is upheld by marriage. At night, the princesses, who are so light that they would drift away if not restrained by heavy clothes, float away to a weightless city and dance. When their father becomes concerned about their exhaustion during the day and their worn slippers, he offers them in marriage as a reward for whoever discovers their secret. They trick all of their possible suitors until the youngest of twelve brothers refuses their sleeping-draught and follows them. The metaphors of light and weight function to suggest the oppressive nature of the heterosexual narrative written for the princesses by their father. Lightness equals woman-centred pleasure, frivolity and freedom whereas heaviness suggests imprisonment (on discovery the princesses' ankles are chained) and enslavement. Dressed in blood-red dresses, the princesses participate in a marriage ceremony which is a sacrificial wake rather than a celebration, taking place, as it does, in a church they have built out of ice soaked with their own blood. Their stories should end with marriage, the process by which they are bartered in exchange for the solution to the dilemma posed by their freedom, and forcibly separated from each other.

Their stories don't end in marriage, however. All but Fortunata, the youngest, actually go through the wedding ceremony and all, we are told, live happily ever after, but not with their husbands. The sisters either kill or leave their spouses and in two cases their stories end in relationships with other women: the first princess lives with a mermaid in a well and the fifth lives with Rapunzel. The seventh princess realises that the man she has married is actually a woman in disguise and when this is discovered, she kills her partner to protect her from being burnt alive. In revising these narratives, Winterson reminds us of the compulsory nature of heterosexuality in fiction, where for women characters marriage and conclusion are usually synonymous. She also hints that if left to their own devices, women revert to their primary orientation with other women. Once the princesses have escaped the institution of heterosexual marriage their sisterly bond is recreated in shared living arrangements and augmented in the case of two sisters with new, infinitely more satisfying partnerships with women.

Jordan's travels make him privy to the existence of this secret lesbian continuum. In his search for Fortunata he eventually finds himself in a brothel where he dresses as a woman in order to be admitted. The prostitutes appear to be content, despite their imprisonment in the house, but Jordan discovers that a secret stream connects it with 'the lodgings of quite a different set of women. Nuns' (p. 30), with whose aid they effect a nightly escape. The prostitutes can leave the brothel whenever they wish and the owner never notices that the women who occupy his house of ill repute are never the same. Winterson suggests here that women's support for each other in their resistance to male oppression is as important in defining them as their sexual behaviour: many women take a turn in the brothel to make their fortunes; some of them have lovers in the convent; some don't. In making this point, she echoes Rich's claim that all women exist on a lesbian continuum which can be defined by feminist identification rather than erotic choice. The nuns aren't so different from the whores after all. After this experience, Jordan continues to dress as a woman for a while and discovers some of the ways in which women use a private language and rule-book to outwit men. He finds this 'conspiracy of women' (p. 32) profoundly shocking but it also suggests to him how women can work to undermine the institution of compulsory heterosexuality.

One 'becomes a woman' in *Sexing the Cherry* when, as Wittig argues, one occupies a subservient economic relation to men, through marriage or prostitution, for example. One way of moving outside these terms is to be a lesbian, as the princesses who engage in partnerships with other women and the whores who have lovers in the convent suggest. The example of the Dog-Woman makes it clear that possessing a body sexed female is not what defines one as a woman. Her huge size and weight is large enough to send an elephant flying into the air and her genitalia confound even an experienced lover. Her monstrosity and heaviness are clearly metaphors for her independence from men and although this resonates quite differently with the reader from the example of the princesses (where heaviness is equated with oppression by compulsory heterosexuality) it is also important to note that the Dog-Woman can 'melt into the night as easily as a thin thing that sings in the choir at church' (p. 14). She thus occupies a privileged place in the text outside what Wittig terms the 'sex-class' of women by virtue of her economic independence and the subsequent redefinition of subjectivity this effects 'beyond the categories of sex' (Wittig, pp. 19–20).

Practice into Theory

Yet how can the lesbian exist in a space, whether imagined as a continuum of woman-identified women (Rich) or as a group of non-women (Wittig), that is completely outside the category of sex, even if we accept that 'sex' is an economic category defined by compulsory heterosexuality? Isn't the lesbian marked by heterosexuality just as much as the heterosexual is marked by lesbianism and male homosexuality? In many ways *Sexing the Cherry* reminds us of Judith Butler's point about their interdependence in *Gender Trouble*. The fact is that when cross-dressed Jordan *is* admitted to the world of women and discovers their secrets. If in Rich's terms this world can be defined as a lesbian continuum then in effect he passes for a lesbian. In doing so he undermines not just the idea that there is anything natural about being female that arises from biology, but also the idea that there can be anything authentic, primary or innate about lesbianism that automatically resists or is uncontaminated by a monolithic heterosexuality. This episode also questions Wittig's version of lesbianism as existing entirely outside the economically subservient category of woman. Jordan discovers that all the women who work in the whore-house are marked by the work they do: they are all prostitutes for the short-sighted owner, whether they have lovers of the same sex or not. To be affected by this economic definition as one who sells sex is not to be totally defined by it, however: as we have already seen, many women in the town spend a short time in the brothel to amass a fortune. In other words, if heterosexuality were really compulsory, lesbianism would not exist: the fact is that the institution of heterosexuality is not all-powerful, but it does affect everybody.

In *Sexing the Cherry* homosexuality is, as Butler suggests, intrinsic in heterosexuality. The Puritan Scroggs, who preaches against all 'deviant' sexual acts, is discovered in a brothel by the Dog-Woman in a homosexual liaison with his neighbour, Firebrace. Ireton and

Bradshaw, the King's prosecutors, are 'frequently found together beneath soiled sheets' (p. 104). Winterson seems to make the general point that the sexually unacceptable and repressed is actually essential to the construction of the normal. The Dog-Woman remarks of Scroggs's ostensible fastidiousness in avoiding lust when making love to his wife that 'what you fear you find' (p. 27). The story of the city where love is forbidden demonstrates that what is repressed becomes even more attractive. As Jordan's singing gradually spreads romance through the entire city, a barmaid puts a Cupid's bow and arrow over the bar: 'she didn't know what it was, but it was forbidden and she liked it' (p. 77). Thus any binaries that operate to police and exclude will necessarily fail because what is excluded was never really absent in the first place. This applies to the binaries male/female and homosexual/heterosexual in *Sexing the Cherry*. Consider, for example, the general point that the Dog-Woman and Jordan are not such deeply antithetical characters in gender terms as they at first appear to be. Each is in fact intrinsic to the other's sense of identity. The opposition between lesbianism and compulsory heterosexuality in Rich and the dichotomy lesbian/woman in Wittig's essay are similarly prone to incipient collapse. As *Gender Trouble* demonstrates, both evoke an implicit binary between essentialism/constructionism and sex/gender which operates widely in feminist theory. Thus lesbianism becomes that which, unfeasibly, entirely resists social construction.

Rich's alignment of lesbianism with heterosexual feminism also seeks to downplay its affiliations with gay male sexuality. She sees lesbian sado-masochism as an unthinking adoption of male homosexual practices that are bound up with domination and inequality and hopes to 'move toward a dissociation of lesbian from male homosexual values and allegiances' (p. 650). Equally, she sees all heterosexual sex as inherently oppressive. Wittig similarly tries to bracket lesbian sexuality off from both heterosexuality and male homosexuality. Indeed, it has been claimed that 'male homosexuality comes to function as a repressed other' in her work. Neither considers the possibilities of the position occupied by gay men, who are oppressed as homosexuals but as men are oppressors. Do they not therefore pose the 'truly subversive category in a heterosexual culture' (Fuss, p. 46)? In fact, lesbianism and gay male sexuality are as entwined with each other as both are with straight sexuality.

In neither Rich's nor Wittig's essays is lesbianism about desire; instead it is about occupying a particular position, a position which, because it is *unchanging* in its opposition to compulsory heterosexuality, itself smoothes out the diversity of lesbian experiences throughout histories and cultures. *Sexing the Cherry*, like *Gender Trouble*, shows sexuality to be more diverse, fragmented and multiple than Rich and Wittig suggest. Neither Winterson not Butler wants to imply that categories like 'homosexual', 'heterosexual', 'masculine' and 'feminine' are meaningless; in fact they analyse how power operates through the construction of such categories. However, they are also concerned to demonstrate that such categories are never entirely watertight because of their cultural and historical variability.

If we abandon Rich's and Wittig's conception of a politics of resistance to the institution of heterosexism based on an identity or position which lies entirely outside that institution with what do we replace it? The answer to this question in *Sexing the Cherry*, as in *Gender Trouble*, lies in an explanation of gender and sexuality as performatively constructed. Practices such as drag and cross-dressing are clearly the most liberating in the text. As Jordan remarks: 'I have met a number of people who, anxious to be free of the burdens of their gender, have dressed themselves men as women and women as men' (p. 31). In female garb, he gains access to the secret world of women and also to the King's trial. The threat of cross-dressing is powerful, as is seen in the case of the princess who marries a woman disguised as a man. The reaction once this is discovered is punitive because the sham marriage hints at the constructedness of heterosexual marriage itself, which is invested with so much institutional power in heterosexist society. The princess and her lover do not merely imitate heterosexual marriage but redefine it. The dissonance between the 'sex' of their bodies, their sexuality, and marriage as an institution (which to be legal requires spouses to be of different sexes) creates a friction which calls into question definitions of biological sex (which is clearly imitable) and marriage itself. As examples of the ultimate illocutionary, or performative, speech act, which 'performs its deed *at the moment* of the utterance',[15] the 'I do' and 'I now pronounce you man and wife' of the marriage ceremony actually bring the marriage into being. If the princess and her female lover are constituted as husband and wife by the ceremony itself, then it is perfectly possible for them to 'perform' within a heterosexist institution and thus subvert it.

The episode where Jordan and his mother discuss the grafting and sexing of a cherry provides the clearest metaphor for a performative conception of gender and sexuality. Grafting is 'the means whereby a plant, perhaps tender or uncertain, is fused into a hardier member of its strain, and so the two take advantage of each other and produce a third kind, without seed or parent' (p. 78). The most explicit resonance here is with identity. Jordan wonders whether 'it was an art I might apply to myself' and wishes to graft some of Tradescant's heroic qualities onto his own. The Dog-Woman comments: '"thou mayest as well try to make a union between thyself and me by sewing us at the hip"', an ironic comment since the novel undertakes precisely this process as it progresses. However, grafting poses such a severe threat because it is an example of non-reproductive, same-sex sexuality, which is 'without seed' and fuses two plants of the same 'strain'. Thus the church condemns it as 'unnatural'. The image here is of a sexuality which is artificial, yet successful (hardy, resistant to disease), biological yet cultural and also subversive by virtue of its artifice. Yet when the cherry grows and is sexed, it is female.

Perhaps Winterson manages to suggest here that the lesbian is more likely to be aware of the performativity of all gender and sexual identities. If this is one implication of the final emphasis on female sex in the passage, then why would this be the case? Would it be because of any inherently oppositional function the lesbian possesses? Or by virtue of her redeployment, or grafting, of aspects of straight male, straight female and gay male sexual practice? Butler's version of gender as a performance, the instability of which leads to continual opportunities for 'trouble', is itself 'troubled' by questions such as these. Is it possible to abandon entirely the material fact of the sexed body? Can we do without conventional notions of identity and agency which have historically formed the basis for oppositional politics such as those of feminism? The Dog-Woman's first act after finding Jordan in the Thames is to wash the mud off to discover his sex. Her neighbour comments that '"He'll break your heart," … "He'll make you love him and he'll break your heart"' (p. 14), equating the male sex with a 'love 'em and leave 'em' philosophy. Winterson seems to suggest here the impossibility of *separating* physical, material, bodily matters from social and cultural factors: even those most visceral experiences such as childbirth, physical pain and sexual desire are marked by prevalent norms, particularly gender norms. To admit this, however, is not the same as saying that such experiences are *entirely* mutable. One of the strengths of *Gender Trouble* is its refusal of the idea that social constructionism necessarily leads to loss of agency and subversive possibilities; one of its weaknesses is a certain imprecision about exactly *when and how* particular gendered performances become subversive and how such resignifying performances can form the basis for oppositional identities and political action. Famously, Butler argues that 'all signification takes place within the orbit of the compulsion to repeat; "agency," then, is to be located within the possibility of a variation on that repetition' (p. 145). How and when does repetition in and of itself become subversive and how does it create the means of intervening to alter the status quo? The example previously mentioned of the princess who has married a woman disguised as a man provides a good way into this debate. As we saw, the marriage performance is a critique of the institution of compulsory heterosexuality, but it only functions effectively as such when it is private. Once someone 'outs' the couple, it is 'too late' (p. 54). The institution brings all its punitive force to bear on the relationship and the princess kills her partner. In forcibly concluding the relationship any power to 'resignify' heterosexual marriage is necessarily lost. All that remains is the textual account of the experience. We could argue that the negative effect of the conclusion to the story does not totally outweigh the potential of the threat within it, which is seen particularly in the celebratory and erotic evocation of lesbian desire and identity in the earlier part of the story. However, it is also possible that Winterson wishes to suggest here the limits of a performative conception of gender identity. If dominant forces range themselves against a reinterpretation or resignification of gender, then those resignifications become ineffectual. Real social and cultural changes are not, according to this view, generated by local performative redeployments of gender conventions. Society is still homophobic, even if terminologies for same-sex sexual practices and orientations change. The forces of Puritanism and multinational environmental pollution still dominate the Dog-Woman and her twentieth-century counterpart's lives in *Sexing the Cherry*.

Conclusion

Writing one chapter on lesbian feminism and queer theory in a book about feminist theory may position the former as subservient to the latter. This book thus potentially repeats a gesture which has been condemned by many lesbian feminists and queer theorists. Yet the examination of *Sexing the Cherry* has suggested that sexuality and gender as fields of study and queer theory and feminism as modes of inquiry are necessarily entwined. If it is impossible to separate them it is equally unwise to conflate them. The truth of the matter is that feminism has both enabled and constrained queer theory. Doubtless this situation demonstrates the mutual involvement of the categories of lesbianism and feminism from the earliest sexological inquiries at the turn of the century. The particular strengths of much lesbian feminist scholarship have been demonstrated in Adrienne Rich's and Monique Wittig's examination of the heterosexual norms that underpin society. In their analyses, sexuality is revealed to be a more complex matter than the popular concepts of free choice or essential orientation would suggest. Patriarchy is no longer the most important system in shaping gender identity and sexuality; heterosexism assumes at least equal importance. Queer theory moves away from a search for a lesbian identity, conceived, in Rich's terms, as a woman-centred continuum or, in Wittig's, as a position outside the economic category of woman. Instead, Butler insists that lesbianism has to be understood in relation to gay male and straight sexual practices and gender identities, a position which makes more sense of bisexual and transgender practices. The historical and cultural diversity of lesbian experience and its place as part of culture is also more fully recognised. What in fact becomes clear is the constructedness of all sexuality and identity, including heterosexual masculinity. Towards the end of *Sexing the Cherry* Jordan ruminates on masculinity:

> When Tradescant asked me to go with him as an explorer I thought I might be a hero after all, and bring back something that mattered, and in the process find something I have lost. The sense of loss was hard to talk about. What could I have lost when I never had anything to begin with?
>
> I had myself to begin with, and that is what I lost. Lost it in my mother because she is bigger and stronger than me and that's not how it's supposed to be with sons. But lost it more importantly in the gap between my ideal of myself and my pounding heart.
>
> (pp. 100–1)

In this passage, Jordan acknowledges the gap between his own ideal of heroic masculine endeavour and his partial, artificial construction of his manhood, an intrinsically failed construction dependent on his relationship with the Dog-Woman. The novel finally reverses the dominant motif of the Dog-Woman's reliance on Jordan and resulting vulnerability but instead of replacing it with one of the Dog-Woman's strength and certitude the message is that all gender and sexual identity is bound up with its opposite. Jordan's mistake is to think that he ever 'had himself to begin with'.

8

Black Feminism and Post-Colonial Theory

Introduction

If lesbians have historically been absent from much feminist theory, so have black women. The title of an important anthology, *All the Women Are White, All the Blacks Are Men, But Some of Us Are Brave*,[1] suggests that this absence is less a matter of the numbers of black women writing and publishing, than it is an issue of ideology and visibility. In other words, as this title implies, femininity is frequently perceived as a white category and blackness is constructed as a masculine category. Of course there are as many examples where the opposite is the case: Freud's famous description of woman as the 'dark continent' equates the task of understanding femininity with an imperialist impulse to dominate and control areas populated by non-white races.[2] Hélène Cixous associates subversive femininity with blackness in 'The Laugh of the Medusa'.[3] My point here is that the category of race cannot merely be 'added on' to those of gender, class and sexuality. In the previous chapter we saw how gender definitions and sexual orientation are mutually involved; this final chapter suggests that gender is always equally marked by racial definitions and vice versa. To take the USA as an example, although early Abolitionist struggles against slavery preceded the fight for women's rights, later suffrage campaigns led by white women polarised around an 'expedient' choice between granting the vote to black *men* or *white* women. In the Civil Rights movements the rights involved were frequently those of black men, with black women assuming a subservient position. At the start of

165

the second wave, the liberal feminist movement centred on the National Organisation for Women was frequently criticised for its ignorance of black women and their different perspectives on, for example, issues such as working outside the home.[4]

Establishing a mutually implicated view of the relationship between gender and race may foreclose a consideration of what 'black' and 'race' actually mean. Does 'black feminism' mean only African-American feminism, or all feminism originating from the African diaspora? (The term 'diaspora' is used here to mean both the historical dispersal around the globe of particular racial or ethnic groups under conditions of colonial domination and oppression and the contemporary cultural identities of such groups.[5]) Is the word 'black' better replaced by more specific, local terms which acknowledge cultural and historical diversity, such as African-American, Latino/a and Chicano/a, or is it important to use 'black' to acknowledge the history of racism based on the institutionalised power of this definition? Some writers choose to capitalise 'Black' in order to signal their anti-racist redeployment of the word. A similar question pertains with regard to the word 'colo[u]r' which has been reappropriated in the phrase 'people/women of colo[u]r'.[6] (Interestingly, the phrase 'men of colo[u]r' is rarely used.) Questions like these are not asked here in a spirit of confusion or impatience. They are included in order to indicate the necessity of making a politically informed choice about terminology and also to raise the issue of the discursive construction of racial categories. Is race less a matter of genetics and biology than of language and semiotics? In no way do I mean to suggest that the concept of race is without powerful material and physical effects. To do so would be to ignore much of history. Instead, I want to argue that the physical and material efficacy of non-white race categorisations arises to some extent from their linguistic multiplicity and mobility. There has been and is much less debate about how to describe white people. Whiteness is conventionally self-evident, neutral, absent, not even requiring discussion. It could be argued that because essential definitions of race based on biological or genetic differences are fictions (albeit powerful ones) the category 'race' should be replaced by that of 'ethnicity', a cultural definition which identifies as groups those who share customs, beliefs and values. However, such a decision ignores the fact that racism polarises around black and white 'racial categories'. Thus it may make sense, when one is part of an oppressed group, to retain an essentialist definition of race for oppositional political purposes. This is a choice which may resemble to a certain degree the deployment of innate sexual orientation as an argument for equal rights in gay politics.

For the pedagogic purposes of this chapter I am reluctant to settle, at this point, for an essential definition of race. More recently, black women's writing has been characterised by its 'migratory' conception of black female subjectivity.[7] Elsewhere a black 'diaspora aesthetic' has been defined by its use of a '"syncretic" dynamic' and 'hybridising tendency'.[8] Both these accounts of black culture move away from arguments couched in terms of an essential difference between black and white towards a more complex conception of racial identity which is necessarily formed by multiple kinds of internal and external diversity and fragmentation. In this sense, these theories are much more typical of contemporary post(-)colonial theory. The brackets around the hyphen indicate a number of points of tension in the term. Colonial cultures and colonised countries are those conquered and controlled by non-indigenous peoples. In what sense, then, do we really live in a 'post-colonial' world where all forms of colonialism have disappeared? Although many countries in the latter half of the twentieth century have dismantled the official structures of colonial rule and achieved independence and self-government, many are still influenced and marked by colonialism. Thus if the prefix means 'after' we may be very premature. The hyphen may inappropriately indicate a clearly contestatory disjunction or break with colonial culture and society in which there may have been, from the start, forms of resistance to oppression. The term itself may suggest that colonialism and its resistance are all that characterised societies and cultures designated as such. Perhaps the prefixes 'neo' or 'de' (as in neocolonialism and decolonisation) make more sense in suggesting both the continuities and the differences between societies and cultures marked by processes of colonisation and their contestation. Clearly both processes must also be seen in relation to imperialism, which can be understood in both economic and ideological terms. Economically, imperialism involved the global spread of capitalism and the destruction of other modes of production and social organisation. Ideologically it involved the spread of an imperialist rhetoric which attempted to create and sustain a belief in European cultural dominance over the rest of the world.

The care over issues of language and terminology in contemporary post-colonial theory demonstrates a willingness to move away from simple dualistic models such as the black/white binary as a way of conceptualising race while still acknowledging the force of such models in racist discourse. Early post-colonial theorists echoed western binarism in creating models like the Self and the Other and the Centre and the Periphery to explain the relationship between the West and the East or the 'first' and the 'third' world.[9] These models were powerful reversals of a conventional way of structuring and ordering perceptions of race, ethnicity, colonialism and/or diaspora but did not necessarily criticise that structure itself. More recently, careful distinctions have been made between, for example, internal, imperial and deep-settler forms of colonisation, partial decolonisation and break-away settler colonies. Such work performs exactly this critical function, but in doing so it begins to express reservations about the utility of the colonial/post-colonial binary itself.[10] However, if we abandon such large-scale attempts to theorise, may we also abandon the critical and oppositional political purchase to which they provide access? As Terry Eagleton put it in a recent review article: 'The line between post-colonial hybridity and Post-Modern anything-goes-ism is embarrassingly thin.'[11] The title of his piece, 'In the Gaudy Supermarket', emphasises the potentially commodified, consumerist tendencies in such a pluralist model of post-coloniality, particularly when associated with the American academy. Indeed, the ambiguous position of the USA in post-colonial theory is emblematic of the ambiguities and potential failings in post-colonial theory itself, which simultaneously needs to account for the USA's history as a break-away settler colony, its contemporary situation of world military dominance (arguably a form of imperialism in itself) and its 'multi-ethnic' population. Perhaps it is not as well placed to do this as movements such as African-American Studies, which have more directly emancipatory agendas.

What has happened to feminism in the preceding discussion? Does a reading of *Sula* in relation to post-colonial theory instead of feminism tend to ignore gender dynamics? Many early post-colonial theorists (perhaps understandably in their particular contexts) paid little attention to how gender complicates and connects with issues of race, ethnicity and decolonisation. It is also true that many African-American feminists working in the USA were more concerned to make a space for race in what they perceived to be an overwhelmingly white, middle-class and straight feminist movement. The complex possibilities created by interaction between black feminist theory and post-colonial theory is one reason why the focus of this chapter is on a black American woman novelist and why two of the theorists discussed are also black American women.

Barbara Smith, 'Toward a Black Feminist Criticism' (1977)

Smith's article has been described as 'the earliest theoretical statement on black feminist criticism'.[12] The piece opens cautiously with the phrase 'I do not know where to begin',[13] but by the end of the first paragraph, where Smith points out the absence of black women writers and black lesbian writers in the literary world, her reconstructive aims begin to be implied. Smith sees politics and literature as mutually implicated sites where black women are ignored, but should be celebrated. She argues that the black literary canon (if it exists at all) is overwhelmingly masculinist and that feminist approaches to black women's writing ignore the specificities of racial difference. To remedy this situation she argues for the creation of a distinctive Black feminist criticism that 'embodies the realization that the politics of sex as well as the politics of race and class are crucially interlocking factors in the works of Black women writers' (p. 170). Black feminist criticism would also work with the assumption that the unique experiences of black women manifest themselves in shared approaches to literature and a distinctive language. These commonalities mean that black women's writing forms, and should be studied as, a specific literary tradition. In examining and supporting this tradition, critics should try to utilise the interpretative strategies and methodologies of other black women. Black feminist criticism should contribute towards and respond to the black feminist movement in a mutually supportive engagement. Much of the remainder of Smith's piece analyses Toni Morrison's *Sula* as a lesbian text; her justification is convincing and persuasively argued. According to Smith, 'many' (p. 175) black women's works can be defined as lesbian 'not because women are "lovers," but because they are the central figures, are positively portrayed and have pivotal relationships with one another. The form and language of these works are also nothing like what white patriarchal culture requires' (p. 175). In many ways her position here closely resembles Adrienne

Rich's in 'Compulsory Heterosexuality and Lesbian Existence', discussed in the previous chapter, where lesbianism is not a matter of sexual desire or object choice, but of an authentically feminist orientation against the institution of heterosexism. Indeed, Smith comments on Morrison's criticism in *Sula* of the heterosexual institutions of marriage and family. One reason why her piece has been chosen for this final chapter is the way in which she complicates and extends Rich's point by introducing the issue of race: 'heterosexual privilege is usually the only privilege that Black women have … Being out, particularly out in print, is the final renunciation of any claim to the crumbs of "tolerance" that nonthreatening "ladylike" Black women are sometimes fed' (p. 182). She implies here that being out as a lesbian is one way of resisting sexism, racism and heterosexism as *interlocking* systems of oppression. The piece concludes with an appeal to white women to recognise and acknowledge 'all the women who write and live on this soil' and a hope that black women and black lesbians will no longer be 'so alone' (p. 183).

Gayatri Chakravorty Spivak, 'Subaltern Studies: Deconstructing Historiography' (1985)

Discussing Spivak's essay here may seem inappropriate. Does it collapse differences to read *Sula*, a novel by an African-American woman writer, alongside Spivak's piece on the Subaltern Studies group, which is a Marxist collective analysing subordinate groups in South Asian culture? Although Spivak has spent much time living and working in the USA, she was born, and partly educated, in India and much, though by no means all, of her work is concerned with South Asian culture. I justify the decision to include her because her influence as a feminist post-colonial critic has been immense. This has been the case, I would suggest, precisely because her work tends to juxtapose western, metropolitan discourses and concepts with their diverse 'others', with startling results. In utilising her text I am following her own practice, not in the sense of placing colonised discourse against colonialist discourse, but in the sense of borrowing a strategic reading process. By reading an African-American woman's text (*Sula*) alongside Spivak's, which focuses for the most part on the theories and practice of a formerly

colonised national culture, I am invoking a process of cultural colli-
sion. Admittedly these categorisations are in themselves questionable, but the larger point is that throughout this book theory and
fiction (to make a simplified distinction) have been read alongside
one another less for their seamless fit than for their points of dis-
continuity and disruption.

Spivak's piece opens with a discussion of the work of the
Subaltern Studies group on the emergence of nationalist resistance
to colonialism in India. The group's theory is that peasant movements for independence failed to be successfully mobilised because
of the insufficient 'level of consciousness' of the peasant class.[14] Thus
the group appears to construct a version of 'subaltern' (or subordinate) consciousness as insufficiently revolutionary in some inherently or essentially failing way. However, Spivak also notes that
'there is always a counterpointing suggestion in the work of the
group that subaltern consciousness is subject to the cathexis of the
elite, that it is never fully recoverable, that it is always askew from
its received signifiers, indeed that it is effaced even as it is disclosed,
that it is irreducibly discursive' (p. 203). In other words, Spivak
points to a central contradiction between a conception of identity
which appears to resemble conventional models of the essential,
asocial, pre-discursive self and a more postmodernist version of the
subject as one constructed by multiple discourses and effects of
power, including (inevitably) those of the coloniser. For Spivak, the
latter account of subaltern consciousness could be taken as a model
for all consciousness: 'the allegory of the predicament of *all* thought,
all deliberative consciousness, though the elite profess otherwise'
(p. 204).

So far, we may feel, so good. Spivak has performed a deconstructive operation on the sick subject. Yet is this not a rather surprising
manoeuvre? Isn't 'curing' the colonised periphery using the 'heal-
ing' techniques of the colonialist, metropolitan centre rather inappropriate, rather out of context? At this point, however, Spivak's
argument extends into a defence of the Subaltern Studies group's
aims as politically useful in their specific context, a '*strategic* use of
positivist essentialism in a scrupulously visible political interest'
(p. 205). In other words, it is possible to equate subaltern consciousness with western postmodernist deconstructions of subjectivity,
but it serves a politically reactionary purpose. It makes much more
sense, from the point of view of radical insurgency, to allot agency
and identity to those who have conventionally never possessed it,

thus resisting the authoritarian dismissal of them as powerless. It also makes sense as a criticism of the universalising tendencies of some postmodernist theory, which, in describing the subject as always and everywhere on *his* white, middle-class deathbed, can reproduce exactly the sort of metanarrative it claims to criticise. (See Chapter 6 for discussion of this issue.) Spivak's essay concludes by grounding her general points in a specific analysis of the status of rumour and the place of woman in the work of the Subaltern Studies group. She argues that rumour functions to mobilise nationalist insurgency, not, as is suggested, by virtue of its direct immediacy (qualities wrongly associated with its spoken quality) but because of its function as 'illegitimate writing' (p. 213) with no original source, which can thus belong to anyone and be utilised for any purpose (however subversive). Spivak links this discussion to Jacques Derrida's suspicion of what he terms 'phonocentrism' (the commonly held view that speech is more authentic than writing because it is closer to a putative source). By choosing to link rumour with writing rather than speech, Spivak severs the link between subaltern consciousness and the phonocentrism of colonial elites and modern philosophy. When she turns to the subject of the exchange of women and territory, Spivak points out the 'blindspot' of subaltern consciousness: 'the simple exclusion of the subaltern as female (sexed) subject' (p. 218). She stresses the crucial structural role of women in mediating patriarchal systems of territorial exchange even while she is entirely absent as a subject in her own right. The essay as a whole exerts a double manoeuvre whereby the claims of the Subaltern Studies group are both undermined and shored up, for reasons which initially appear to be tangential to the project of the group itself but are revealed to be entirely relevant to it.

bell hooks, 'Postmodern Blackness' (1991)

bell hooks adopted her great-grandmother's name to 'show that women could trace their lineage through the matriarchal line' and uses the lower case to 'move away from the notion of iconic figures' in the American feminist movement.[15] 'Postmodern Blackness' comes from her book *Yearning: Race, Gender, and Cultural Politics*. It opens with the contention that some versions of postmodernism can be exclusive of minorities and argues that 'very few African-

American intellectuals have talked or written about postmodernism'.[16] Of the few that have, even fewer have discussed black women. However, hooks is equally suspicious of associating blackness with 'concrete gut level experience' (p. 23). Instead of taking recourse to essentialist models of black identity, whether strategically or otherwise, she advocates anti-essentialism as a way of attacking racism. Racism works by creating models of unified, 'authentic' black identity and pathologising them, so anti-essentialism would be a 'serious challenge' (p. 28) to it and allow for the ways in which class and gender complicate any notion of 'collective black experience' (p. 28). hooks turns to the notion of the 'authority of experience' (p. 29) to combat the concern that forgoing an essential black identity will necessarily lead to the loss of black history, culture and tradition. She argues that 'there is a radical difference between a repudiation of the idea that there is a black "essence" and recognition of the way black identity has been specifically constituted in the experience of exile and struggle' (p. 29). Only by accepting this distinction and working with the simultaneously deconstructive and reconstructive strategies hooks describes is it possible to deal with the 'yearning' of many subordinate groups for a 'critical voice' in a postmodernist context (p. 27). hooks argues that it is necessary for black intellectuals working with postmodernist ideas to extend their work beyond the confines of the academy towards the arena of popular culture and the black underclass. However, she also acknowledges the difficulties many black writers, including herself, face when they try and publish postmodernist work which fails to correspond to the realism expected of black art and culture.

Toni Morrison, *Sula* (1973)

In 1993 Toni Morrison became the first African-American woman writer to win the Nobel Prize for Literature. A British broadsheet newspaper article commented: 'it was inevitable that the Swedish Academy would be accused of overweening political correctness'.[17] It is unclear exactly why controversy should 'inevitably' surround the decision to award Morrison what is arguably the most prestigious of literary prizes. If we read carefully enough, however, the use of the loaded term 'political correctness' suggests that the decision may have been made on grounds other than abstract literary merit. As earlier chapters have suggested, we need to be suspicious of any conception of literature as entirely unaffected by politics, particularly when such an absence is associated with aesthetic value. Such judgements deliberately ignore the ways in which all writing is political by recognising only minority, subordinate or subversive political content and making dominant or elite political values invisible because they merely reflect the status quo. Like Winterson's sexuality, Morrison's race and gender mark out her work as somehow less 'neutral' than that of white male writers whose race and gender are perceived to be normative. A review of *Sula* quoted by Barbara Smith remarked:

> Toni Morrison is far too talented to remain only a marvelous recorder of the black side of provincial American life. If she is to maintain the large and serious audience she deserves, she is going to have to address a riskier contemporary reality than this beautiful but nevertheless distanced novel. *And if she does this, it seems to me that she might easily transcend that early and unintentionally limiting classification 'black woman writer' and take her place among the most serious, important and talented American novelists now working.*
> (Smith, p. 171; italics as in original)

Yet Morrison has kept writing about the 'black side of provincial American life'. She has deconstructed the opposition between 'black woman writer' and 'serious, important and talented American novelist', not just by being both at once, but by showing how these categories are falsely opposed in the first place. Her work reconstructs an African-American cultural tradition which the white literary canon has attempted to marginalise; in so doing it also demonstrates how white history and culture necessarily depend on their black 'other(s)'.

Sula, Morrison's second novel, is the story of two black girls, Nel and Sula, who grow up together in the small town of Medallion. Marked in different ways by a series of formative childhood experiences, many shared with each other, the two drift apart when Sula leaves town and Nel marries Jude. When Sula returns ten years later she and Nel resume their friendship but their long-standing relationship is challenged when Nel discovers that Sula has slept with Jude. Although three years later Nel visits Sula on her deathbed, the two women are never reconciled. Only after her funeral does Nel realise that her grief is not at losing her husband, but at losing Sula. The novel is a searching examination of the formation of Sula and

Nel's identity as black women. Of primary importance in creating their sense of subjectivity are their relationships with their mothers and grandmothers, each other and black men, which are set against the wider, but no less significant, context of white racism. Morrison uses two central characters to create a text which functions through dialogue; the 'conversation' between Sula and Nel's judgements, reactions and decisions, which are compared and contrasted by the reader. The action encompasses the years 1919 to 1965 and specific dates are used to separate sections of the text into smaller units. This device suggests that the story being told has wider cultural and social significance. Indeed, this shifting between the general and the specific is also present in the narrative style. Although told in the third person, the narrating voice modulates from the quality of orally told black folklore to a narrower focus on particular characters' thoughts and feelings. The plot generally follows the story, but there are some important flashbacks and significant lapses, for example the ten years when Sula leaves Medallion. These features create a distinctive quality which Morrison has described as follows: 'To make the story appear oral, meandering, effortless, spoken – to have the reader *feel* the narrator without *identifying* that narrator, or hearing him or her knock about, and to have the reader work *with* the author in the construction of the book – is what's important.'[18] Here Morrison acknowledges both the oral and the dialogic quality of her writing.

Theory and Practice

This final chapter complicates the adversarial, binary structure of previous chapters by abandoning the simple opposition between theory into practice and practice into theory. The intention is to conclude by questioning the usefulness of a distinction which was, from the start, merely a pragmatic and pedagogic one. The attentive reader may have noticed that this structure was beginning to 'fail' in the previous chapter, where discussion of *Sexing the Cherry* in relation to Judith Butler's *Gender Trouble* took place only in the final 'practice into theory' section instead of in both of the last sections. Modifying the book's conceptual structure now is not meant to imply that it is entirely inappropriate in the context of black feminism and post-colonial theory, but it is meant to suggest to the reader, amongst other things, the culturally specific nature of that structure. Instead of using *Sula* first to 'prove' and then to 'disprove' the theories of Smith, Spivak and hooks I want to set all four of the texts in this chapter into play in a more fluid and ambivalent manner.

My reading of Smith's 'Toward a Black Feminist Criticism' is thus already 'against the grain'. Smith herself provides a perceptive interpretation of Morrison's *Sula* as a lesbian text and it would be pointless to recapitulate that work here. What is of more interest is the sense of disjunction some readers have perceived between this part of the article and the early part on the necessity for defining a black feminist criticism and tradition of black women's writing. In what sense can reading *Sula* as a lesbian novel be related to interpreting it as a black woman's novel? Frequently Smith uses the phrase 'Black women and Black lesbians' as if to suggest (to borrow from Monique Wittig, discussed in the previous chapter) that black lesbians are *not* black women; elsewhere her position seems to be that the out lesbian is the only authentically feminist black woman, by virtue of her critical and oppositional position in relation to patriarchy, heterosexism and direct and institutional racism. Smith has frequently been criticised for constructing an essentialist account of black female identity and an overly homogenised version of black women's writing. The texts of black women, according to some accounts of Smith's position, constitute a tradition because they reflect in a simple way the shared experiences of black women. Smith contradicts herself, it is suggested, by castigating white female and black male critics for ignoring black women's writing and simultaneously suggesting that only black female critics are well equipped to analyse their work.[19] All of these contradictions can be subsumed in the over-arching one of whether there is or is not such a thing as an essential black female identity which provides a source for writing, politics and sexuality. What I want to suggest is that Smith's position is not usefully characterised as self-contradictory, but is better understood as a dialogic one, which works by establishing a conversation between apparently opposed positions. In other words, some of Smith's contentions – that black lesbians are and are not black women; that black women do and do not share the same experiences and that black women's writing should and should not be analysed only by black feminists – are put *alongside* one another rather than *against* each other. In making this point I am using the same kind of 'strategic' reading strategy that Spivak advocates when analysing the work of the Subaltern Studies group. This strategy is also claimed by Deborah Chay in her analysis of Smith. Approaching Smith's piece strategically allows readers, in her words, to 'recognize that her universal claims for black women are themselves historically specific and have a variety of political effects *without* compromising their/our strong opposition to her essentialist/essentializing tendencies' (p. 644). However, this assumes that we *are* opposed to Smith's 'essentialising tendencies' and merely want to excuse them as an unfortunate lapse. Surely essentialism is absolutely justifiable and necessary in certain circumstances? Smith's reply to Chay makes exactly this point: 'If by essentialist you mean that when I look in the mirror and see a Black woman I think it means something, then I suppose I am essentialist.'[20] She is equally concerned, however, to establish the specific non-academic and politically active readership for which her piece was written and thus justify and contextualise her essentialism. Unlike Chay's reading of Smith, then, my own seeks to keep in conversational play the two poles of essentialism and anti-essentialism in relation to black female identity.

When we turn to Spivak and hooks, we see that their strategies resemble this reading of Smith's. Both are anxious to harness the reconstructive efficacy of essentialist models of identity to the critical force of anti-essentialism. Spivak plays around with western postmodernist discourses about the death of the subject, but finally considers them inappropriate in the context of South Asian culture. However, she does not lose the deconstructive force she has brought to bear on the question of nationalist insurgency in India. The two approaches embed themselves in each other as the text progresses. hooks also utilises both. Although her piece may appear to be the most obviously supportive of anti-essentialism she retains its opposite in her commitment to 'the authority of experience' (p. 29). She remarks:

> The unwillingness to critique essentialism on the part of many African-Americans is rooted in the fear that it will cause folks to lose sight of the specific history and experience of African-Americans and the unique sensibilities and culture that arise from that experience. An adequate response to this concern is to critique essentialism while emphasizing the significance of 'the authority of experience'. There is a radical difference between a repudiation of the idea that there is a black 'essence' and recognition of the way black identity has been specifically constituted in the experience of exile and struggle. (p. 29)

hooks wants to abandon essential black identity but not essential black experience, which, it seems, it always and everywhere formed by 'exile and struggle'. This may seem like having it both ways, but perhaps that is a sensible and (more importantly) politically useful approach to take for a subordinate group working within a racist, heterosexist, patriarchal context. The other advantage of the position taken in my reading of Smith, Spivak and hooks is that it can be seen to contain a number of potential criticisms. Purists who wish to take a purely deconstructive, anti-essentialist position find it represented, as do those who argue on behalf of the essentialist cause. Of course neither perspective remains unchallenged in such a strategic reading and it is possible that such an approach may uncomfortably remind us of an old-fashioned liberal-humanist pluralism. However, I would claim that these pieces do provoke more than a response of 'anything goes' because they force the reader to establish *in what contexts* certain positions are appropriate.

What of *Sula*, which seems to have temporarily vanished from this chapter? Morrison's novel brings into operation exactly the kinds of context-specific interpretations of black female identity that we have been discussing in the work of Smith, Spivak and hooks. What is most striking about the novel is its consideration of friendship between black women as the possible source of an essential black female self. In two crucial scenes early in the book, Morrison relates black female identity to the body and to the bonds of friendship between black women. In one episode Nel and Sula share a wordless, instinctive game where they strip the bark from twigs, dig holes in the earth with them and bury rubbish inside. This is described as a sensuous communion arising from their adolescent bodies' awareness of an emerging sexuality. From this immediately physical experience a strong sense of shared identity is created, yet this moment is quickly succeeded by one which is predicated on division, loss and fear: the death of Chicken Little. It is Sula who lets go of Chicken when swinging him so that he falls in the river and drowns. Despite Nel's attempts to comfort her and their unspoken decision to keep the event a secret, at the funeral 'Nel and Sula did not touch hands or look at each other ... There was a space, a separateness, between them'.[21] They join hands again after the service like 'any two young girlfriends' (p. 66), which strongly implies that the experience unites them in a firm resolve to support each other. However, their unity seems to be, if not spurious or illusory, founded on division and absence. Later in the novel it is suggested that

Chicken's death taught Sula 'that there was no self to count on' and left her with no feeling of internal consistency: 'no compulsion to verify herself'(p. 119).

In another early episode, Nel is bullied by some white Irish boys. She takes merely evasive action until Sula confronts her assailants by cutting off the tip of her finger in front of them, commenting '"If I can do that to myself, what you suppose I'll do to you?"' (pp. 54–5). Instead of directing violence outwards against the boys, her public self-mutilation shocks and frightens them by evoking an old association between blackness, femaleness and immediate physical experience. However, this clichéd association is strategically deployed by Sula to protect the girls. Morrison recognises that identity is founded on loss, division and absence, but sees this as politically problematic. Thus she tends to take essentialist and anti-essentialist accounts of black female identity and show them accompanying, rather than opposing, each other. She also encourages us to consider when and where these conceptions of identity are appropriate or politically useful. Nel and Sula's first meeting, for example, is described as follows: 'Because each had discovered years before that they were neither white nor male, and that all freedom and triumph was forbidden to them, they had set about creating something else to be. Their meeting was fortunate, for it let them use each other to grow on' (p. 52). The understanding that black female identity is profoundly relational is seen both negatively (formed in response to white male identity) and positively (formed in response to a black female soul-mate). The sisterly bonds between women can recover the innate, authentic black female self which has been temporarily lost and allow it to 'grow' and 'be' – both are verbs which blend change and stability, essence and transience.

Anti-essentialist accounts of subjectivity are placed alongside essentialist ones in another important episode early in the novel when Nel and her mother Helene visit Nel's grandmother. The long journey south to New Orleans starts badly when Helene and Nel get into the whites-only carriage of the train by mistake. A white conductor stops them just as Helene opens the door of the 'colored-only' carriage and questions her. Her position between the two carriages reflects her ambiguous racial categorisation as the 'custard-colored' (p. 22) daughter of a 'Creole whore' (p. 17) who doubtless has some white ancestry. The conductor's concern to place and position her is obvious in his refusal to accept her excuse that she made a mistake and unintentionally got in the wrong car.

His sour reply: '"We don't 'low no mistakes on this train. Now git your butt on in there"' (p. 21) attempts to deny her 'impure' existence by forcing her to occupy the black carriage without 'polluting' the white one. Helene's position in the black carriage is no more comfortable, however. She responds to the conductor's abuse by suddenly smiling, 'like a street pup that wags its tail at the very doorjamb of the butcher shop he has been kicked away from only moments before' (p. 21). This attempt to placate or conciliate her abuser destroys any communion the other black people in the carriage may have felt for her: 'The two black soldiers, who had been watching the scene with what appeared to be indifference, now looked stricken' (p. 21). Nel senses that 'they were bubbling with a hatred for her mother' (p. 22) for her betrayal of black pride. At the root of this betrayal is Helene's attempt to separate her femininity from her race. Her smile is 'dazzling' and 'coquettish' (p. 21), as if she wishes to protect herself from racial abuse by encouraging the conductor to see her as an attractive woman, 'regardless' of her racial category. Thus the soldiers punish her by denying her that femininity: they refuse to help her with her luggage. By the end of the trip, however, Helene has been forced to admit the connection between her race and her gender. When there are no lavatories for coloured women at the small southern stations, Helene and Nel, like the other women on the train, have to squat in the nearby grass. Thus the reconnection of Helene's race and gender takes place in an immediately physical way as she finally gives in to her body's needs. In New Orleans, Nel meets her grandmother, who is beautiful, disreputable and talks an exotic French Creole. The embarrassment of the train journey makes her afraid that 'if *she* [her mother] were really custard, then there was a chance that Nel was too' (p. 22), but the trip as a whole allows her to understand her essential uniqueness:

> 'I'm me,' she whispered. 'Me.'
> Nel didn't know quite what she meant, but on the other hand she knew exactly what she meant.
> 'I'm me. I'm not their daughter, I'm not Nel. I'm me. Me.'
> Each time she said the word *me* there was a gathering in her like power, like joy, like fear.   (p. 28)

The trip shows Nel that essential black femininity is a fiction but a necessary one. Helene attempts to emphasise that identity is founded on difference – the 'difference' of white ancestry and attractive 'feminine' refinements, for example – but her strategy fails to counter the refusal to recognise such distinctions on the part of white men. Finally accepting and using their definition of her as essentially black and female gives her power, not to resist, but to remain unmoved by this racism. By the end of the trip, Helene not only is 'able to fold leaves as well as the fat woman' but also 'never felt a stir as she passed the muddy eyes of the men' (p. 24) on her way to pee in the grass. Nel recognises that creating a version of herself as black and female in a unique and precious way gives her the 'strength to cultivate a friend in spite of her mother' (p. 29). That friend is Sula.

As we have already seen, Nel and Sula's relationship sustains both women when they are 'two throats and one eye' and have 'no price' (p. 147), in other words, when they maintain the belief that they share essential qualities founded on being black and female. As the novel progresses, Morrison shows the dangers for both women of abandoning or being persuaded out of this belief. Nel's marriage and reaction to Jude's infidelity entails her separation from Sula through the acknowledgement of difference:

> She had clung to Nel as the closest thing to both an other and a self, only to discover that she and Nel were not one and the same thing. She had no thought at all of causing Nel pain when she bedded down with Jude. They had always shared the affection of other people ... Marriage, apparently, had changed all that, but having had no intimate knowledge of marriage, having lived in a house with women who thought all men available, and selected from among them with a care only for their tastes, she was ill-prepared for the possessiveness of the one person she felt close to.
>
> (p. 119)

Marriage makes Nel 'different' from Sula by making her sexually possessive and by forcing her to transfer her deepest affections from Sula to Jude. It marks her as the property of a man. What we are encouraged to perceive as Nel's betrayal of Sula forces Sula into a more definite occupation of the role of threat, outsider and 'other' in Medallion. Putting her in this position demonises and pathologises her, allowing the townspeople to blame her as the source of all misfortune and thus behave better themselves. On her death this is made clear: 'mothers who had defended their children from Sula's malevolence (or who had defended their positions as mothers from Sula's scorn for the role) now had nothing to rub up against. The tension was gone and so was the reason for the effort they had made' (p. 153).

At the novel's poignant conclusion, even Nel is brought to a realisation of the necessity for black women to focus on their essential similarity in certain contexts. When she visits Eva Peace, Sula's grandmother, Eva questions her about Chicken Little's death and refuses to recognise a distinction that Nel has held dear since the event: the distinction between her own innocence and Sula's guilt. Eva comments: '"You, Sula. What's the difference? You was there. You watched, didn't you? Me, I never would've watched"' (p. 168). Nel begins to wonder whether the pleasure she felt as Chicken drowned implicates her as much as, if not more than, Sula, who had always assumed all the responsibility for the event. This recognition also links her with Sula in another way. Eva believed Sula watched her mother, Hannah, burn to death out of 'interest', instead of trying to save her. Nel realises that in distancing herself from Sula at the point of Chicken's death she began the process of splitting that fractured their relationship and forcibly separated Sula from her community. After her funeral, a grief-stricken Nel finally realises that '"all that time, I thought I was missing Jude ... We was girls together ... O Lord, Sula...girl, girl, girlgirlgirl"' (p. 174). She recognises that a childhood friendship could, in different circumstances, have been the source of a mutually sustaining relationship which challenged the status quo. The disappearing punctuation between the repeated word 'girl' enacts an imaginary textual process of bringing the girlfriends closer together.

Morrison's message about black female identity is clear. Like Smith, Spivak and hooks she admits that all identity is founded on loss and difference, but she also shows that such knowledge is politically useless in the context of a subordinated group, such as black women. White heterosexist patriarchy is more effectively challenged, she implies, by working within essentialist definitions of black female identity and making them positive, supportive and enriching. She also shows that this strategy is context-specific: it is inappropriate when considering the situation of black men, for example. Morrison develops a firmly anti-essentialist version of black male identity. Jude decides to marry Nel, for example, as a way of shoring up his sense of failed masculinity. When he understands that he will never be hired to work on the New River Road because he is black, he realises that 'the two of them together will make one Jude' (p. 83). Marriage to Nel, whose inferior gender appears to 'ballast' his sense of superiority, in fact reveals that his identity is predicated on failure and reliance on a subordinated, but necessary, 'other'. On her return to Medallion, Sula unsettles Jude's conception of himself as a struggling victim of white racism:

> everything in the world loves you. White men love you. They spend so much time worrying about your penis they forget their own. The only thing they want to do is cut off a nigger's privates. And if that ain't love and respect I don't know what is. And white women? They chase you all to every corner of the earth, feel for you under every bed. I knew a white woman wouldn't leave the house after 6 o'clock for fear one of you would snatch her. Now ain't that love? ... Colored women worry themselves into bad health just trying to hang onto your cuffs. Even little children – white and black, boys and girls – spend all their childhood eating their hearts out 'cause they think you don't love them. And if that ain't enough, you love yourselves. Nothing in this world loves a black man like another black man.   (pp. 103–4)

Sula suggests that white racist repudiation and rejection of black masculinity conceal a secret dependence on and fascination with it. This in fact resembles the more obvious adulation of black men by black women and children. She shows that attraction and repulsion, dependence and independence are linked processes and thus implicitly questions how those processes function in Jude's treatment of Nel. This anti-essentialist critique is powerful in an appropriate context: that of black male identity. However, when Sula, after Nel's rejection of her, takes it to its extremes and describes 'being a woman and colored' as 'the same as being a man' (p. 142), she forgets that she is speaking in a different context. Her version of anti-essentialist identity politics is shown to be counter-productive when applied to the situation of black women.

Conclusion

Morrison works with essentialist and anti-essentialist versions of identity that closely resemble those Smith, Spivak and hooks use. Like them, she puts both in dialogue rather than opposition and shows how each is appropriate or politically useful in particular contexts. The risks, for black women, of abandoning an essential explanation of black female identity are made clear, as are the advantages of anti-essentialist interpretations, in relation to black men, for example. Morrison suggests that basing black female identity on physical experience and friendship between women may be strategically essential to combat racism and small-mindedness, but her criticism of essentialist positions is never far away. Margaret Homans describes the work of Patricia Williams and Alice Walker as establishing 'constructive dialogue between poststructuralist and humanist views of identity rather than either reducing the black woman's body to sheer ground or matter or, to the contrary, using that body to validate disembodiment'.[22] She describes this position as one of 'pragmatic ambivalence' (p. 90). In applying notions of dialogue and conversation to the work of black women writers she is not alone.[23] However, it may be inappropriate to interpret the work of an African-American woman writer using terms that will immediately call to mind, for some readers, the work of Mikhail Bakhtin on the European novel.[24] Doing so raises similar concerns about cultural specificity to those mentioned when discussing Spivak's essay in relation to Morrison's work. After all, to expand Terry Eagleton's acerbic statement, 'There is a great deal of timely good sense ... in pointing out to the more idealist employees of the Western post-colonial industry ... that ethnic minorities within metropolitan countries are not the same as colonised peoples' and an African-American woman writer is not writing from the same tradition as a white European novelist or a historian of South Asian culture. However, we can find evidence that dialogue is commonly utilised in black feminist thought. Patricia Hill Collins argues that 'for Black women, new knowledge claims are rarely worked out in isolation from other individuals and are usually developed through dialogue with other members of a community ... The use of dialogue has deep roots in an African-based oral tradition and in African-American culture'.[25] Thus dialogue and conversation are appropriate models to use to interpret Morrison's writing practice and restructure this chapter. While I acknowledge the relevance of other interpretative models I choose to read her work, to borrow Smith's words, 'look[ing] first for precedents and insights in interpretation within the works of other Black women' (p. 175). This is a strategic choice that resembles Morrison's own position in *Sula*.

In doing so, this book may be guilty of what Kaminsky calls 'fetishizing, and therefore immobilizing, race in the desire to engage in responsible feminist practice'.[26] She goes on to castigate 'anthologies of feminist literary criticism which consist of large numbers of essays on white women writers that pay little attention to race, overshadowing a single article on a racially identified writer or subject' (p. 9). Obviously this book is guilty of using such a structure. In its defence, it does so to try and suggest, but then question, the subordinate position that black feminism has traditionally had in feminist theory, so that readers are able to understand and criticise the trajectory of feminist thinking this century, which has been very white-oriented. Kaminsky argues that 'only when we conceptualize race as mutable and multivalenced can we hope to make sense of the ways in which it interacts with the differently nuanced category of gender' (p. 9). This chapter has sought to acknowledge the intrinsic instability of race as a category, discuss the importance of its discursive construction and suggest some of the ways in which this intermeshes with power effects. It has also demonstrated a number of different strategic responses to racism, heterosexism and patriarchy in particular political and discursive contexts. It attempts to put black feminism in dialogue with post-colonial theory while recognising its importance as a separate tradition.

Concluding Note

Feminist theory has traditionally pointed out the absence of explicit consideration of gender issues in other theories. It has analysed the ways in which interpretations are unconsciously dependent on particular constructions of masculinity and femininity. Marxist feminism, for example, as discussed in Chapter 3, argues that in a conventionally sexually segregated society women's reproductive and domestic labour in the home is as crucial in sustaining capitalism as the productive work of men in the wage labour force. More recently, as Chapters 7 and 8 indicate, feminism has itself been criticised for its inattention to issues of sexuality, race and ethnicity. The terms 'third-wave feminism' and 'postfeminism' acknowledge the fracture of crude definitions of women's identity based on a shared oppression resulting from gender alone. Simple definitions of feminist theory and politics based on this conception of woman have also been complicated. It is clear that feminism has always been in dialogue with other transformative theories like liberalism, Marxism, psychoanalysis, and (more recently) poststructuralism and postmodernism. In these situations feminism is in the position of irritant, chafing at the conventions of a particular theory; on other occasions it is in the defensive position, acknowledging and attempting to incorporate challenges such as those of queer theory and post-colonial theory to the interpretations it holds dear. One obvious way of perceiving these two impulses is as the beginning and end of a story, or narrative. It is equally obvious, though, that both impulses have always been present in feminism. The terms 'first', 'second' and 'third' wave imply a story of progress, suggesting that there is scope for further development using the same metaphor or frame of reference. The term 'postfeminism' is more clearly conclusive; it indicates a break with preceding work. However, the extent to which the prefix 'post' is contestatory has been debated in relation to the terms 'poststructuralism', 'postmodernism' and 'postcolonialism'. One may, or may not, wish to place a hyphen in these words, to indicate a conceptual break with what has gone before. 'Postfeminism' may not, then, imply the 'end', or inappropriateness, of feminism as clearly as it appears to do.

It is clear that the terms one chooses to use create different narratives, or stories. In her article 'Sexual Difference and Collective Identities: The New Global Constellation', Seyla Benhabib argues that it is this capacity to generate stories about oneself which is distinctive of identity. She argues that such a model of subjectivity is not to be confused with the traditional modern account of the pre-social, unified self who possesses the ability to act rationally and morally. What she defines as a 'dialogic narrative' (p. 344) view of identity is one that is shaped and formed by historical and cultural context and inflected (inevitably) by otherness and difference. However, identity is not entirely *determined* by those things, as it is in some postmodernist and poststructuralist versions of the death of the subject. She thus allows for *'the conditions of possible human agency'*.[1] In other words, it is the capacity to 'keep telling a story about who one is that makes sense to oneself and to others' (p. 347) that characterises human identity, even if that story alters, is confused, or temporarily breaks down. Such narratives take place in continual conversation with other narratives; they inevitably acknowledge other perspectives and voices since to do otherwise is impossible. One implication of Benhabib's argument is that we can understand collective political identities in a similar way. To elaborate her argument in relation to feminist theory and politics would mean that feminism acquires identity and agency (or power to act) because of its ability to generate multiple and diverse narratives about itself, some of which have been discussed in this book. These narrative versions of feminism include difference and otherness; they exist in dialogue with other theories. Indeed they have shaped other theories as much as they have been formed by those theories; in other words, they constitute each other. Equally, feminist theory has always been in conversation with both universalist perceptions of women's essential shared identity and dispersed, fragmented views of women's difference.

Benhabib's article discusses one novel at some length to support her points about identity. That novel is Virginia Woolf's *Orlando*. She describes her use of the text as an 'excursus', an 'interesting convergence of literary and philosophical perspectives' (p. 341) and writes that 'her own views of narrativity develop in interlocution' (p. 341) with Woolf's novel. Her use of the novel is not then, simply illustrative, but is in itself dialogic: the literary text converses with her more 'philosophical' and 'theoretical' sources. This book has suggested just such a model for the relationship between the concerns of twentieth-century women novelists and feminist theorists. It also argues that those novelists have occupied a similar conversational, ambivalent position in relation to the genre in which they write. Their innovations in that genre resemble those innovations feminist theorists have made when discussing gender identity, the body, politics and writing. As Julia Kristeva suggests, women occupy a marginal position, which is not to say that such a position is always and everywhere identical: margins can shift and move.[2] Benhabib acknowledges that 'the codes of established narratives in various cultures define our capacity to tell the story in very different ways; they limit our freedom to "vary the code"' (p. 344). A position of marginality will have a similar limiting effect. To support her point about the importance of these limits she again uses a woman novelist, footnoting the work of Toni Morrison and praising the way it suggests cultural variability and 'demonstrates the indispensability of narrative for the *empowerment* of oppressed and marginal groups' (p. 345). She argues that even in such an oppressed or marginal position: 'it is always possible in a conversation to drop the last remark and let it crash on the floor in silence, or to carry on and keep the dialogue alive and going, or to become whimsical, ironic, and critical and turn the conversation on itself, so too do we always have options in telling a life story that makes sense to us' (pp. 344–5). This book demonstrates that women novelists and theorists have continually used such a strategy, making apparent those fictional or philosophical conventions which have conventionally functioned to marginalise them. In doing so they have created a space in which they can tell a story which 'makes sense' to them and to others.

Notes

Notes to the Introduction

1. Doris Lessing's 'To Room Nineteen' can be read quickly and is widely available. It is included in *The Norton Anthology of English Literature*, 6th edn, vol. 2, ed. M. H. Abrams (New York: Norton, 1993), pp. 2301–23, as well as in Doris Lessing, *To Room Nineteen: Collected Stories*, vol. 1 (London: Flamingo, 1994), pp. 352–86. The reader will therefore be able to make a swift assessment of how this book works and what it does with literary texts.
2. This phrase borrows from Rosalind Coward's excellent 'Are Women's Novels Feminist Novels?', in *The New Feminist Criticism: Essays on Women, Literature and Theory*, ed. Elaine Showalter (London: Virago, 1986), pp. 225–39.
3. See Ian Watt, *The Rise of the Novel: Studies in Defoe, Richardson and Fielding* (London: Chatto and Windus, 1957) for this standard version of eighteenth-century fiction.
4. See, for example, Janet Todd, *The Sign of Angellica: Women, Writing and Fiction, 1660–1800* (London: Virago, 1989); Dale Spender, *Mothers of the Novel: 100 Good Women Writers before Jane Austen* (London: Pandora, 1986); Jane Spencer, *The Rise of the Woman Novelist: From Aphra Behn to Jane Austen* (Oxford: Blackwell, 1986).
5. See, for example, Sandra M. Gilbert and Susan Gubar, *The Madwoman in the Attic: The Woman Writer and the Nineteenth-Century Literary Imagination* (New Haven, Conn.: Yale University Press, 1979).
6. Virginia Woolf, *A Room of One's Own* (Harmondsworth: Penguin, 1945), p. 77.
7. See Toril Moi's discussion of Kristeva and marginality in *Sexual/Textual Politics: Feminist Literary Theory* (London: Routledge, 1985), pp. 163–7.
8. Rosemary Hennessey and Rajeswari Mohan, 'The Construction of Woman in Three Popular Texts of Empire: Towards a Critique of Materialist Feminism', *Textual Practice*, 3 (1989), 323–57 (p. 325).
9. Some of the various and subtle distinctions between the terms 'modern', 'postmodern', 'modernity', 'postmodernity', 'modernism', 'postmodernism', 'modernist' and 'postmodernist' are discussed in Chapters 5 and particularly 6 of this book.
10. A footnote about footnotes! After the first reference, page numbers are given in the text. Where there is any ambiguity the author's name and/or the title of the work are included.
11. Doris Lessing, Preface to *The Golden Notebook* (London: Flamingo, 1993), p. 21.

Notes to Chapter 1: First-Wave Feminism

1. *Reassessments of 'First Wave' Feminism*, ed. Elizabeth Sarah (Oxford: Pergamon Press, 1982), p. 520.
2. Olive Banks's book *Faces of Feminism: A Study of Feminism as a Social Movement* (Oxford: Martin Robertson, 1981) covers these years in Part III, which is called 'The Intermission'. She does, however, suggest that feminism split into its 'constituent parts' (p. 150) in this period so that this is only an 'apparent break in continuity' (p. 154). For a study of this period in the USA see Leila J. Rupp and Verta Taylor, *Survival in the Doldrums: The American Women's Rights Movement, 1945–1960s* (New York: Oxford University Press, 1987).
3. Olive Banks discusses the impact of evangelical Christianity, Enlightenment philosophy and the socialist tradition on first-wave feminism in Chapters 2, 3 and 4 of *Faces of Feminism*.
4. See Barbara Caine, 'Feminism, Suffrage and the Nineteenth-Century English Women's Movement', in *Reassessments of 'First Wave' Feminism*, ed. Elizabeth Sarah (Oxford: Pergamon Press, 1982), pp. 537–50.
5. Olive Banks, *Becoming a Feminist: The Social Origins of 'First Wave' Feminism* (Brighton: Wheatsheaf, 1986).
6. See Banks, *Faces of Feminism*, p. 149, and Barbara Caine, p. 550, for rather different accounts of this issue.
7. See Banks, *Faces of Feminism*, and Ellen Dubois, *Feminism and Suffrage: The Emergence of an Independent Women's Movement in America, 1848–1869* (Ithaca, N.Y.: Cornell University Press, 1978), for accounts of the first wave in the USA, and see Sarah, *Reassessments of 'First Wave' Feminism*, for non-'first world' discussion.
8. Interview with Deirdre Bair, quoted in Deirdre Bair, 'Simone de Beauvoir: Politics, Language, and Feminist Identity', *Yale French Studies*, 72 (1986), 149–62 (p. 154).
9. See Elaine Showalter, *A Literature of Their Own: British Women Novelists from Brontë to Lessing*, new edition (London: Virago Press, 1982), p. 282.
10. For full details of the different manuscript versions of the essay see Virginia Woolf, *Women and Fiction: The Manuscript Versions of 'A Room of One's Own'*, ed. S. P. Rosenbaum, Shakespeare Head Press edition (Oxford: Blackwell, 1992).
11. Virginia Woolf, *A Room of One's Own* (Harmondsworth: Penguin, 1945), p. 102.
12. Readers of the English translation should be aware that it has its problems, including the cutting of a number of sections detailing the lives of important women in history. See Deirdre Bair, ' "Madly Sensible and Brilliantly Confused": From *Le Deuxième sexe* to *The Second Sex*', in *Dalhousie French Studies*, 13 (1987), 23–35.
13. Simone de Beauvoir, *The Second Sex*, ed. and trans. H. M. Parshley (London: Picador, 1988), p. 295.
14. Doris Lessing, 'To Room Nineteen', in *To Room Nineteen: Collected Stories*, vol. 1 (London: Flamingo, 1994), pp. 352–86 (p. 375).
15. See Hermione Lee, *Virginia Woolf* (London: Vintage, 1997), p. 557 for this estimate.

16. See Carl Gustav Jung, 'The Syzygy: Anima and Animus', in *The Collected Works of C. G. Jung*, vol. 9, Part II: *Aion Researches into the Phenomenology of the Self*, ed. Herbert Read, Michael Fordham and Gerhard Adler, trans. R. F. C. Hull (London: Routledge and Kegan Paul, 1959), pp. 11–22.

17. See Toril Moi's introduction in her *Sexual/Textual Politics: Feminist Literary Theory* (London: Routledge, 1985) for this view.

18. See Elaine Showalter, *A Literature of Their Own* and Toril Moi, *Sexual/Textual Politics* for expositions of these different views. Moi also discusses Showalter's position in her book.

19. See Virginia Tiger, '"Taking Hands in (Dis)Unity": Story to Storied in Doris Lessing's "To Room Nineteen" and "A Room"', *MFS*, 36 (1990), 421–33 for a more detailed examination of some of these points.

20. Jane Marcus, 'Thinking Back Through Our Mothers', in *New Feminist Essays on Virginia Woolf*, ed. Jane Marcus (London: Macmillan, 1981), pp. 1–30 (p. 1).

21. See, for example, Dorothy Kaufmann, 'Simone de Beauvoir: Questions of Difference and Generation', *Yale French Studies*, 72 (1986), 121–31 for a discussion of this position in relation to de Beauvoir.

22. See Linda M. G. Zerilli, 'A Process without a Subject: Simone de Beauvoir and Julia Kristeva on Maternity', *Signs*, 18 (1992), 111–35 for this view. See also Kristana Arp, 'Beauvoir's Concept of Bodily Alienation' and Julie K. Ward, 'Beauvoir's Two Senses of "Body" in *The Second Sex*', 161–78 and 223–43, in *Feminist Interpretations of Simone de Beauvoir*, ed. Margaret A. Simons (University Park, Penn.: Pennsylvania State University Press, 1995).

23. Jean-Paul Sartre, *Being and Nothingness: An Essay on Phenomenological Ontology*, trans. Hazel E. Barnes, introd. Mary Warnock (London: Methuen, 1958).

24. See Michèle Le Doeuff, 'Simone de Beauvoir and Existentialism', *Feminist Studies*, 6 (1980), 277–89; Margaret A. Simons, 'Beauvoir and Sartre: The Philosophical Relationship', *Yale French Studies*, 72 (1986), 165–79; Sonia Kruks, 'Gender and Subjectivity: Simone de Beauvoir and Contemporary Feminism', *Signs*, 18 (1992), 89–110; Karen Vintges, '*The Second Sex* and Philosophy', Michèle Le Doeuff, 'Simone de Beauvoir: Falling into (Ambiguous) Line', Sonia Kruks, 'Simone de Beauvoir: Teaching Sartre About Freedom', Kate Fullbrook and Edward Fullbrook, 'Sartre's Secret Key', 45–58, 59–66, 79–96, 97–112, in *Feminist Interpretations of Simone de Beauvoir*, ed. Margaret A. Simons (University Park, Penn.: Pennsylvania State University Press, 1995).

25. See Toril Moi, *Simone de Beauvoir: The Making of an Intellectual Woman* (Oxford: Blackwell, 1994), pp. 146–7, pp. 177–8, and Judith Okely, *Simone de Beauvoir: A Re-Reading* (London: Virago, 1986), pp. 105–6 for these different views.

26. See Margaret A. Simons, 'Lesbian Connections: Simone de Beauvoir and Feminism', *Signs*, 18 (1992), 136–61.

27. Claudia Card, 'Lesbian Attitudes and *The Second Sex*', *Women's Studies International Forum*, 8 (1985), 209–14, reprinted in *Hypatia Reborn: Essays*

in Feminist Philosophy, ed. Azizah Y. al-Hibri and Margaret A. Simons (Bloomington, Ind.: Indiana University Press, 1990), pp. 290–9.

28. See Mary Evans, *Simone de Beauvoir: A Feminist Mandarin* (London: Tavistock, 1985), pp. 67–8.
29. See Moi, *Simone de Beauvoir*, p. 209; and Jane Heath, *Simone de Beauvoir, Key Women Writers* (Hemel Hempstead: Harvester Wheatsheaf, 1989), p. 5.
30. Alice Schwartzer, *Simone de Beauvoir Today: Conversations, 1972–1982* (London: Chatto).

Notes to Chapter 2: Liberal Feminism

1. See, for example, Zillah Eisenstein, *The Radical Future of Liberal Feminism* (New York: Longman, 1981), p. 177; Margaret Andersen, *Thinking about Women: Sociological Perspectives on Sex and Gender*, 2nd edn (New York: Macmillan, 1988), pp. 292–3, 298–9.
2. See Betty Friedan, *It Changed My Life: Writings on the Women's Movement* (New York: W. W. Norton, 1985), p. xxiii.
3. Judith Stacey, 'Are Feminists Afraid to Leave Home? The Challenge of Conservative Pro-Family Feminism', in *What is Feminism?*, ed. Juliet Mitchell and Ann Oakley (Oxford: Basil Blackwell, 1986), pp. 219–48.
4. Juliet Mitchell, *Woman's Estate* (Harmondsworth: Penguin, 1971), p. 11.
5. There is a great deal of debate about the extent and nature of Mill's collaboration with Taylor on a variety of his published works.
6. See Eisenstein, *The Radical Future of Liberal Feminism* for a study of feminism's roots in liberal philosophy and economics.
7. See Mitchell, *Woman's Estate*, p. 52, and Barbara Ryan, 'Ideological Purity and Feminism: The US Women's Movement from 1966 to 1975', *Gender and Society*, 3 (1989), 239–59, for consideration of these different causes of the emergence of the second wave in the USA.
8. See Rachel Bowlby, '"The Problem with No Name": Rereading Friedan's *The Feminine Mystique*', *Feminist Review*, 27 (1987), 61–75 (p. 61) for the suggestion that the book opens 'like a thriller'.
9. Betty Friedan, *The Feminine Mystique* (Harmondsworth: Penguin, 1992), p. 38.
10. Betty Friedan, *The Second Stage* (London: Abacus, 1983), p. 49.
11. See Malcolm Bradbury, 'The Paleface Professor', *The Times*, Saturday, 19 January 1985, p. 6.
12. Lurie is a part-time Professor of English Literature at Cornell University.
13. Alison Lurie, *The War between the Tates* (London: Abacus, 1993), p. 55.
14. See Judie Newman, 'Sexual and Civil Conflicts: *The War between the Tates*', in *University Fiction*, ed. David Bevan (Amsterdam: Rodopi, 1990), pp. 103–23 for a discussion of the influence of the writing of George Kennan on Brian Tate's opinions.

15. Leila J. Rupp and Verta Taylor, *Survival in the Doldrums: The American Women's Rights Movement, 1945–1960s* (Oxford: Oxford University Press, 1987), p. 14.
16. Sandra Dijkstra, 'Simone de Beauvoir and Betty Friedan: The Politics of Omission', *Feminist Studies*, 6 (1980), 294–303 (p. 295).

Notes to Chapter 3: Marxist Feminism

1. Donna Landry and Gerald MacLean, *Materialist Feminisms* (Oxford: Blackwell, 1993), p. 32.
2. See Clara Connolly, Lynne Segal et al., 'Feminism and Class Politics: A Round-Table Discussion', *Feminist Review*, 23 (1986), 13–30.
3. For an introduction to Marxist theory and its application to literary texts see Terry Eagleton, *Criticism and Ideology: A Study in Marxist Literary Theory* (London: Verso, 1978) and *Marxism and Literary Criticism* (London: Routledge, 1992).
4. Karl Marx and Friedrich Engels, *The German Ideology* (London: Lawrence and Wishart, 1974), p. 64.
5. See Annette Kuhn and AnnMarie Wolpe (eds), *Feminism and Materialism: Women and Modes of Production* (London: Routledge, 1978), p. 8.
6. Louise C. Johnson, 'Socialist Feminisms', in *Feminist Knowledge: Critique and Construct*, ed. Sneja Gunew (London: Routledge, 1990), pp. 304–31 (p. 326).
7. See the chapters in the section entitled 'Towards Feminist Marxism', in *The Politics of Diversity: Feminism, Marxism and Nationalism*, ed. Roberta Hamilton and Michèle Barrett (London: Verso, 1986), which all consider the domestic labour debate.
8. See Veronica Beechey, 'Women and Production: A Critical Analysis of Some Sociological Theories of Women's Work', in *Feminism and Materialism: Women and Modes of Production*, ed. Annette Kuhn and AnnMarie Wolpe (London: Routledge, 1978), pp. 155–97.
9. See Heidi Hartmann, 'Capitalism, Patriarchy and Job Segregation by Sex', in *Capitalist Patriarchy and the Case for Socialist Feminism*, ed. Zillah R. Eisenstein (New York: Monthly Review Press, 1979), pp. 206–47.
10. See Zillah Eisenstein, 'Some Notes on the Relations of Capitalist Patriarchy', in *Capitalist Patriarchy and the Case for Socialist Feminism*, ed. Zillah Eisenstein (New York: Monthly Review Press, 1979), pp. 41–55.
11. See Zillah Eisenstein, 'Developing a Theory of Capitalist Patriarchy and Socialist Feminism', in *Capitalist Patriarchy and the Case for Socialist Feminism*, ed. Zillah Eisenstein (New York: Monthly Review Press, 1979), pp. 5–40.
12. See Heidi Hartmann, 'The Unhappy Marriage of Marxism and Feminism: Towards a More Progressive Union', in *Women and Revolution: A Discussion of the Unhappy Marriage of Marxism and Feminism*, ed. Lydia Sargent (London: Pluto Press, 1981).

13. See, for example, Michèle Barrett and Mary McIntosh, 'Ethnocentrism and Socialist-Feminist Theory', *Feminist Review*, 20 (1985), 23–47 for an early exposition of this view.
14. Sheila Rowbotham, *Woman's Consciousness: Man's World* (Harmondsworth: Penguin, 1973), p. 5.
15. Michèle Barrett, *Women's Oppression Today: The Marxist/Feminist Encounter*, revised edn (London: Verso, 1988), p. 1. First published as *Women's Oppression Today: Problems in Marxist Feminist Analysis* (London: Verso, 1980).
16. Gayle Greene, *Doris Lessing: The Poetics of Change* (Ann Arbor, Mich.: University of Michigan Press, 1994), pp. 16–19.
17. Doris Lessing, *The Golden Notebook* (London: Flamingo, 1993), p. 20.
18. Rachel Bowlby, 'For the Etruscans', in *The New Feminist Criticism: Essays on Women, Literature, and Theory*, ed. Elaine Showalter (London: Routledge, 1989), pp. 271–91 (pp. 279–80).
19. See Anne Mulkeen, 'Twentieth-Century Realism: The "Grid" Structure of *The Golden Notebook*', *Studies in the Novel*, 4 (1972), 262–74.
20. The phrase is Jean-François Lyotard's, from *The Postmodern Condition: A Report on Knowledge*, trans. Geoff Bennington and Brian Massumi (Manchester: Manchester University Press, 1984), p. xxiv.

Notes to Chapter 4: Psychoanalytic Feminism

1. *Women and Revolution: A Discussion of the Unhappy Marriage of Marxism and Feminism*, ed. Lydia Sargent (London: Pluto Press, 1981).
2. Rachel Bowlby, 'Still Crazy After All These Years', in *Between Feminism and Psychoanalysis*, ed. Teresa Brennan (London: Routledge, 1989), pp. 40–59 (p. 42).
3. A useful introduction to psychoanalysis is Freud's own: *An Outline of Psychoanalysis*, trans. and ed. James Strachey (London: The Hogarth Press, 1969). Interesting applications of psychoanalytic theory to literature are contained in Sue Vice, *Psychoanalytic Criticism* (London: Polity Press, 1995).
4. Juliet Mitchell, *Psychoanalysis and Feminism* (Harmondsworth: Penguin, 1990), p. xv.
5. Nancy Chodorow, *The Reproduction of Mothering: Psychoanalysis and the Sociology of Gender* (Berkeley, Cal.: University of California Press, 1978), p. 142.
6. Margaret Atwood, *Lady Oracle* (London: Virago, 1982), p. 103.
7. See Elizabeth Wilson, 'Psychoanalysis: Psychic Law and Order?', *Feminist Review*, 8 (1981), 63–78 for further discussion of this point.
8. Before writing *Psychoanalysis and Feminism* Mitchell was better known for her Marxist feminist work such as *Woman's Estate* (Harmondsworth: Penguin, 1971).
9. See Roisin McDonough and Rachel Harrison, 'Patriarchy and Relations of Production', in *Feminism and Materialism: Women and Modes of*

Production, ed. Annette Kuhn and AnnMarie Wolpe (London: Routledge, 1987), pp. 14–25.

10. Jane Gallop, *Feminism and Psychoanalysis: The Daughter's Seduction* (Basingstoke: Macmillan, 1982), p. 9.
11. See Sigmund Freud, 'Fragment of an Analysis of a Case of Hysteria' ('Dora'), in *Case Histories I: 'Dora' and 'Little Hans'*, The Penguin Freud Library, vol. 8 (Harmondsworth: Penguin, 1990).
12. Toril Moi, 'Patriarchal Thought and the Drive for Knowledge', in *Between Feminism and Psychoanalysis*, ed. Teresa Brennan (London: Routledge, 1989), pp. 189–205 (p. 191).
13. Elizabeth Grosz, *Jacques Lacan: A Feminist Introduction* (London: Routledge, 1990), pp. 22–3.

Notes to Chapter 5: Poststructuralist Feminism

1. See, for example, Elaine Marks and Isabelle de Courtivron, *New French Feminisms: An Anthology* (Hemel Hempstead: Harvester Wheatsheaf, 1981); Hester Eisenstein and Alice Jardine, *The Future of Difference* (Boston, Mass.: G. K. Hall, 1980); Toril Moi, *Sexual/Textual Politics: Feminist Literary Theory* (London: Routledge, 1985).
2. See Christine Delphy, 'The Invention of French Feminism: An Essential Move', *Yale French Studies*, (1993), 190–221.
3. In discussing linguistics and psychoanalysis at the expense of philosophy I am repeating an interpretative manoeuvre which has been questioned in recent criticsm, particularly of Irigaray and Kristeva. (See, for example, Tina Chanter, *Ethics of Eros: Irigaray's Rewriting of the Philosophers* (London: Routledge, 1995), p. 3; John Lechte, *Julia Kristeva* (London: Routledge, 1990), p. 14.) However, I think the choice is justified precisely because of the significance of that interpretative manoeuvre in appropriations of their work in English as a discipline which has emphasised the linguistic and psychoanalytic as more directly relevant to a process of textual interpretation.
4. See, for example, Toril Moi, pp. 104–8 for discussion of Cixous's debt to Derrida, Margaret Whitford, *Luce Irigaray: Philosophy in the Feminine* (London: Routledge, 1991), p. 123 for discussion of how Irigaray moves beyond Derrida, and Lechte, pp. 95–9 for discussion of Derrida's influence on Kristeva.
5. On structuralism see Robert Scholes, *Structuralism in Literature* (New Haven, Conn.: Yale University Press, 1974) and Jonathan Culler, *Structuralist Poetics: Structuralism, Linguistics and the Study of Literature* (London: Routledge, 1975). On poststructuralism see *Untying the Text: A Post-Structuralist Reader*, ed. Robert Young (London: Routledge and Kegan Paul, 1981).
6. Luce Irigaray trained with Lacan at the Ecole Freudienne, from which she was expelled after the publication of *Speculum of the Other Woman*.

A large proportion of commentators on Cixous, Irigaray and Kristeva situate them in relation to Lacan, or explain explicitly why they are not doing so. See, for example, Moi (pp. 99–101), Jane Gallop, *Feminism and Psychoanalysis: The Daughter's Seduction* (Basingstoke: Macmillan, 1982) and Elizabeth Grosz, *Sexual Subversions: Three French Feminists* (Sydney: Allen and Unwin, 1989).

7. Jacques Lacan, *The Seminar. Book III: The Psychoses, 1955–56*, trans. Russell Grigg (London: Routledge, 1993), p. 167.

8. A useful introduction to the work of Lacan in relation to feminism is Elizabeth Grosz, *Jacques Lacan: A Feminist Introduction* (London: Routledge, 1990).

9. See particularly Jacques Derrida, *Spurs: Nietzsche's Styles/Eperons: Les Styles de Nietzsche*, trans. Barbara Harlow (Chicago, Ill.: University of Chicago Press, 1979).

10. Hélène Cixous, 'The Laugh of the Medusa', *New French Feminisms: An Anthology*, ed. Elaine Marks and Isabelle de Courtivron (Hemel Hempstead: Harvester Wheatsheaf, 1981), 245–64 (p. 255).

11. Sigmund Freud, 'Medusa's Head', in *The Standard Edition of the Complete Psychological Works of Sigmund Freud*, vol. 18, ed. James Strachey (London: Hogarth Press, 1940), pp. 273–4.

12. Luce Irigaray, 'When Our Lips Speak Together', in *This Sex Which is Not One*, trans. Catherine Porter with Carolyn Burke (Ithaca, N.Y.: Cornell University Press, 1985), 205–18 (p. 205).

13. Maggie Berg, 'Luce Irigaray's "Contradictions": Poststructuralism and Feminism', *Signs*, 17 (1991), 50–70 (65).

14. Julia Kristeva, 'From One Identity to an Other', in *The Portable Kristeva*, ed. Kelly Oliver (New York: Columbia, 1997), pp. 93–115 (p. 101).

15. See Virginia Woolf, 'Modern Fiction', in *The Common Reader*, First Series (London: The Hogarth Press, 1968), pp. 184–95.

16. Peter Faulkner, *Modernism* (London: Routledge, 1990), p. 2.

17. See for example Bonnie Kime Scott, *Refiguring Modernism*, vol. 1: *The Women of 1928* (Bloomington, Ind.: Indiana University Press, 1995) and *The Gender of Modernism: A Critical Anthology* (Bloomington, Ind.: Indiana University Press, 1990), and Joseph Boone, *Libidinal Currents: Sexuality and the Shaping of Modernism* (Chicago, Ill.: University of Chicago Press, 1998).

18. Virginia Woolf, *Orlando*, ed. Rachel Bowlby, World's Classics (Oxford: Oxford University Press, 1992), p. 13.

19. Sherron Knopp, '"If I Saw You Would You Kiss Me?": Sapphism and the Subversiveness of Virginia Woolf's *Orlando*', *PMLA*, 103 (1988), 24–34.

20. See for example Moi's judgements of Cixous and Irigaray.

21. Jacqueline Rose, 'Julia Kristeva – Take Two', in *Ethics, Politics and Difference in Julia Kristeva's Writing*, ed. Kelly Oliver (New York: Routledge, 1993), pp. 41–61 (pp. 52–3).

22. Woolf refers to it as 'all a joke; & yet gay & quick reading I think; a writers' holiday', *The Diary of Virginia Woolf, 1925–1930*, vol. 3, ed. Anne Olivier Bell (London: Hogarth, 1980). For contemporary reviews see

Virginia Woolf: The Critical Heritage, ed. Robin Majundar and Allen McLaurin (London: Routledge, 1975), pp. 222–54.

23. See Elizabeth Abel, *Virginia Woolf and the Fictions of Psychoanalysis* (Chicago, Ill.: University of Chicago Press, 1989).

24. Gayatri Chakravorty Spivak, 'French Feminism in an International Frame', in *In Other Worlds: Essays in Cultural Politics* (London: Methuen, 1987), pp. 134–53 (p. 144).

25. Elizabeth Grosz, 'The Hetero and the Homo', in *Engaging with Irigaray: Feminist Philosophy and Modern European Thought*, ed. Carolyn Burke, Naomi Schor and Margaret Whitford (New York: Columbia University Press, 1994), pp. 335–50 (p. 339).

26. Judith Butler, 'The Body Politics of Julia Kristeva', in *Ethics, Politics and Difference in Julia Kristeva's Writing*, ed. Kelly Oliver (New York: Routledge, 1993), pp. 164–78 (p. 177).

27. Judith Butler, *Bodies that Matter: On the Discursive Limits of 'Sex'* (London: Routledge, 1993), p. 51.

28. See, for example, Irigaray, *An Ethic of Sexual Difference*, trans. Carolyn Burke and Gillian C. Gill (Ithaca, N.Y.: Cornell University Press, 1993) and *Marine Lover of Friedrich Nietzsche*, trans. Gillian C. Gill (New York: Columbia University Press, 1993).

29. See, for example, Teresa de Lauretis, *The Practice of Love: Lesbian Sexuality and Perverse Desire* (Bloomington, Ind.: Indiana University Press, 1994).

Notes to Chapter 6: Postmodernism and Feminism

1. Steven Best and Douglas Kellner, *Postmodern Theory: Critical Interrogations* (Basingstoke: Macmillan, 1991), p. 25.

2. The dates have been chosen to associate the beginning of the modern period with the onset of industrialisation and the emergence of Enlightenment philosophies, and its end with the creation of a consumerist and post-industrial society and the questioning of Enlightenment philosophies. This is obviously a crude account. For discussion of these issues see *Theories of Modernity and Postmodernity*, ed. Brian S. Turner (London: Sage, 1990).

3. Jean-François Lyotard, *The Postmodern Condition: A Report on Knowledge*, trans. Geoff Bennington and Brian Massumi, Foreword by Fredric Jameson (Minneapolis, Minn.: University of Minnesota Press, 1984), p. xxiv.

4. Jean Baudrillard, 'Simulacra and Simulations', in *Jean Baudrillard: Selected Writings*, ed. Mark Poster (Cambridge: Polity Press, 1988), pp. 166–84.

5. See Fredric Jameson, *Postmodernism; or, the Cultural Logic of Late Capitalism* (London: Verso, 1991).

6. See Linda Hutcheon, *The Politics of Postmodernism* (London: Routledge, 1989), pp. 23–6.

7. See, for example, David Lodge, 'Modernism, Antimodernism and Postmodernism', in *Working with Structuralism: Essays and Reviews on Nineteenth- and Twentieth-Century Literature* (London: Routledge, 1981), pp. 3–16.
8. See, for example, the essays in *Feminism/Postmodernism*, ed. Linda J. Nicholson (London: Routledge, 1990).
9. Alice Jardine, *Gynesis: Configurations of Woman and Modernity* (Ithaca, N.Y.: Cornell University Press, 1985), p. 15.
10. Seyla Benhabib, 'Feminism and the Question of Postmodernism', in *Situating the Self: Gender, Community and Postmodernism in Contemporary Ethics* (Cambridge: Polity Press, 1992), 203–41 (pp. 212–13).
11. John Bayley, 'Fighting for the Crown', *New York Review of Books*, 23 April 1992, pp. 9–11 (p. 9).
12. Andrea Dworkin's *Pornography: Men Possessing Women* (London: Women's Press, 1981) which takes this view, was published two years after *The Sadeian Woman*. For discussion of *The Sadeian Woman* in relation to the contemporary and subsequent feminist debates about pornography see Sally Keenan, 'Angela Carter's *The Sadeian Woman*: Feminism as Treason', in *The Infernal Desires of Angela Carter: Fiction, Femininity, Feminism*, ed. Joseph Bristow and Trev Broughton (London: Longman, 1997), 132–148.
13. Angela Carter, *Nights at the Circus* (London: Picador, 1985), p. 32.
14. John Haffenden, *Novelists in Interview* (London: Methuen, 1985), p. 87.
15. See Michel Foucault, *The History of Sexuality*, vol. 1: *An Introduction*, trans. Robert Hurley (New York: Vintage, 1978).
16. See, for example, Sarah Gamble, *Angela Carter: Writing from the Front Line* (Edinburgh: Edinburgh University Press, 1997), p. 162.
17. Aidan Day, *Angela Carter: The Rational Glass* (Manchester: Manchester University Press, 1998), p. 169.
18. See Carol Gilligan, *In a Different Voice: Psychological Theory and Women's Development* (Cambridge, Mass.: Harvard University Press, 1982).
19. Clearly the name is a reference to Toussaint l'Ouverture, the black leader of the Haitian rebellions against the French of 1791–1801. See C. L. R. James, *The Black Jacobins: Toussaint L'Ouverture and the San Domingo Revolution*, 2nd edn (New York: Vintage, 1963).
20. See Foucault's account in *Discipline and Punish: The Birth of the Prison*, trans. Alan Sheridan (London: Allen Lane, 1977), pp. 200–9.
21. Judith Butler, 'Contingent Foundations: Feminism and the Question of Postmodernism', *Praxis International*, 11 (1991), 150–65.

Notes to Chapter 7: Lesbian Feminism and Queer Theory

1. Teresa de Lauretis, 'Queer Theory: Lesbian and Gay Sexualities: An Introduction', *differences*, 3 (1991), iii–xviii (viii).
2. For a subtle and illuminating analysis of this process see Judith Butler, 'Against Proper Objects', in *Feminism Meets Queer Theory*, ed. Elizabeth

Weed and Naomi Schor (Bloomington, Ind.: Indiana University Press, 1997), pp. 1–30.

3. See Diana Fuss, *Essentially Speaking: Feminism, Nature and Difference* (London: Routledge, 1990), pp. 107–8 for a useful summary of critical opinion on the construction of the category of the homosexual.

4. Alan Sinfield, *Cultural Politics: Queer Reading* (London: Routledge, 1994), p. 19.

5. Michel Foucault, *The History of Sexuality*, vol. 1: *An Introduction*, trans. Robert Hurley (New York: Vintage, 1978).

6. Quoted in Lillian Faderman, *Surpassing the Love of Men: Romantic Friendship and Love Between Women from the Renaissance to the Present* (London: The Women's Press, 1985), p. 242.

7. Esther Newton, 'The Mythic Mannish Lesbian: Radclyffe Hall and the New Woman', *Signs*, 9 (1984), 557–75.

8. Adrienne Rich, 'Compulsory Heterosexuality and Lesbian Existence', *Signs*, 5 (1980), 631–60 (632).

9. Monique Wittig, 'One is Not Born a Woman', in *The Straight Mind and Other Essays* (Hemel Hempstead: Harvester Wheatsheaf, 1992), pp. 9–20 (p. 20).

10. Judith Butler, *Gender Trouble: Feminism and the Subversion of Identity* (London: Routledge, 1990), p. 7.

11. Hilary Hinds, '*Oranges Are Not the Only Fruit*: Reaching Audiences Other Lesbian Texts Cannot Reach', in *New Lesbian Criticism: Literary and Cultural Readings*, ed. Sally Munt (Hemel Hempstead: Harvester Wheatsheaf, 1992), pp. 153–72.

12. Rosellen Brown, 'Fertile Imagination', *Women's Review of Books*, 7 (1990), 9–10 (10).

13. Laura Doan, 'Jeanette Winterson's Sexing the Postmodern', in *The Lesbian Postmodern*, ed. Laura Doan (New York: Columbia University Press, 1994), pp. 137–55 (p. 153).

14. Jeanette Winterson, *Sexing the Cherry* (London: Vintage, 1990), p. 23.

15. Judith Butler, *Excitable Speech: A Politics of the Performative* (London: Routledge, 1997), p. 3.

Notes to Chapter 8: Black Feminism and Post-Colonial Theory

1. *All the Women Are White, All the Blacks Are Men, But Some of Us Are Brave*, ed. Gloria T. Hull, Patricia Bell Scott and Barbara Smith (Old Westbury: The Feminist Press, 1982).

2. Sigmund Freud, 'The Question of Lay Analysis: Conversations with an Impartial Person', in *The Standard Edition of the Complete Psychological Works of Sigmund Freud*, vol. 20, trans. and ed. James Strachey (London: Hogarth, 1953), pp. 183–250 (p. 212).

3. See Hélène Cixous, 'The Laugh of the Medusa' in *New French Feminisms: An Anthology*, ed. Elaine Marks and Isabelle de Courtivron

(Hemel Hempstead: Harvester Wheatsheaf, 1981), pp. 245–64 (pp. 247–8).

4. See Deborah K. King, 'Multiple Jeopardy, Multiple Consciousness: The Context of a Black Feminist Ideology, *Signs*', 14 (1988), 42–72.

5. See Stuart Hall, 'Cultural Identity and Diaspora', in *Colonial Discourse and Post-Colonial Theory: A Reader*, ed. Patrick Williams and Laura Chrisman (Hemel Hempstead: Harvester Wheatsheaf, 1993), pp. 392–403.

6. See, for example, *This Bridge Called My Back: Writings by Radical Women of Color*, ed. Cherrie Moraga and Gloria Anzaldua (Kitchen Table: Women of Color Press, 1983).

7. Carole Boyce Davies, *Black Women, Writing and Identity: Migrations of the Subject* (London: Routledge, 1994), p. 3.

8. Kobena Mercer, 'Diaspora Culture and the Dialogic Imagination: The Aesthetics of Black Independent Film in Britain', in *Blackframes: Critical Perspectives on Black Independent Cinema*, ed. Mbye B. Cham and Claire Andrade Watkins (Cambridge, Mass.: The MIT Press, 1988), pp. 50–61 (p. 57).

9. See, for example, Edward Said, *Orientalism* (London: Routledge, 1978).

10. Anne McClintock, 'The Angel of Progress: Pitfalls of the Term "Post-colonialism"', in *Colonial Discourse and Post-Colonial Theory: A Reader*, ed. Patrick Williams and Laura Chrisman (Hemel Hempstead: Harvester Wheatsheaf, 1993), pp. 291–304 (p. 295).

11. Terry Eagleton, 'In the Gaudy Supermarket', Review of Gayatri Chakravorty Spivak, *A Critique of Post-Colonial Reason: Toward a History of the Vanishing Present*, *London Review of Books Online*, 21, 10 (31 May 1999), <http.www.lrb.co.uk.>

12. Deborah E. McDowell, 'New Directions for Black Feminist Criticism', *Black American Literature Forum*, 14 (1980), 153–9 (p. 154).

13. Barbara Smith, 'Toward a Black Feminist Criticism', in *The New Feminist Criticism: Essays on Women, Literature, and Theory*, ed. Elaine Showalter (London: Virago, 1986), pp. 168–85 (p. 168).

14. Gayatri Chakravorty Spivak, 'Subaltern Studies: Deconstructing Historiography', in *In Other Worlds: Essays in Cultural Politics* (London: Methuen, 1987), pp. 197–221 (p. 200).

15. Sian Griffiths, 'A Class Sister Act', *The Times Higher Education Supplement*, 13 October 1995, p. 20.

16. bell hooks, 'Postmodern Blackness', in *Yearning: Race, Gender, and Cultural Politics* (London: Turnaround, 1991), pp. 23–31 (p. 23).

17. Peter Pringle, 'Victims of Slavery Find Their Voice', *Independent on Sunday*, 10 October 1993, p. 18.

18. Toni Morrison, 'Rootedness: The Ancestor as Foundation', in *Literature in the Modern World: Critical Essays and Documents*, ed. Dennis Walder (Oxford: Oxford University Press, 1990), pp. 326–32 (p. 328).

19. For a detailed discussion of these points see Deborah G. Chay, 'Rereading Barbara Smith: Black Feminist Criticism and the Category of Experience', *New Literary History*, 21 (1993), 635–52.

20. Barbara Smith, 'Reply to Deborah Chay', *New Literary History*, 24 (1993), 653–6 (p. 654).

21. Toni Morrison, *Sula* (London: Picador, 1991), p. 64.
22. Margaret Homans, '"Women of Color" Writers and Feminist Theory', *New Literary History*, 25 (1994), 73–94 (p. 87).
23. See for example Mae Gwendolyn Henderson, 'Speaking in Tongues: Dialogics, Dialectics and the Black Woman Writer's Literary Tradition', in *Reading Black, Reading Feminist: A Critical Anthology*, ed. Henry Louis Gates, Jr (New York: Meridian Press, 1990), pp. 116–42.
24. Mikhail Bakhtin, *The Dialogic Imagination: Four Essays*, ed. Michael Holquist, trans. Caryl Emerson and Michael Holquist (Austin: University of Texas Press, 1981).
25. Patricia Hill Collins, 'The Social Construction of Black Feminist Thought', *Signs*, 14 (1989), 745–73 (p. 763).
26. Amy Kaminsky, 'Gender, Race, Raza', *Feminist Studies*, 20 (1994), 7–31 (p. 9).

Notes to the Concluding Note

1. Seyla Benhabib, 'Sexual Difference and Collective Identities: The New Global Constellation', *Signs*, 24 (1999), 335–61 (p. 346).
2. See Toril Moi's discussion of Kristeva's association of femininity with marginality in her *Sexual/Textual Politics: Feminist Literary Theory* (London: Routledge, 1985), pp. 163–7.

Bibliography

Books

Abel, Elizabeth, *Virginia Woolf and the Fictions of Psychoanalysis* (Chicago, Ill.: University of Chicago Press, 1989).

Abrams, M. H., *The Norton Anthology of English Literature*, 6th edn, vol. 2 (New York: Norton, 1993).

Andersen, Margaret, *Thinking about Women: Sociological Perspectives on Sex and Gender*, 2nd edn (New York: Macmillan, 1988).

Atwood, Margaret, *Lady Oracle* (London: Virago, 1982).

Bakhtin, Mikhail, *The Dialogic Imagination: Four Essays*, ed. Michael Holquist, trans. Caryl Emerson and Michael Holquist (Austin, Tx: University of Texas Press, 1981).

Banks, Olive, *Faces of Feminism: A Study of Feminism as a Social Movement* (Oxford: Martin Robertson, 1981).

——, *Becoming a Feminist: The Social Origins of 'First Wave' Feminism* (Brighton: Wheatsheaf, 1986).

Barrett, Michèle, *Women's Oppression Today: The Marxist/Feminist Encounter*, revised edn (London: Verso, 1988).

Baudrillard, Jean, *Selected Writings*, ed. Mark Poster (Cambridge: Polity Press, 1988).

Beauvoir, Simone de, *The Second Sex*, ed. and trans. H. M. Parshley (London: Picador, 1988).

Benhabib, Seyla, *Situating the Self: Gender, Community and Postmodernism in Contemporary Ethics* (Cambridge: Polity Press, 1992).

Best, Steven and Douglas Kellner, *Postmodern Theory: Critical Interrogations* (Basingstoke: Macmillan, 1991).

Bevan, David, *University Fiction* (Amsterdam: Rodopi, 1990).

Boone, Joseph, *Libidinal Currents: Sexuality and the Shaping of Modernism* (Chicago, Ill.: University of Chicago Press, 1998).

Brennan, Teresa, *Between Feminism and Psychoanalysis* (London: Routledge, 1989).

Bristow, Joseph and Trev Broughton, *The Infernal Desires of Angela Carter: Fiction, Femininity, Feminism* (London: Longman, 1997).

Burke, Carolyn, Naomi Schor and Margaret Whitford, *Engaging with Irigaray: Feminist Philosophy and Modern European Thought* (New York: Columbia University Press, 1994).

Butler, Judith, *Bodies that Matter: On the Discursive Limits of 'Sex'* (London: Routledge, 1993).

——, *Excitable Speech: A Politics of the Performative* (London: Routledge, 1997).

——, *Gender Trouble: Feminism and the Subversion of Identity* (London: Routledge, 1990).

Carter, Angela, *Nights at the Circus* (London: Picador, 1985).

Cham, Mbye B. and Claire Andrade-Watkins, *Blackframes: Critical Perspectives on Black Independent Cinema* (Cambridge, Mass.: MIT. Press, 1988).

Chanter, Tina, *Ethics of Eros: Irigaray's Rewriting of the Philosophers* (London: Routledge, 1995).

Chodorow, Nancy, *The Reproduction of Mothering: Psychoanalysis and the Sociology of Gender* (Berkeley, Cal.: University of California Press, 1978).

Culler, Jonathan, *Structuralist Poetics: Structuralism, Linguistics and the Study of Literature* (London: Routledge, 1975).

Davies, Carole Boyce, *Black Women, Writing and Identity: Migrations of the Subject* (London: Routledge, 1994).

Day, Aidan, *Angela Carter: The Rational Glass* (Manchester: Manchester University Press, 1998).

Derrida, Jacques, *Spurs: Nietzsche's Styles/Eperons: Les Styles de Nietzsche*, trans. Barbara Harlow (Chicago, Ill.: University of Chicago Press, 1979).

Doan, Laura, *The Lesbian Postmodern* (New York: Columbia University Press, 1994).

Dubois, Ellen, *Feminism and Suffrage: The Emergence of an Independent Women's Movement in America, 1848–1869* (Ithaca, N.Y.: Cornell University Press, 1978).

Dworkin, Andrea, *Pornography: Men Possessing Women* (London: Women's Press, 1981).

Eagleton, Terry, *Criticism and Ideology: A Study in Marxist Literary Theory* (London: Verso, 1978).

——, *Marxism and Literary Criticism* (London: Routledge, 1992).

Eisenstein, Hester and Alice Jardine, *The Future of Difference* (Boston, Mass.: G. K. Hall, 1980).

Eisenstein, Zillah R., *Capitalist Patriarchy and the Case for Socialist Feminism* (New York: Monthly Review Press, 1979).

——, *The Radical Future of Liberal Feminism* (New York: Longman, 1981).

Evans, Mary, *Simone de Beauvoir: A Feminist Mandarin* (London: Tavistock, 1985).

Faderman, Lillian, *Surpassing the Love of Men: Romantic Friendship and Love between Women from the Renaissance to the Present* (London: The Women's Press, 1985).

Faulkner, Peter, *Modernism* (London: Routledge, 1990).

Foucault, Michel, *Discipline and Punish: The Birth of the Prison*, trans. Alan Sheridan (London: Allen Lane, 1977).

——, *The History of Sexuality*, vol. I: *An Introduction*, trans. Robert Hurley (New York: Vintage, 1978).

Freud, Sigmund, *An Outline of Psychoanalysis*, trans. and ed. James Strachey (London: The Hogarth Press, 1969).

——, 'Fragment of an Analysis of a Case of Hysteria' ('Dora'), in *Case Histories I: 'Dora' and 'Little Hans'*, The Penguin Freud Library vol. 8 (Harmondsworth: Penguin, 1990).

——, 'Medusa's Head', in *The Standard Edition of the Complete Psychological Works of Sigmund Freud*, vol. 18, ed. James Strachey (London: The Hogarth Press, 1940), pp. 273–4.

——, 'The Question of Lay Analysis: Conversations with an Impartial Person', in *The Standard Edition of the Complete Psychological Works of Sigmund Freud*, vol. 20, ed. James Strachey (London: The Hogarth Press, 1953), pp. 183–250.

Friedan, Betty, *It Changed My Life: Writings on the Women's Movement* (New York: W. W. Norton, 1985).

——, *The Feminine Mystique* (Harmondsworth: Penguin, 1992).

——, *The Second Stage* (London: Abacus, 1983).

Fuss, Diana, *Essentially Speaking: Feminism, Nature and Difference* (London: Routledge, 1990).

Gallop, Jane, *Feminism and Psychoanalysis: The Daughter's Seduction* (Basingstoke: Macmillan, 1982).

Gamble, Sarah, *Angela Carter: Writing from the Front Line* (Edinburgh: Edinburgh University Press, 1997).

Gates, Henry Louis, Jr, *Reading Black, Reading Feminist: A Critical Anthology* (New York: Meridian Press, 1990).

Gilbert, Sandra M. and Susan Gubar, *The Madwoman in the Attic: The Woman Writer and the Nineteenth-Century Literary Imagination* (New Haven, Conn.: Yale University Press, 1979).

Gilligan, Carol, *In a Different Voice: Psychological Theory and Women's Development* (Cambridge, Mass.: Harvard University Press, 1982).

Greene, Gayle, *Doris Lessing: The Poetics of Change* (Ann Arbor, Mich.: University of Michigan Press, 1994).

Grosz, Elizabeth, *Jacques Lacan: A Feminist Introduction* (London: Routledge, 1990).

——, *Sexual Subversions: Three French Feminists* (Sydney: Allen and Unwin, 1989).

Gunew, Sneja, *Feminist Knowledge: Critique and Construct* (London: Routledge, 1990).

Haffenden, John, *Novelists in Interview* (London: Methuen, 1985).

Hamilton, Roberta and Michèle Barrett, *The Politics of Diversity: Feminism, Marxism and Nationalism* (London: Verso, 1986).

Heath, Jane, *Simone de Beauvoir*, Key Women Writers (Hemel Hempstead: Harvester Wheatsheaf, 1989).

hooks, bell, *Yearning: Race, Gender, and Cultural Politics* (London: Turnaround, 1991).

Hull, Gloria T., Patricia Bell Scott and Barbara Smith, *All the Women Are White, All the Blacks Are Men, But Some of Us Are Brave* (Old Westbury: The Feminist Press, 1982).

Hutcheon, Linda, *The Politics of Postmodernism* (London: Routledge, 1989).

Irigaray, Luce, *An Ethic of Sexual Difference*, trans. Carolyn Burke and Gillian C. Gill (Ithaca, N.Y.: Cornell University Press, 1993).

——, *Marine Lover of Friedrich Nietzsche*, trans. Gillian C. Gill (New York: Columbia University Press, 1993).

——, *This Sex Which Is Not One*, trans. Catherine Porter with Carolyn Burke (Ithaca, N.Y.: Cornell University Press, 1985).

James, C. L. R., *The Black Jacobins: Toussaint L'Ouverture and the San Domingo Revolution*, 2nd edn (New York: Vintage, 1963).

Jameson, Fredric, *Postmodernism; or, the Cultural Logic of Late Capitalism* (London: Verso, 1991).

Jardine, Alice, *Gynesis: Configurations of Woman and Modernity* (Ithaca, N.Y.: Cornell University Press, 1985).

Jung, Carl Gustav, *Aion: Researches into the Phenomenology of the Self – The Collected Works of C. G. Jung*, vol. 9, part II, ed. Herbert Read, Michael Fordham and Gerhard Adler, trans. R. F. C. Hull (London: Routledge and Kegan Paul, 1959), pp. 11–22.

Kristeva, Julia, *The Portable Kristeva*, ed. Kelly Oliver (New York: Columbia, 1997).

Kuhn, Annette and AnnMarie Wolpe, *Feminism and Materialism: Women and Modes of Production* (London: Routledge, 1978).

Lacan, Jacques, *The Seminar. Book III: The Psychoses, 1955–56*, trans. Russell Grigg (London: Routledge, 1993).

Landry, Donna and Gerald MacLean, *Materialist Feminisms* (Oxford: Blackwell, 1993).

Lauretis, Teresa de, *The Practice of Love: Lesbian Sexuality and Perverse Desire* (Bloomington, Ind.: Indiana University Press, 1994).

Lechte, John, *Julia Kristeva* (London: Routledge, 1990).

Lee, Hermione, *Virginia Woolf* (London: Vintage, 1997).

Lessing, Doris, *The Golden Notebook* (London: Flamingo, 1993).

——, *To Room Nineteen: Collected Stories*, vol. 1 (London: Flamingo, 1994).

Lodge, David, *Working with Structuralism: Essays and Reviews on Nineteenth- and Twentieth-Century Literature* (London: Routledge, 1981).

Lurie, Alison, *The War between the Tates* (London: Abacus, 1993).

Lyotard, Jean-François, *The Postmodern Condition: A Report on Knowledge*, trans. Geoff Bennington and Brian Massumi (Manchester: Manchester University Press, 1984).

Majundar, Robin and Allen McLaurin, *Virginia Woolf: The Critical Heritage* (London: Routledge, 1975).

Marcus, Jane, *New Feminist Essays on Virginia Woolf* (London: Macmillan, 1981).

Marks, Elaine and Isabelle de Courtivron, *New French Feminisms: An Anthology* (Hemel Hempstead: Harvester Wheatsheaf, 1981).

Marx, Karl and Friedrich Engels, *The German Ideology* (London: Lawrence and Wishart, 1974).

Mitchell, Juliet, *Psychoanalysis and Feminism* (Harmondsworth: Penguin, 1990).

——, *Woman's Estate* (Harmondsworth: Penguin, 1971).

Mitchell, Juliet and Ann Oakley, *What is Feminism?* (Oxford: Basil Blackwell, 1986).

Moi, Toril, *Sexual/Textual Politics: Feminist Literary Theory* (London: Routledge, 1985).

——, *Simone de Beauvoir: The Making of an Intellectual Woman* (Oxford: Blackwell, 1994).

Moraga, Cherrie and Gloria Anzaldua, *This Bridge Called My Back: Writings by Radical Women of Color* (Kitchen Table: Women of Color Press, 1983).

Morrison, Toni, *Sula* (London: Picador, 1991).

Munt, Sally, *New Lesbian Criticism: Literary and Cultural Readings* (Hemel Hempstead: Harvester Wheatsheaf, 1992).

Nicholson, Linda J., *Feminism/Postmodernism* (London: Routledge, 1990).

Okely, Judith, *Simone de Beauvoir: A Re-Reading* (London: Virago, 1986).

Oliver, Kelly, *Ethics, Politics and Difference in Julia Kristeva's Writing* (New York: Routledge, 1993).

Rowbotham, Sheila, *Woman's Consciousness: Man's World* (Harmondsworth: Penguin, 1973).

Rupp, Leila J. and Verta Taylor, *Survival in the Doldrums: The American Women's Rights Movement, 1945–1960s* (Oxford: Oxford University Press, 1987).

Said, Edward, *Orientalism* (London: Routledge, 1978).

Sarah, Elizabeth, *Reassessments of 'First Wave' Feminism* (Oxford: Pergamon Press, 1982).

Sargent, Lydia, *Women and Revolution: A Discussion of the Unhappy Marriage of Marxism and Feminism* (London: Pluto Press, 1981).

Sartre, Jean-Paul, *Being and Nothingness: An Essay on Phenomenological Ontology*, trans. Hazel E. Barnes, introd. Mary Warnock (London: Methuen, 1958).

Scholes, Robert, *Structuralism in Literature* (New Haven, Conn.: Yale University Press, 1974).

Schwartzer, Alice, *Simone de Beauvoir Today: Conversations, 1972–1982* (London: Chatto, 1984).

Scott, Bonnie Kime, *The Gender of Modernism: A Critical Anthology* (Bloomington, Ind.: Indiana University Press, 1990).

——, *Refiguring Modernism*, vol. I: *The Women of 1928* (Bloomington, Ind.: Indiana University Press, 1995).

Showalter, Elaine, *A Literature of Their Own: British Women Novelists from Brontë to Lessing*, new edn (London: Virago Press, 1982).

——, *The New Feminist Criticism: Essays on Women, Literature, and Theory* (London: Routledge, 1989).

Simons, Margaret A., *Feminist Interpretations of Simone de Beauvoir* (University Park, Penn.: Pennsylvania State University Press, 1995).

Sinfield, Alan, *Cultural Politics: Queer Reading* (London: Routledge, 1994).

Spencer, Jane, *The Rise of the Woman Novelist: From Aphra Behn to Jane Austen* (Oxford: Blackwell, 1986).

Spender, Dale, *Mothers of the Novel: 100 Good Women Writers Before Jane Austen* (London: Pandora, 1986).

Spivak, Gayatri Chakravorty, *In Other Worlds: Essays in Cultural Politics* (London: Methuen, 1987).

Todd, Janet, *The Sign of Angellica: Women, Writing and Fiction, 1660–1800* (London: Virago, 1989).

Turner, Brian S., *Theories of Modernity and Postmodernity* (London: Sage, 1990).

Vice, Sue, *Psychoanalytic Criticism* (London: Polity Press, 1995).

Walder Dennis, *Literature in the Modern World: Critical Essays and Documents* (Oxford: Oxford University Press, 1990).

Watt, Ian, *The Rise of the Novel: Studies in Defoe, Richardson and Fielding* (London: Chatto and Windus, 1957).

Weed, Elizabeth and Naomi Schor, *Feminism Meets Queer Theory* (Bloomington, Ind.: Indiana University Press, 1997).

Whitford, Margaret, *Luce Irigaray: Philosophy in the Feminine* (London: Routledge, 1991).

Williams, Patrick and Laura Chrisman, *Colonial Discourse and Post-Colonial Theory: A Reader* (Hemel Hempstead: Harvester Wheatsheaf, 1993).

Winterson, Jeanette, *Sexing the Cherry* (London: Vintage, 1990).

Wittig, Monique, *The Straight Mind and Other Essays* (Hemel Hempstead: Harvester Wheatsheaf, 1992).

Woolf, Virginia, *A Room of One's Own* (Harmondsworth: Penguin, 1945).

——, *Orlando*, ed. Rachel Bowlby, World's Classics (Oxford: Oxford University Press, 1992).

——, *The Common Reader*, First Series (London: The Hogarth Press, 1968).

——, *The Diary of Virginia Woolf, 1925–1930*, vol. 3, ed. Anne Olivier Bell (London: The Hogarth Press, 1980).

——, *Women and Fiction: The Manuscript Versions of 'A Room of One's Own'*, ed. S. P. Rosenbaum, Shakespeare Head Press edn (Oxford: Blackwell, 1992).

Young, Robert, *Untying the Text: A Post-Structuralist Reader* (London: Routledge and Kegan Paul, 1981).

Articles

Bair, Deirdre, '"Madly Sensible and Brilliantly Confused": From *Le Deuxième sexe* to *The Second Sex*', *Dalhousie French Studies*, 13 (1987), 23–35.

——, 'Simone de Beauvoir: Politics, Language, and Feminist Identity', *Yale French Studies*, 72 (1986), 149–62.

Barrett, Michèle and Mary McIntosh, 'Ethnocentrism and Socialist-Feminist Theory,' *Feminist Review*, 20 (1985), 23–47.

Bayley, John, 'Fighting for the Crown', *New York Review of Books*, 23 April 1992, pp. 9–11.

Benhabib, Seyla, 'Sexual Difference and Collective Identities: The New Global Constellation', *Signs*, 24 (1999), 335–61.

Berg, Maggie, 'Luce Irigaray's "Contradictions": Poststructuralism and Feminism', *Signs*, 17 (1991), 50–70.

Bowlby, Rachel, '"The Problem with No Name": Rereading Friedan's *The Feminine Mystique*', *Feminist Review*, 27 (1987), 61–75.

Bradbury, Malcolm, 'The Paleface Professor', *The Times*, Saturday, 19 January 1985, p. 6.

Brown, Rosellen, 'Fertile Imagination', *Women's Review of Books*, 7 (1990), 9–10.

Butler, Judith, 'Contingent Foundations: Feminism and the Question of Postmodernism', *Praxis International*, 11 (1991), 150–65.

Card, Claudia, 'Lesbian Attitudes and *The Second Sex*', *Women's Studies International Forum*, 8 (1985), 209–14.

Chay, Deborah G., 'Rereading Barbara Smith: Black Feminist Criticism and the Category of Experience', *New Literary History*, 21 (1993), 635–52.

Collins, Patricia Hill, 'The Social Construction of Black Feminist Thought', *Signs*, 14 (1989), 745–73.

Connolly, Clara, Lynne Segal et al.,'Feminism and Class Politics: A Round-Table Discussion', *Feminist Review*, 23 (1986), 13–30.

Delphy, Christine, 'The Invention of French Feminism: An Essential Move', *Yale French Studies*, 87 (1993) 190–221.

Dijkstra, Sandra, 'Simone de Beauvoir and Betty Friedan: The Politics of Omission', *Feminist Studies*, 6 (1980), 294–303.

Eagleton, Terry, 'In the Gaudy Supermarket', Review of Gayatri Chakravorty Spivak, *A Critique of Post-Colonial Reason: Toward a History of the Vanishing Present*, London *Review of Books Online*, 21, 10, 31 May 1999, <http.www.lrb.co.uk.>

Griffiths, Sian, 'A Class Sister Act', *The Times Higher Educational Supplement*, 13 October 1995, p. 20.

Hennessey, Rosemary and Rajeswari Mohan, 'The Construction of Woman in Three Popular Texts of Empire: Towards a Critique of Materialist Feminism', *Textual Practice*, 3 (1989), 323–57.

Homans, Margaret, '"Women of Color": Writers and Feminist Theory', *New Literary History*, 25 (1994), 73–94.

Kaminsky, Amy, 'Gender, Race, Raza', *Feminist Studies*, 20 (1994), 7–31.

Kaufmann, Dorothy, 'Simone de Beauvoir: Questions of Difference and Generation', *Yale French Studies*, 72 (1986), 121–31.

King, Deborah K., 'Multiple Jeopardy, Multiple Consciousness: The Context of a Black Feminist Ideology', *Signs*, 14 (1988), 42–72.

Knopp, Sherron, '"If I Saw You Would You Kiss Me?": Sapphism and the Subversiveness of Virginia Woolf's *Orlando*', *PMLA*, 103 (1988), 24–34.

Kruks, Sonia, 'Gender and Subjectivity: Simone de Beauvoir and Contemporary Feminism', *Signs*, 18 (1992), 89–110.

Lauretis, Teresa de, 'Queer Theory: Lesbian and Gay Sexualities: An Introduction', *differences*, 3 (1991), iii–xviii.

Le Doeuff, Michèle, 'Simone de Beauvoir and Existentialism', *Feminist Studies*, 6 (1980), 277–89.

McDowell, Deborah E., 'New Directions for Black Feminist Criticism', *Black American Literature Forum*, 14 (1980), 153–9.

Mulkeen, Anne, 'Twentieth-Century Realism: The "Grid" Structure of *The Golden Notebook*', *Studies in the Novel*, 4 (1972), 262–74.

Newton, Esther, 'The Mythic Mannish Lesbian: Radclyffe Hall and the New Woman', *Signs*, 9 (1984), 557–75.

Pringle, Peter, 'Victims of Slavery Find Their Voice', *Independent on Sunday*, 10 October 1993, p. 18.

Rich, Adrienne, 'Compulsory Heterosexuality and Lesbian Existence', *Signs*, 5 (1980), 631–60.

Ryan, Barbara, 'Ideological Purity and Feminism: The US Women's Movement from 1966 to 1975', *Gender and Society*, 3 (1989), 239–59.

Simons, Margaret A., 'Beauvoir and Sartre: The Philosophical Relationship', *Yale French Studies*, 72 (1986), 165–79.

——, 'Lesbian Connections: Simone de Beauvoir and Feminism', *Signs*, 18 (1992), 136–61.

Smith, Barbara, 'Reply to Deborah Chay', *New Literary History*, 24 (1993), 653–6.

Tiger, Virginia, '"Taking Hands in (Dis)Unity": Story to Storied in Doris Lessing's "To Room Nineteen" and "A Room"', *MFS*, 36 (1990), 421–33.

Wilson, Elizabeth, 'Psychoanalysis: Psychic Law and Order?', *Feminist Review*, 8 (1981), 63–78.

Zerilli, Linda M. G., 'A Process without a Subject: Simone de Beauvoir and Julia Kristeva on Maternity', *Signs*, 18 (1992), 111–35.

Index